'Myler's ability to dig deep, gather plenty of background information, coupled with his easy-flowing style of writing, paints a fascinating scene building up to the contests. We urge you to add this book to your collection.'

Boxing News

'Myler just doesn't deal with what happened inside the ropes but also provides a balanced overview of the controversies, personalities and historical contexts that make these fights worth reading about.'

Ring

Boxing's Hall of Shame

'Boxing scribe Thomas Myler shares with the reader a ringside seat for the sport's most controversial fights. It's an engaging read, one that feeds our fascination with the darker side of the sport.'

Bert Sugar, author and broadcaster

'Well written and thoroughly researched by one of the best boxing writers in these islands, Myler has a keen eye for the story behind the story. A must read for all fight fans.'

Yorkshire Post

Ringside With The Celtic Warriors

'This latest offering from this highly-respected boxing writer is well up to the standard we expect from him. Myler is really someone who has been there, done that.'

Boxing News

'Thomas Myler has come up with another gem. His credentials and easy, readable style make this a must book for fight fans.'

The Sun

'As a ring historian, Thomas Myler has few peers.'

Belfast Telegraph

CLOSE
ENCOUNTERS
WITH THE GLOVES OFF

Boxing's Greats Recall the Inside Stories
of Their Biggest Fights

Thomas Myler

First published by Pitch Publishing, 2016

Pitch Publishing
A2 Yeoman Gate
Yeoman Way
Durrington
BN13 3QZ
www.pitchpublishing.co.uk

© 2016, Thomas Myler

A CIP catalogue record is available for this book
from the British Library.

ISBN 978-1-78531-122-2

Typesetting and origination by Pitch Publishing

Printed by Bell and Bain Ltd, Glasgow.

Contents

*To Betty, who was always
in my corner, win or lose*

'Boxing is the ultimate challenge. There's nothing that can compare to testing yourself the way you do every time you step into a ring.'

Sugar Ray Leonard

Acknowledgements

THIS book would not have been possible without the help and kindness of many people who gave their time and energy to assist with the project. All of them are too numerous to be named individually but particular reference should be made of many.

The invaluable team at *Boxing News*, past and present, deserve special mention such as various editors over the years like Graham Houston, Harry Mullan, Claude Abrams and Tris Dixon who could never do enough, whether checking facts and figures, supplying photographs or publishing reviews and plugs for my books. Not for nothing is *Boxing News* called the world's best fight magazine.

Special mention must also be made of the Press Association news agency, Getty Images and *Ring* magazine for immeasurable assistance including supplying photographs. The *Irish Independent* and *Dublin Evening Herald* have to be mentioned in this context too, as does freelance photographer Aidan Walsh. Where, too, would writers and chroniclers be without the indispensable website boxrec.com, an invaluable source of information? Columnist, chronicler and author Bob Mee also lent his expertise whenever a fact needed clarification. My family too were always there to help.

Sadly, my dear and beloved wife Betty passed away before I started the project but she would have fully approved of the project, unquestionably.

Without the help and co-operation of the boxers themselves, this book in any event would not have seen the light of day. Their time and full co-operation was always evident and while many have sadly left us, they, and those happily still with us, deserve my heartfelt thanks and gratitude.

Last and by no means least, my sincere thanks to Pitch Publishing for having the foresight, dedication and care for getting the book into print. Credit here must go to publishing executives Paul and Jane Camillin, editor Gareth Davis, typesetter Graham Hales and proofreader Dean Rockett, with Derek Hammond in charge of marketing.

Thank you all.

Introduction

C ALL it what you will, the noble art, the sweet science, the fight game, showbusiness with blood but boxing has an excitement, a drama, a charisma all its own. True, it has its do-gooders and its abolishers because of its very nature. But the most incontrovertible piece of evidence that its critics can never ignore or deny it that boxing, in some form, has been with us as long as man can remember. Fist-fighting, as a sporting competition, has been part of our culture for thousands of years.

To set the scene for this book, it would seem appropriate to take a brief look at boxing history down the years and establish where the sport has been and where it is at the present time.

It has certainly come a long, long way since its beginnings in ancient Greece where excavations at Knossos on the island of Crete have revealed that a form of the sport was known among its inhabitants as early as 1500 BC. But it was not until the early 19th century that a boxing dynasty was established in England and later in America.

The first recognised rules were set up by the English champion Jack Broughton in 1743 and were in operation until 1838 when the London Prize Ring Rules, or the New Rules of Prizefighting as they were initially called, were introduced. These were revised in 1853 and again in 1866. In 1867 John Sholto Douglas, the ninth Marquis of Queensberry, sponsored new rules compiled by his friend John Chambers, a keen follower of prizefighting. They had first met at Magdelene

College in Cambridge and the marquis, who had only a sketchy knowledge of boxing, agreed to lend the new rules his name and patronage. Thus the Queensberry Rules came into force.

In the early years of the 18th century, a typical contest had been an unregulated, no-holds-barred battle watched by a circle of spectators, hence 'the ring' as we know it today. There was no referee, or any set rounds or time limits. Beyond the fighters' personal sense of sportsmanship, there were simply no rules. The object was to fight until one contestant could no longer carry on. Battles generally lasted for hours, and while fists were considered the primary weapon, no tactic was forbidden. These included gouging, throwing, kicking, strangling and often the use of a cudgel, a short thick stick.

For many years, no consideration was given to the relative weight of the contestants, and no organisation existed to give official recognition to champions or challengers. To set up a title battle, a fighter would issue, often in writing, a challenge or response to an open invitation by the so-called champion to take on worthy rivals.

In time bare-knuckle fighting went into decline and by the time the Queensberry Rules were drawn up, they were considered more in keeping with the times. America fell in line and boxing had entered a whole new era.

Wrestling tackles and other dangerous practices were banned, the length of rounds limited to three minutes with a rest of 60 seconds in between, and contestants had to wear 'fair-sized boxing gloves of the best quality and new'.

The Queensberry Rules are basically the same today as the ones in operation a century and a half ago, although naturally with changes and modifications over the years to bring them up to date with conditions at the time. With safety at the core of all changes, these included the shortening of championship fights from 45 rounds to 25, then to 20, subsequently to 15 and today to 12. Other changes were extra weight classes, the methods of scoring fights and as recently as 1990 the changing of the weigh-in from the day of the fight to 24 hours earlier.

Even when the Queensberry Rules were introduced, old habits died hard.

There were still fights to a finish but gradually promoters saw the commercial sense in using a maximum number of rounds and, if no knockout or intervention had been achieved, having a points verdict based on which participant had done the better work over the whole fight.

Through it all, boxing has survived over the centuries in spite of some rough passages. It has fallen a victim of reformers, lawmakers, expungers, and so often the ineptitude of its own administrators. For example, take the so-called alphabet boys, or alphabet soup. This refers to the abbreviations of the various sanctioning bodies that have proliferated since the 1980s, and creating what aficionados of the sport consider 'cheap' world titles. These continue to be handed out like coupons at a supermarket.

Up to the 1950s there were only eight divisions, with only one champion per division, for a total of eight world champions at once. Sometimes fewer, if one boxer was the champion in two or more divisions at the one time. A contender became *the* world champion only by beating the then-champion or by defeating other leading contenders in elimination tournaments for a vacant title.

In those days, there were only a handful of world sanctioning bodies, the National Boxing Association, the New York State Athletic Commission, the European Boxing Union and the British Boxing Board of Control. By the 1980s many new boxing organisations had sprung up to the point where it seemed if the manager or promoter paid the requisite sanctioning fee, the boxer could fight for a somewhat dubious 'world' title even if his record was not generally considered by most fans and commentators as world class.

Currently there are no fewer than 17 weight divisions and, at the last count, six major sanctioning organisations for a total of 102 world champions no less. This figure could be doubled to almost 200 when one adds in 'world' titles variously labelled as interim, silver, diamond, emeritus, super and recess. Many boxing fans and critics belittle these 'world' championships and have labelled them alphabet soup titles or trinkets.

'The situation has got to be sorted out,' Barry McGuigan, the former world featherweight champion, said to me in a recent interview. 'It is going to take time because it means cutting out people who at the moment are earning money. But it needs to be done. There is competition too from the Ultimate Fighting Championship, or mixed martial arts or whatever you like to call it. However, I don't think this form of fighting involves the same level of skill as boxing. That is because in boxing you are only able to strike with your upper body, not your legs. For me, boxing at its best is the greatest skill of all. It is an art.'

In the final analysis, it can be said that boxing, with all its faults, is the great survivor. It has come through, though certainly not unscathed, to remain one of the world's premier sports – certainly the richest. The 2015 big fight in Las Vegas between Floyd Mayweather and Manny Pacquiao for the undisputed world welterweight title grossed more than $600m, with Mayweather picking up a cheque for over $200m, both all-time records. Those figures are mind-boggling in any currency.

The actual attendance was 16,507, puny compared to the 100,000-plus gates of the Roaring 20s and small even into the 1950s and 1960s, but promoters don't need to depend on ticket sales anymore. Boxing has long since moved into totally different eras. For many years now, the television executives are the people who call the shots, and will continue to do so.

Meanwhile boxing goes on. Promoters make matches, publicists spread the news, managers get the best deals for their boxers, and trainers ensure that the contestants are in the best possible physical and mental condition. In the end, it is the boxers themselves who make the difference between winning and losing. They are on their own as they walk out to the centre of the ring under the bright lights to receive last-minute instructions from the referee.

In the following pages, you will read the views and opinions of boxers themselves, in this case legendary figures in the sport whose names are familiar to even the most casual of boxing fans and who have made an indelible mark in their chosen profession. So without any further delay, enjoy the journey by having some close encounters with many of the all-time greats. There goes the first bell. Settle back.

1

Sugar Ray Robinson
Night of the Big Heat

IT was the night of 25 June 1952 and New York City was sweltering in a record heatwave with the temperature reaching 90 degrees Fahrenheit. Conditions for the big fight at the Yankee Stadium 'might have made Dante's Inferno seem like a refrigerator,' said Jim Jennings of the *New York Mirror,* noting that under the blazing ringside lights it was 104 degrees.

The big open-air stadium in the South Bronx was traditionally the home base of the New York Yankees baseball team but on this night Joey Maxim was defending his world light-heavyweight title against the middleweight champion Sugar Ray Robinson who was attempting to become only the third triple champion in the Queensberry Rules era, having earlier held the welterweight title.

Maxim, a solid fighter of Italian parentage who used solid boxing skills rather than punching power throughout his career, was born Giuseppe Antonio Bernardinelli in Cleveland, Ohio. He took his boxing name from the rapid-fire Maxim machine gun invented in 1884 and said to have played a large part in Britain's imperial conquests. Maxim, too, had the capacity to rapidly throw a consistent number of left jabs at opponents.

As the sweating crowd of 47,968 passed through the turnstiles in the scorching heat, the receipts would total $421,000, the highest gross for a title fight in the 175lb division for 26 years. No wonder James D. Norris, boss of the promoting organisation the International Boxing Club, was smiling at ringside.

The remarkable fight, scheduled for 15 rounds, would end dramatically and sensationally at the end of the 13th with Robinson slumped on his stool, head on his sweating chest and mumbling he could not go on any further. As Jesse Abramson reported in the *New York Herald Tribune*, 'The brilliant middleweight champion, with an unbeatable points lead, had made all the fight for the 13 rounds, outpunching and outboxing Maxim and exhausting himself on this roasting, burning night.'

When I had the pleasure of interviewing Robinson in a hotel in Glasgow during his British tour in 1964, his final year in the ring, he gave me the full story of that incredible night and much more besides.

'The original date was 23 June but heavy rain forced the IBC to postpone it for 48 hours because a big baseball match was scheduled for the next night at the nearby Polo Grounds and the promoters had an agreement that there could not be a clash of events,' he said, taking occasional sips of his orange juice.

'I weighed 157 lb and Maxim 173, giving him an advantage of 15 lb but I wasn't too worried. I'd fought and beaten heavier men before, including Jake LaMotta, and I felt I could do the same again. This wasn't a boast but you've got to feel that way in boxing. Any negative feelings and you shouldn't be in there.

'A strange thing happened the night before the fight. I dreamt I died in the ring and there was a doctor bending over me saying, "He's dead, he's dead." When I woke up I was really scared and I thought of calling off the fight. I was reminded of what had happened five years earlier when I knocked out the Irish-American Jimmy Doyle and he died after the fight. A few nights earlier I had dreamt Doyle had fallen dead at my feet.

'The paramedics were taking him out on a stretcher and when I woke up I couldn't see his face but somehow I knew it was him. Doyle had been injured in a previous fight and maybe he shouldn't have been in the ring at all with me that night. But there you go. The press were very hard on me after the fight. When I had been asked by the coroner at the inquest if I had anything to say, I said it was my business to hurt people. I was just telling the truth about boxing but the press labelled me an insensitive person with no real feelings.

'I didn't box again for a few months as I was completely broken up. Later on at a charity show I gave my entire purse of $13,000 to Doyle's mother and set up a $10,000 trust fund for her. Then, when I knocked out Flashy Sebastian in the first round and he lay still on the canvas I thought I'd killed him too. But thankfully he just had concussion. I breathed a sigh of relief.

'But to get back to Maxim. I didn't tell anybody about my dream of dying in the ring. I just wanted to get on with the fight. The plan worked out between my manager George Gainford and my trainers Harry Wiley and Pee Wee Beale was that I would keep the pressure on Maxim, mix up my shots, move in and out and collect the points. That's how it worked out.'

The *Press Association* reported that Robinson made full use of his speed by darting in and out of Maxim before the light-heavyweight champion could set himself up for counter shots. A terrific left hook in the seventh rocked Maxim back on his heels before Robinson tore in for the kill but the heavier man held on. Still, Robinson had a commanding lead on points.

'I was going for that light-heavyweight title and nothing was going to stop me. I don't honestly think that Maxim hit me solidly once in the first ten rounds. He landed but not to any great extent. He was working when we clinched but on the outside he didn't land a thing. But by tenth I felt I was getting weaker. I was breathing hard like a man in a desert needing a drink.

'It was so hot that the referee Ruby Goldstein had to be helped out of the ring at the end of the round and Ray Miller took his place. I guess it was one of the few times two referees were ever used in a championship fight. Probably the first time ever. You could check it out but I'm fairly sure I'm right. I personally never heard of two referees in the one fight anyhow.

'I don't recall much about the 11th or 12th rounds and the heat was really getting to me and I was in a kind of fog but I do remember Harry Wiley shouting in my ear and telling me I only had to stay on my feet for another few rounds and I'd win. I have a vague memory of throwing a right hand in the 13th round, missing and falling flat on my face.

'They emptied a bucket of water over me at the bell but I was all in. When the bell rang for the 14th I just couldn't get up off my stool and I said I couldn't go on. It was the only time I had been stopped in my career. I heard later that all officials had me well in front. One judge marked it nine for me, three for Maxim and one even. The second had it ten for me and three for Maxim. Before his collapse, referee Goldstein had it 5-2 in my favour with three even and the new referee Miller had it two for me and one for Maxim. I could not have lost the decision.

'I think they may have carried me to the dressing room. I couldn't remember much of what happened. In the dressing room I do recall the commission doctor sticking a needle into me and through the haze I saw the mayor of New York and I mumbled something to him about Maxim not being able to knock me out. When one of my handlers took me to the shower I dragged the mayor in along with me, fully clothed.

'It was crazy. I kept repeating, "He didn't beat me. It was God's will." I heard somebody behind me saying I was crazy from the heat but I said I wasn't crazy. The next day I was feeling much better and I went to see the movies of the fight and the gloom came over me again. I had come so close to that title but that's how it goes. You win some, you lose some,' he shrugged with a smile. 'Incidentally, we both lost around 20lb each in the fight. That gives you some idea of the conditions.'

A.J. Liebling of the *New Yorker* saw the dramatic finish like this, 'After the 12th round, all Sugar Ray had to do was to finish the fight on his feet and he would win on points. But when he came out for the 13th, he walked as if he had the gout in both feet and dreaded putting them down. When he punched, which was infrequently, he was as late and as wild as an amateur, and when he wasn't punching, his arms hung by his sides.

'Maxim landed one or two fairly good shots, I thought where I sat. And then Robinson, the complete boxer, the epitome of ring grace, swung wildly and, like a child, missed his man completely and fell hard on his face. When he got up, Maxim backed him against the ropes and hit him a couple of times. The round ended and Robinson's seconds half dragged, half carried him to his corner. He couldn't get off the stool at the end of the one-minute interval and Maxim was declared the winner in the 14th round because the bell had rung for the beginning of the round.'

Ironically, the 15-round distance in championship fights would be officially shortened to 12 in the 1980s. Had that been the case in 1952, Robinson would have been a clear points winner and taken a third world title. Up to then, this had only been achieved by two boxers, Henry Armstrong, who won the featherweight, lightweight and welterweight titles and earlier by Bob Fitzsimmons who was champion at middleweight, light-heavyweight and heavyweight.

Over 60 years on, Robinson is rated as the greatest boxer of all time. His outstanding ability as a superb ring craftsman and hard, accurate puncher plus his flamboyant persona made him a hero to boxing fans all over the world. At his peak, and even in the closing years of his 25-year career, he was as flashy outside the ring as he was inside it. A sleek, handsome man with a ready smile, his clothes were always impeccable, with expensive rings on his perfectly manicured fingers and his black hair pomaded to a bright sheen.

I asked Robinson about his early life. While he said he was born in Detroit, a fact long accepted by several writers including his official biographer Dave Anderson of the *New*

York Times in 1969, Herb Boyd wrote a book on Robinson in 2005 and maintained the boxer's birth certificate showed Ailey, Georgia as his birthplace. His parents, however, were born in Dublin, Georgia, but soon moved to Detroit and later New York.

'Things were tough in Detroit, even though it was the place to be because it was the centre of the automobile industry,' he said. 'My dad had a serious drink problem and he wasn't able to hold down a job. He drifted from one job to another, ending up with nothing better than unskilled work, although other black people were getting good jobs in factories which seemed to be mushrooming all over the place.

'Money was always a problem around the house and my mother got a job as a seamstress with a local linen company but cash was still a problem. We moved house several times but always managed to survive. It was in Detroit that I first met my idol Joe Louis, who would go on to win the world heavyweight title and hold it for nearly 12 years. I heard he trained at the Brewster Gym and I would go over and carry his gym kit for him. It was a real thrill.

'Later on mom took me and my two sisters to New York City, but left dad behind. She explained to us that he had never really settled down and with his drink problem, we would be better off on our own. We moved house a bit in the city when the rent would go up. It was in New York that I got into boxing seriously.

'A friend of mom's suggested as I liked boxing that I should drop down to the Salem Crescent Athletic Club in the cellar of a Methodist church. It was there I met the chief trainer George Gainford who would later become my manager all throughout my career. He got me into amateur boxing and I won two Golden Gloves titles, at featherweight and lightweight. I might have made the US team for the 1940 Olympics in Tokyo but Japan was involved in the war and they were cancelled. I turned pro that year and I guess it all took off from there.'

Gainford organised Robinson's fights and schedules as his official manager on record but it was Sugar Ray himself who always worked out the financial details and had the final say over contracts. 'Yes, I suppose I was a tough guy with promoters but they can sit back and count the cash but it's the boxers themselves to take the blows,' he said. 'I reckoned from early on that if I'm owed a dollar, then why should I take 50 cents? It makes sense if you think about it.'

Robinson's financial dealings with promoter James D. Norris, particularly for his first fight with the rugged Carmen Basilio for Sugar Ray's world middleweight title on 23 September 1957, was the work of legend, and deserves a place in any boxing anthology. As *Time* magazine reported at the time, 'Robinson's fierce pride as a boxing craftsman has been matched by his curious pride in being a slick man with a buck. Last week Sugar Ray the businessman employed a merciless hard sell to peddle Robinson the athlete.'

In the early stages of negotiations Norris suffered a near-fatal heart attack when protracted talks had broken down. Robinson had heard that the television rights had been sold to a particular network and that Sugar Ray himself had already received a higher offer from a different broadcaster.

Norris insisted that Robinson had no say in the matter but at a hastily-called meeting of the New York State Athletic Commission which was sanctioning the fight, Robinson said that if there were any TV cameras positioned at ringside he was walking back to his dressing room and going home.

'When the chairman Julius Helfand said I was contracted for the fight and that I had better see my lawyer, I stood up and said that if their action meant taking my title away I would sue the commission for taking away my rights as a citizen. Helfand barked, "Don't threaten us. We don't want to hear any more of your threats." I left the meeting but three days later I got my way and came away with the best contract of my career – $228,000 as my 45 per cent of the gate, $255,000 from theatre and TV rights and $30,000 from the movie and radio rights.

'I heard that Basilio was complaining, having to settle for 20 per cent of the live gate, but with theatre and TV rights, he came out of it very well but remember he was the challenger and I was the champion. That made all the difference.

'During the early negotiations Norris, the promoter, assigned Joe Louis, the former world heavyweight champion, to try and talk me into cutting my demands. Mind you, Louis was himself hitting hard times financially. When he called into my office in Harlem, I said to him, "How can you ask me to do this? These guys, look at what they've done to you. If I go along with them, I'll end up just as broke. You ought to be on my side instead of doing this." In the end, Louis had to agree.'

In a thriller, which *Ring* magazine called 'a brilliant chapter in boxing history', Robinson was beaten on a split decision, with the referee marking it for Sugar Ray and the two judges calling it for Basilio. The two clashed again six months later and this time Robinson upset the form book by regaining his title. Again, the verdict was split. This time Sugar Ray won on the cards of the two judges, with the referee marking it for Basilio.

There were plans for a third meeting but preliminary talks quickly broke down. Promoter Norris told the press, 'Robinson is looking for 45 per cent of the gate and Basilio wants 30 per cent. To hand both boxers a total of 75 per cent is simply unreasonable. We want to forget about these two and move on to other boxers and other fights.'

What about another great rivalry, Robinson's two clashes with Randolph Turpin? The Britisher, a former navy cook, caused a stunning upset in their first fight on 10 July 1951 when he outpointed Sugar Ray and took away his world middleweight title in London before a capacity crowd of 18,000 at the Earls Court Arena. In their return match two months later at the open-air Polo Grounds in New York, Robinson regained the championship by stopping Turpin in ten rounds before a crowd of 61,370 who paid $767,000, a record up to then for a fight below the heavyweight division.

Turpin was arguably the best British boxer of the post-Second World War era. His father was from British Guiana, now the independent state of Guyana, and his mother was from the English Midlands town of Leamington Spa in

Warwickshire. A heavy hitter and one of three fighting brothers, he had compiled a record of 43 fights, with two losses and a draw but entered the ring as a 6/1 underdog, with some bookies making him 10/1.

Robinson, on the other hand, had 132 fights with just one loss, reversed two weeks later. But Turpin's supporters pointed out that at 31, Sugar Ray was seven years older than their man and this could tell over the 15 rounds. There were also stories that Sugar Ray was not as fit as he should have been and that his constant travelling all over Europe with an entourage of 14 and taking in six fights in seven weeks in six different cities had tired him out.

'I was never one for making excuses and I won't make them to you now but the fighting doesn't make you tired,' he said. 'All the running around from country to country does. But Turpin whipped me square. He had a style I found hard to figure out. He was doing all boxing things wrong, jerking his head up when punching.

'In the seventh round we were in a clinch when his forehead smacked against my left eyebrow and split it open. That didn't help. I knew at the end of the 14th round that I'd lost. At the bell to end the 15th and the fight, I went over to Turpin's corner and congratulated him. I told him I was beaten by a better man.

'Luckily I had a return fight clause in the contract which allowed me to fight him within 64 days and get the champion's end of the purse, 30 per cent of the gate, even though I was the challenger. Some people criticised me for leaving Turpin only 25 per cent but he and his team agreed to that before the first fight and now he was the champion.

'I felt much fresher and sharper in the return fight. I was slightly ahead after nine rounds but George and I had planned it that way. I would pace myself in the middle rounds then step up the pace in the last five or six rounds. But the plan suddenly changed in the tenth round when Turpin butted me and the blood came out from the scar over my left eye.

'I knew I had to get him out of there fast because the referee Ruby Goldstein was casting anxious glances at the injury and he could decide to stop the fight any minute. In desperation I lashed out with a hard right which dropped Turpin. He lay flat on his back for three seconds and took a count of nine.

'When he got to his feet I went all out and trapped him on the ropes. I must have landed at least 20 hard blows and he looked like falling on his face to the canvas when Goldstein jumped in, wrapped his arms around Turpin and led him to his corner. I was champion of the world again after 64 days without the title and it felt real good.'

Robinson would win and lose the world middleweight title in seven championship fights, first taking it from his old rival Jake LaMotta in 13 rounds on 14 February 1951, St Valentine's Day. The previous November he had gone on his first European tour and won all his five fights against some of the continent's best boxers. In between the fights, he partied a lot and didn't his manager George Gainford warn him to be taking too many chances of losing his edge?

'George worried about everything but he needn't have had any fears on that count,' said Robinson. 'I think I knew best. I was up at six o'clock every morning for a five-mile training run and I worked a lot in the gym. Even though there was no title at stake in any of the fights, I didn't want a loss on my record which might affect my chances of getting a shot at LaMotta's title back in the US.

'I took eight people with me on that first European tour – my wife, George and his wife, two trainers, a golf pro, a barber and a secretary, and added a bodyguard/interpreter when we got to Paris. We had 53 pieces of luggage. I never realised I was so popular in Paris and letters arrived by the sack-load. They were for autographs, personal appearances, social functions, dinner parties, business lunches and so on.

'My wife Edna Mae and I visited several nightclubs in the city and though neither of us drank alcohol we liked to get out on the dance floor. On one occasion the MC asked me to join the band and I sat down and played first the drums and then the piano and got a round of applause. I made around $50,000 for five fights in Europe and I think we spent half of it. Edna

Mae spent a lot of time shopping in Paris. But I'd no regrets. It was worth it. I remembered when I hadn't got two cents to rub together and now I was making up for it.

'For the record I beat Jean Stock in two rounds in Paris and Luc van Dam in four in Brussels. In Geneva Jean Walzack went the full ten rounds and back in Paris I stopped Robert Villemain in nine rounds. My final fight was in Frankfurt and I knocked out Hans Stretz in five. That fight was on Christmas Day, an unusual day for fans to come out and see a boxing match. I smiled later when somebody showed me an American newspaper with the heading "Hans stretched". I liked that one.'

Robinson had a larger party with him on his second tour of Europe but not the 20 as reported in several British newspapers. Their writers were calling it 'a travelling circus'. There were 13 in all. This time however there was an additional item, his 17-foot-long flamingo pink Cadillac embellished with 'Sugar Ray' painted in his own handwriting on the side. 'Several papers said this was sheer extravagance but I had my reputation as an artiste to maintain,' he said. 'That car was the symbol of my reputation. I loved to drive it around Paris with the top down, the radio on loud and me wearing a beret.'

Such was that reputation that when the Cadillac pulled away from the hotel and headed up the Champs-Elysees, gendarmes waved other traffic to a standstill. Cyclists followed, like seagulls after a fishing boat, shouting his name, 'Ehh-Ro-bean-soan' while he acknowledged in French, 'Ca marche.'

Whenever important people gathered, Sugar Ray was bound to be there. The big and expensive Lido nightclub opened a new show and the next day the newspapers gave a big play to Robinson dancing with the movie star Martine Carol. When photographers had asked him if he would take the floor with the glamorous woman, he looked up from his Coca-Cola and said, "Sure, if she wants to. You go ask her." She agreed and we danced.

'The papers were saying I was the biggest celebrity in Paris. I had several cheques, each for $100,000, to donate to cancer organisations in Europe. That made me feel real good. Lots of invitations poured in and I did the most worthy causes. I managed to raise a sizeable amount at the Palais De Chaillot for retired comedians. I unveiled a plaque in honour of the great French boxer and former world middleweight champion Marcel Cerdan.

'I turned out to receive an award from a French magazine as "Boxer of the Year" and met France's First Lady, Madame Auriol. She thanked me publicly for a donation to a cancer fund and I played golf at St Cloud outside Paris and attracted a gallery. I heard back in the US that *Time* magazine had put me on the cover and I felt good about that.

'But I never forgot what I came to Europe for and that was to box. George never failed to remind me about that. I had six fights before the title defence against Randolph Turpin. I stopped Kid Marcel in Paris in five rounds and outpointed Jean Wanes in Zurich over ten. I beat Jan de Bruin in eight in Antwerp and Jean Walzack in six in Liege. I finished off Cyrille Dellanoit in three in Turin and had a no-contest with Gerhard Hecht in West Berlin.

'Let me tell you about the Hecht fight as it was a controversial one, to say the least. It was held in the open air at the Waldbuehne Stadium on a Sunday afternoon and there was a crowd of 30,000 in attendance. Among them were a few thousand US servicemen but the German fans out-cheered them in welcoming me into the ring. I was the first world champion to appear in a Berlin ring for 25 years.

'Hecht was a local in his early 20s and it was said he was promising. I made up my mind not to carry him but to get down to work straight away. After all, a lucky punch, or rather an unlucky punch, could end everything. In the opening round I aimed a right hook at his ribs but he spun around and the punch landed on his side. He went down and the referee Otto Nispel pushed me away and took up the count from the timekeeper and counted out Hecht who was writhing in apparent pain on the canvas, holding his back.

'He was carried to his corner and the crowd, angry at the short duration of the contest which they had paid good money to see, started to chant "Foul! Foul!" A doctor was brought into the ring and after examining Hecht decided that he had in fact been fouled but decided that after a minute's rest he would be able to continue, even though the referee had officially counted him out. What are rules for, only to be adhered to!

'At the bell for the second round I moved in fast and dropped him with a right to the ribs as he came in sideways. Suddenly the referee shouted at me, "Go to your corner, you're disqualified." By now the big crowd were getting very angry at the second termination of the contest and they started throwing bottles, stones, chairs and anything that they could find towards the ring. Everybody ducked for cover. George grabbed me and pulled me down the ring steps and under the ring for protection. The boxing writers and ringsiders were diving for cover.

'Eventually heavily-armed police were brought in to help bring some kind of control to the situation and more importantly, as far as we were concerned, to take us out of the arena and into waiting cars to get us quickly back to our hotel. To add to an already confused situation, the West Berlin Boxing Commission convened a special meeting the next day and announced in a statement that they were suspending the referee "for handling the contest in an improper manner".

'They said the official verdict was now no contest, and that's the way it went into the record books. I told George I never wanted to box in Germany again and I never did. Once was more than enough. I was tired by the time I got to London for the Turpin fight but I never want to use that as an excuse. Randy beat me fair and square.'

On the gangster element in boxing, particularly in the 1940s and 1950s, Robinson said he could have been a much richer man had he gone along with the underworld and agreed to their offers to either lose fights deliberately or carry opponents he could have knocked out or stopped.

'After I signed to fight Jake LaMotta for the world middleweight title scheduled for 14 February 1951 I had a visit in my training camp at Pompton Lakes, New Jersey from

Frankie Carbo, the underworld tsar of boxing who controlled several world champions' contracts, including LaMotta's. Carbo had several aliases but most people referred to him as "Mr Big" or "Mr Grey". He was usually dressed in grey.

'He said he was representing LaMotta and that he wanted me to have three fights with Jake. He said, "You win the first, LaMotta wins the second and the third is on the level. That's the way it would have to be, and in that way we would make a lot of money. I'll leave it with you." I told George Gainford, my manager, and we agreed to turn the offer down. When Carbo came back to my camp I told him we weren't interested and he said that was fine and I never heard from him again. Not many boxers turned down Carbo so I guess he respected me for it.

'It was common knowledge in boxing circles that Carbo was the man behind the infamous fixed fight between Jake LaMotta and "Blackjack" Billy Fox at Madison Square Garden in New York in 1947, even though Frank "Blinky" Palermo, Fox's manager, did all the dirty work, having strong connections with the underworld too. That fight was stopped in the fourth round as LaMotta allowed Fox to pummel him on the ropes, with the crowd, sensing a fake, booing and jeering.

'LaMotta confirmed before the Kefauver Senate Commission 13 years later in a probe to clean up boxing that, under direct orders from Carbo, he did in fact deliberately lose to Fox so as to get a world middleweight title fight with Marcel Cerdan, a fight he would win in ten rounds. By losing too, he allowed Fox to be manoeuvred into a world light-heavyweight title fight against Gus Lesnevich. Fox lost that one, with Lesnevich knocking him out in ten rounds and in the first round in a return fight.'

Interestingly, the Kefauver Commission found that Carbo's police record showed 22 arrests, 17 for offences such as grand larceny, felonious assault, vagrancy, suspicious character and violation of New York's boxing laws as well as five murder charges for which he served time in Alcatraz. Obviously he was not a man to cross and he once said in an interview, 'I always got along with Robinson, a real champ and a swell guy.'

A few weeks before Sugar Ray defended his world middle-weight title on 16 April 1952 at the Chicago Stadium against the former champion Rocky Graziano, who himself had earlier been involved with gangsters and was suspended for a time, Robinson was approached by representatives of the Chicago Mafia to throw the fight.

'The deal was that I would get a flat $3m if Graziano won the first fight, me win the second and with the third fight on the level,' said Sugar Ray. 'But as I had earlier done with Carbo, I turned it down and again I heard nothing more about it.

'Back in 1942, my second year in professional boxing, I was in my hotel in Chicago before a fight with Tony Motisi, a small-time fighter, when I got a call from reception to say that three men wanted to see me in the lobby. Gainford asked to send them up and when George asked them to take off their coats, one of them had a gun in a holster. The guy with the gun said if I carried Motisi for the ten rounds I would get a good payment. He said they were betting a lot of money on Motisi going the full distance.

'George said he was glad to know the three men but we couldn't do business and he showed them the door. I knocked out Motisi in the first round.'

Robinson did get into trouble with the New York State Athletic Commission which controlled boxing in the state following a press conference at his training camp at Greenwood Lake before his first world middleweight title fight with Carmen Basilio at the Yankee Stadium in New York on 23 September 1957. He sent shock waves through the sport when he told reporters that he had offered to buy out the promoters, the International Boxing Club, known as the IBC, for $300,000 and was turned down.

Sugar Ray also said he was on the way out as a boxer and that he would be retiring soon. But it was his remarks about bribe offers that upset the commission as boxers were expected, at least at the time, to report any such dealings with the underworld in a bid to clean up the sport and help rid it of undesirable elements.

Robinson told the international gathering of newspapermen, 'I may as well tell you guys that I received hundreds of thousands of dollars, once a $3m offer, to lose fights. I don't want to mention the last time I got such an offer because it would involve a man very prominent in boxing. The gangsters and the hoodlums are there if you want to deal with them. I simply rejected the bribes. I never reported them because I never wanted to cause any trouble.'

When Julius Helfand, chairman of the commission, read Robinson's statements the next day, he ordered him to substantiate his remarks under oath or risk suspension. Sugar Ray repeated what he had said but as the fight was only two days away and a suspension out of the question, he got away with a stern warning to report all bribes or offers in the future.

'I don't want to paint myself as a kind of goody-two-shoes, Thomas, but I was never interested in that kind of thing. I don't think anybody could ever question my honesty in the ring. Yes, of course there is crookedness in boxing as there is in many other activities where there is big money but you have to stand by your principles. Yes, I received big offers to take dives, not only against LaMotta and Graziano but other fights. But the mobsters soon got to know I wouldn't play ball.

'I could have been a richer man had I gone along with them. You must remember I was often 5/1, 6/1, often higher in the betting and I could have made a packet by losing. The temptation was there but you must stand by your principles in life. It's all you've got, if you think about it.'

The two fights with Basilio were wars, particularly the first one. Carmen was considered in the trade 'a pretty tough customer' and while he was expected to give Robinson a good run, the experts plumped for Sugar Ray to hold on to his title. Born in Canastota in Upper State New York to Italian parents who were part of a community of onion farmers, Basilio was one of ten children and grew up to be a lean, craggy individual who looked as if his 5ft 6.5in in physique had been carved out of rock. Going into the Robinson fight, his lumpy, hammered face showed he had been in the ring wars. In 70 professional contests, the former US Marine had never been knocked out or stopped, and had only once been off his feet.

'I figured Basilio was going to be tough and I expected a hard fight,' said Robinson, 'and I was right on both counts. He kept coming forward like a tank on the battlefield but I was generally able to pick him off with left jabs, hooks and uppercuts. After 15 rounds I thought I had done enough to win but while the referee Al Berle gave it to me by nine rounds to six, which I thought was about fair generally, the two judges saw it differently.

'Artie Aidala had it 9-5 for Basilio with one round even. Bill Recht also gave it to Basilio by 8-6 and one even. I was no longer world middleweight champion but I had no squawks. "There were two judges and a referee out there and I'll abide by their decision," I told a packed dressing room. "You win some, you lose some. I lost this one." That's just it.'

Ring magazine described the fight as 'a brilliant chapter in ring history', with editor Nat Fleischer recording, 'The affair was a throwback to the days when ringmen fought their hearts out to gain their objective, and because of that, it will take its place among ring classics.' Peter Wilson of the *Daily Mirror* wrote, 'In all my life, so much of which has been spent at the ringsides of the world, I cannot recall a better fight than this one. The skill, the tormenting devilry of the matador was all Robinson's but this was one fight the bull won.'

The return fight was held six months later, on 25 March 1958, and this time at the Chicago Stadium, a familiar venue for Robinson as he had achieved many of his greatest victories there including his title win over Jake LaMotta in February 1951. A crowd of 17,979 paid $351,955 to see how it would all work out.

'I always felt in control,' said Robinson. 'I closed Basilio's left eye with a good right hand in the fourth and by the sixth it was shut tight. As the rounds went by, it puffed up and naturally this hampered him although in fairness he didn't use it as an excuse afterwards. At the finish I felt I had done enough to win. I was right. I was world middleweight champion again and it felt good.'

It was a split decision, like in the first fight. Under the Chicago points system, referee Frank Sikora called it 69-66 for Basilio which was booed, judge John Bray marking it 71-64 for Sugar Ray and judge Spike Adams giving the casting vote for Robinson 72-65. Joseph C. Nichols of the *New York Times* scored it on the New York system of rounds won, lost or drawn by having it for Robinson by 11-4. 'True, many of the rounds were exceedingly close but any margin was Robinson's creation,' he reported.

Sugar Ray would lose the title on 22 January 1960 to the Boston fireman Paul Pender over 15 rounds and failed to regain it in three subsequent fights, once against Pender and twice against Gene Fullmer, all going the full 15 rounds. Sugar Ray finally retired on 10 December 1965 with a record of 202 fights, with 175 wins, 19 defeats mainly coming towards the end of his 25-year career, six draws and two no-contests. In 1969 he set up the Sugar Ray Robinson Youth Foundation in Los Angeles to help the underprivileged. Robinson died in Los Angeles on 12 April 1989 at the age of 67 due to natural causes brought about by diabetes and hypertension. He was also a victim of Alzheimer's.

Over 2,000 mourners attended Sugar Ray's funeral, among them several past and present world champions as well as movie stars including Elizabeth Taylor. Giving the eulogy, the Rev. Jesse Jackson said, 'Robinson was born at the bottom but left at the top. Ray had charisma and special gifts from God. He was an original art form.' Tributes came in from all over the world. Mike Tyson, former heavyweight champion of the world, said, 'When you think of the name Sugar Ray Robinson you think of class and style and dignity.'

The former world champion at two weights and almost a third was inducted into the International Boxing Hall of Fame in New York in 1990 and was featured on a commemorative stamp by the US Postal Service in 2006.

2

George Foreman
The Jungle and other Rumbles

IT seemed like a work of fiction, something straight out of the pages of a novel – a world heavyweight championship fight in 1974 planned for a country that had never staged a major boxing match before, Zaire in Central Africa, formerly the Belgian Congo and later, as today, the Democratic Republic of the Congo. Not only would big boxing be new there, but Zaire was one of the poorest countries in the world, with no infrastructure whatsoever, certainly not in a position to put on such an important event, a contest for boxing's biggest prize, the heavyweight championship of the world, which would attract universal interest.

This was the Third World at its most extreme. Kinshasa, the capital, where the fight was due to be held, had an old dilapidated stadium built by the Belgians in 1917 and which for many years had thick underbrush growing wildly inside and outside. The old seats were cracking and crumbling. The roads to it were merely dirt tracks. It all looked like the set for a movie about the land that time forgot.

Even Zaire's political framework was suspect. Its 71 million population was ruled by a dictator, president Mobutu Sese Seko, who had come to power in 1965 after a bloody war of independence from colonial rule and who frequently removed his detractors and settled disputes with the help of a firing squad. Now promoter Don King was throwing out feelers to boxing writers and sports editors across America that he planned to have George Foreman defend his world heavyweight title against the former champion Muhammad Ali in Zaire.

King would put the proposition to both boxers and felt confident they would accept, even if it meant them travelling to 'no man's land'. Ali had been stripped of his heavyweight title in April 1967 when he refused to enlist in the US Army over the Vietnam war issue but he was now the top contender and anxious to get back on top.

Foreman had since won the title and ruthlessly disposed of his two challengers, Joe Roman, the Puerto Rican champion, in one round in Tokyo and the skilful Ken Norton, noted for his awkward if effective crossed-arm style, in two in Venezuela. Ali could be number three. King would label the big fight the 'Rumble In The Jungle' and it would put not only Zaire on the map but the whole of Central Africa. It would be the start of something new, something exciting.

Foreman got news that King was planning the Zaire fight when he heard it on the radio while having breakfast one morning at his ranch in Livermore, California, shortly after returning from Venezuela in March 1974. 'King hadn't approached me at this stage but I would be interested at least in talking to him,' George told this writer when he was in Dublin in November 2004 to promote his indoor electrically heated grill, or as it was known, George Foreman's Lean, Mean Fat Reducing Grilling Machine, or simply George Foreman's Grill. It has since sold over 100 million worldwide.

'Ali was at ringside for the Norton fight in Caracas,' he said, 'and when the referee called it off after I'd floored Ken in the first and again in the second, I glared down at him and shouted, "I'm going to kill you." Ali did not respond, which was unusual for him as he was always the most talkative of guys as you well know. I sensed a kind of fear in his eyes. I knew then that if we ever fought each other I would beat him. After all, I had just put Ken Norton away in two rounds, and Ali, in two fights with Norton, lost the first and won the second, both going the full 12 rounds. Many people felt Ken should have got the decision in the second fight, which was split.

'The big fight was scheduled for 24 September 1974 and it was officially announced on the day we signed contracts. Every major newspaper and magazine in the country sent their writers to interview me at my ranch and get my views. Some come from abroad. There was no doubt that interest was enormously high and that it was going to be a worldwide event, even if it was taking place in far-off Central Africa. I told them I felt very confident that I would be able to turn back the challenge as Ali was clearly past his best. Though he had recently outpointed the former champion Joe Frazier, he wasn't really that impressive against Ken Norton in either fight.'

The Foreman–Ali fight was Don King's first big promotion and it would be his legacy. A few years ago when I was writing a boxing column for the *Irish Independent*, I contacted him about a middleweight title fight he was promoting in Las Vegas. During the conversation I asked him if he had any particular memories of the Rumble In The Jungle. 'Enough to fill a book, Thomas,' he quipped. 'Someday I may well get around to it.'

Shock-haired and something of a larger-than-life character, the Foreman–Ali fight turned King into the most recognisable and flamboyant figure in big-time modern boxing. A monarch among the world's great hustlers, a fact he himself readily admitted, The Don reinvented himself so successfully that in the space of two years he went from being an ex-con with a prison record for manslaughter to a powerhouse in the fight game, staging some of the world's most hyped sporting events. 'Never count me out,' he told one reporter. 'I just get back up there and fight – and more importantly, to win.'

King had not been the only promoter anxious to put on the Ali–Foreman fight when it became known that both boxers were anxious for it. Teddy Brenner of Madison Square Garden was after it, as was Ali's former attorney Bob Arum of Top Rank Promotions. Jerry Perenchino, a Hollywood booking agent with strong boxing connections was also in the frame. But it was King who had the trump cards.

Don had the backing of Hank Schwartz, a prominent businessman and president of Video Techniques in New York, an electronics and satellite company with all the advanced technology at his disposal, an important factor in the untested wilderness of Central Africa. King flew to Zaire and told president Mobuto he would put on 'the biggest and richest fight of all time that would put his country, all Africa, on the world map'. King would also produce a three-day jazz festival, and entertainers including Stevie Wonder, Ray Charles, Aretha Franklin, BB King and James Brown had already signed up. There would be revelry all over the place. Mobuto would back the whole thing financially.

'I understood that King, Mobuto and their associates worked around the clock to get everything in working order,' recalled Foreman. 'A new runway was built so that jumbo jets could land. The stadium was cleaned up and lights were put on top of it. I learned that an asphalt parking lot was constructed in the midst of thick green foliage. A special bar was built for the media and system for the TV signal was set up. All seemed ready for the "Rumble In The Jungle".'

Suddenly, disaster. On 15 September, nine days before the scheduled fight date, Foreman was sparring with Bill McMurray, a 33-year-old journeyman heavyweight and part-time truck driver who had lost almost half of his 75 fights. McMurray raised his elbow to protect his face and Foreman's right eyebrow accidentally collided with the bone of the elbow. A gash over the eye immediately began to drip blood and George grabbed a towel, pressing it against the slice on his skin. The freak accident caused the fight to be postponed, a major setback particularly for those who had a large financial interest in the event.

'The new date was 30 October. The injury had cleared but by then I was miserable, not least because of the food. My cook and long-time friend Tyree Lyons scoured Kinshasa for edible chow and found little. I really missed my cheeseburgers. Even my first quarters were an old army barracks infested with rats, lizards and insects. They were surrounded by cyclone fencing and barbed wire and inhabited by rowdy soldiers. Finally I found a suite at the Intercontinental Hotel but I was worried about somebody coming in and messing with me so I hired guards to keep a 24-hour watch outside the room.

'This was clearly Muhammad Ali country. Sentiment in his favour coloured how everyone looked at me. Most people wanted him to win back the title. I realised that I couldn't win whatever happened. If I knocked him out, I would get grudging respect for beating a legend. If I lost, there would be a big crowd at the railway station, jeering me back to Palookaville. It really was a no-win situation.'

Ali may have been the sentimental favourite but the hard money was on Foreman, with the betting 3/1 on him to hold on to his title. After all, George had won all his 44 professional fights, only three going the scheduled distance. He looked unbeatable, with a jackhammer punch in both gloves. Ali had 44 wins and two losses, 31 by the short route, but he had only been able to finish off one of his last six opponents. Ali was 32 and Foreman 26, an age difference which could be an important factor the longer the fight went.

A fanfare of African music, including the Zaire national anthem, had heralded the arrival of Ali into the ring, his right hand extended above his head and encouraging the crowd of 70,000 to cheer and keep cheering. Foreman stood in his corner looking sombre with his handlers.

Seconds before the opening bell, Zack Clayton, refereeing his third world heavyweight title fight, called both men to the centre of the ring for instructions. Ali talked over the referee's words, saying to Foreman, 'You have heard of me since you were young. You've been following me since you were a little boy. Now you must meet me, your master.' It was a brilliant psychological stroke and would give Ali a mind advantage. Foreman ignored the taunts and kept staring at Ali eye to eye.

'Ali's plan apparently was to keep moving, not swaying back and he had done against Sonny Liston when he won the title but moving from side to side,' remembered George. 'He wasn't hitting me hard in that first round but more or less flicking jabs at me, perhaps sounding me out on the advice of his cornermen, trainer Angelo Dundee, his man-of-all-jobs Bundini Brown and his doctor Ferdie Pacheco. They were all good boxing men but the most important thing was what would happen in the ring itself, not in the corner.

'In the second, third and fourth rounds I had let go a torrent of heavy punches and while most of them connected, Ali was still on his feet, moving and jabbing and hooking. I could hear Brown shouting "Dance man, dance" and I heard later that Dundee kept warning Ali to stay off the ropes but Ali ignored him saying, "Shut up, I known what I'm doing." This tactic became known as his "rope-a-dope". Apparently one of the top ropes was loose which allowed Ali to lean way out of the ring. Whether the loose rope was by accident or design I don't know. Nobody checks the ropes before a fight, do they? You just want that bell to ring and get down to business.

'By the fifth round I was beginning to feel exhausted but my trainer Archie Moore, the former light-heavyweight champion of the world, and my manager Dick Sadler told me to keep punching and that I'd get to Ali. I was now beginning to wonder. My punches, no matter how hard I threw them, were connecting but he was still on his feet. What was I to think? Was my corner telling me that I would eventually catch him and put him down just to boost my confidence? Did they secretly know that the writing was on the wall for me? I don't know.

'Every time I did hit Ali he would cover up, fire a jab and move away. He seemed to be putting his punches together better now, mixing them up by jabbing, hooking and uppercutting. However, my corner told me I was ahead on points and that was somewhat encouraging I guess. Maybe I would land the big one. But when? Just when? I connected with some good shots in the seventh but they were not hard or solid enough to drop him. I could hear Dundee yelling when Ali lay back on the ropes and letting me attack him, "Not too far back, Muhammad, or you'll fall out of the ring."

'In the eighth I beckoned Ali to come to me. I dropped my hands to see if he would come into my web but he was still on the move. I did nab him on the ropes and started pounded him with whatever strength I had remaining in my tired body. We got tangled up a bit and as I was extricating myself I leaned forward to get a good shot at him when he fired a fast, hard left-right combination to my chin and jaw and I went down awkwardly as I had been a bit off balance. I was not all that hurt and I decided to stay down and get up at eight.

'I kept a watch on Clayton's count…six, seven…and Sadler in my corner motioned me to get up. It seemed all of a sudden he counted nine, ten and waved his hands wide. It was all over and I was no longer champion of the world. It seemed a quick count but to be fair maybe it wasn't. It just seemed quick to me, that's all. There was talk after the fight that the drinking water in my corner was medicinal and it did taste very strange.

'Sugar Ray Robinson watched the fight back in the States and he was quoted as saying that I seemed drugged. Jim Murray, the reporter, said I fought like "a drunk trying to find a keyhole". Who knows? The facts were that boxing had a new heavyweight champion and I was in Palookaville. I really felt bad, down in the dumps. As for Ali, he had said bad things about me but I felt he was a real gentleman and still is. The bad-mouthing was all for publicity. That was his way of doing things. Nothing more.

'I used to hate talking about the fight but no more. I was sure I was going to beat him. When he put me down I should have been able to jump up. I would wake up at night for years, sweating, thinking I should have gotten up. I think I could have beaten the count. I'm not saying I could have won but I could have continued and you never know what could have happened then. But there you are. You should have done this. You should have done that. It's all history now.

'The defeat did hurt me for a long time, though, because I was devastated. When you're the heavyweight champion of the world and you lose the title, it's not really the fight you lose, it's yourself. He certainly tricked me that night with his rope-a-dope tactics, laying on the ropes and letting me punch myself out. I guess it just wasn't my night.

'You get to a point when you think you're invincible. I kept on winning, winning, winning then I lost in Zaire. It really devastated me. It changed my life. One day people are walking by you and afraid to even ask you a question, and the next day they are patting you on the back with pity. It's funny, you know. I have achieved great things as a boxer but the world chooses what it wants to remember. Look at the great plays Shakespeare wrote, but most people only ever remember *Hamlet* and *Romeo and Juliet*.

'That fight in Africa is what most people want to remember and you shouldn't ride against that. It's an important part of boxing history but it's all in the past now. I would still achieve great things in boxing. As for Ali, I've seen quite a lot of him since and we've come great friends over the years. Although he has Parkinson's, he still has great days.'

Ring magazine headlined its story in the following month's issue, 'Ali outfought, outlasted and outwitted Foreman in a classic upset.' Nat Loubet, who took over the editorship on the death of Nat Fleischer in 1972, wrote, 'The consensus was that Ali would slow down after five rounds or so of body punching by Foreman and then would be caught up with it and quickly destroyed. It didn't work out quite like that, with a crashing left hook followed by a solid right cross finishing the fight.

'The fight was a slugfest, a real pier six bangaroo and one of the better heavyweight fights from the standpoint of action. Of the two, Foreman was the more tired. Ali took all Foreman could deliver, and although he looked tired he never went down. Foreman lost steam in his punches and became an open target for the eighth round, a turn of events that spewed forth a flurry of Ali punches that decided the situation, ending all speculation.'

The definitive work on the fight would be by the acclaimed author Norman Mailer who wrote a superb book in 1975 about it. Simply called *The Fight*, the work is now something of a collector's item and this writer is very fortunate in having the book in his library. Graphically describing Foreman pursuing Ali throughout the fight 'like a man chasing a cat', Mailer wrote of that defining eighth round, 'A big projectile the size of a fist in a glove drove into the middle of Foreman's mind, the best punch of the startled night, the blow Ali saved for a career. Foreman's arms flew out to the side like a man with a parachute jumping out of a plane.

'All the while his eyes were on Ali and he looked up with no anger as if Ali, indeed, was the man he knew best and would see him on his dying day. Foreman started to tumble and topple and went down in sections. The referee took Ali to a corner and Foreman, like a drunk hoping to get out of bed and go to work, rolled over. Whether he heard the count or not, he was on his feet a fraction after the count of ten and whipped. Back in America everybody was yelling that the fight was fixed. Yes. So was Rembrandt's *The Night Watch* and Joyce's *Portrait of the Artist as a Young Man*.'

Boxing followers were first alerted to the prowess of Foreman when he won the gold medal at the 1968 Olympics in Mexico City. These were the Games in which two American athletes, Tommie Smith and John Carlos, staged 'black power' demonstrations when they went up on the rostrum at the medal ceremonies. As they turned to face the flag and hear the national anthem, they each raised a black-gloved fist in the most overtly political statement in the history of the Games. Foreman got himself noticed on the rostrum later with a patriotic waving of a small Stars and Stripes and instantly became a national hero.

The fifth of seven children of a railroad worker, Foreman was born in Marshall, Texas and moved to Houston while still a young child. The Foremans were poor with barely enough food to go around. Young George did not do too well in school and dropped out as soon as he could. Getting himself involved in a group of wayward youths like himself in the deprived Fifth Ward district where crime was a way of life, it was not long before he got into trouble with the police over robberies, muggings and the like.

'You could say I lived on the wild side in those early days, and I certainly did,' he recalled. 'I was never really out of trouble. You name it, I did it, and it was all around me in Fifth Ward where I became well known to the neighbourhood kids and the cops. One week I smashed about 200 windows and never got caught. I went back the next day to break more glass. Our district was full of baddies – ex-cons, dope addicts, thieves, criminals of just about every description you can think of.

'I was heading down that path, and fast, until the day I saw one of my pro football heroes, Jim Brown of the Cleveland Browns, talking abut the Jobs Corps. This program, administered by the Department of Labor was established by President Lyndon B. Johnson and offers free education and academic training to youths between 16 and 24, improving the quality of their lives. I was impressed and promised to do something about joining up. I forgot about it then but it was always at the back of my mind. I certainly wasn't happy with the way my life was taking me.

'A little while later while I was watching sports on the wall television in the pool hall with several members of the gang, I got into conversation with one guy. He told me he was once a down-and-outer himself, rarely came into the hall now and had just joined the Jobs Corps where he was learning a trade which would lead to a job. He said he was finally doing something constructive instead of always getting into trouble with the police. "Why don't you give it a try, George?" he said. "You've nothing to lose, have you?" That did it. The next day I went down and signed up. Jobs Corps turned my life around and I never looked back.

'Besides learning a trade, there was some money in it too, $30 a month and they would put $50 in the bank for me as well as sending some to my mother. The Jobs Corps would take me out of the jungle I was in. However, though I liked the Jobs Corps I still found that I was struggling with my temper and often got into fights. Nevertheless, after six months, I got myself a qualification as an electronics engineer. I also learned Latin and was introduced to history and anthropology.

I graduated to their parks unit in Pleasanton, California where they had first-rate physical education facilities including a bona fide boxing programme.'

Foreman came under the tutelage of Charles Broadus, the recreational instructor. Everybody called him Doc Broadus. He turned George over to the boxing instructor James Jackson and together they steered George on the road that would lead to Olympic fame and the heavyweight championship of the world. Jackson had been a middleweight boxer himself while in the army and he had 18 amateur bouts and five professional contests before joining the Jobs Corps.

Jackson could see that Foreman had power but boxing was more than knocking people down and out. There were the basic boxing skills, how to jab, hook, uppercut, move around, keep your chin out of the way of the opponent's punches and generally look after yourself in the ring. Foreman learned fast and under Jackson's expert guidance he had his first amateur bout, an impressive win, in February 1967. Twenty months later he qualified as the US heavyweight in the 1968 Mexico Olympics after winning the trials, and won the gold medal by knocking out Russia's formidable Iones Cepulis in the second round.

Offers from all over America, and a number from abroad, came for Foreman to turn professional but he decided to wait and get the best deal possible. After all, it wasn't every day that an Olympic gold medallist in the heavyweight division, especially a talented American, was knocking around weighing up his options. He boxed several exhibitions, cashing in on his Mexico success and both trained and sparred with the brooding Sonny Liston, who had lost his world heavyweight championship to Muhammad Ali a few short years earlier. Foreman wanted to get the feel of mixing with the professionals.

'I liked Sonny, a real good guy who just got the wrong end of the stick,' said George. 'He was a far better fighter than he ever got credit for. Most people remember him for the two fights with Muhammad Ali, which he lost as you know in controversial circumstances. But it must not be forgotten that he had some good wins too. Outside of knocking out Floyd Patterson in the first round in both of their fights, he walloped some top contenders on the way up, like finishing off Cleveland Williams, the "Big Cat", in three rounds and then in two and Zora Folley in three. Sonny never shook off the cloak of the ex-con. A great pity.'

It was while working out with Liston that Foreman got to know Sonny's trainer Dick Sadler, a former vaudeville song-and-dance man. Impressed with George's power, Sadler forecast that the Olympic champion would make progress in the pro game and became his manager. Sadler brought in Archie Moore, the former world light-heavyweight champion and heavyweight challenger as one of the trainers. When Ancient Archie, as he was known, saw Foreman in the gym, he exclaimed, 'My, God bless the puncher. There is a lot to be smoothened out but with his power he can go all the way to the stars, and let me tell you, it will be stars his opponents will be seeing. Mark my words.'

With an amateur record of 22 wins and four losses behind him, Foreman finally made his debut in the paid ranks in June 1969 when he stopped Donald Waldheim in the third round at Madison Square Garden on a card headlined by Joe Frazier's world heavyweight title defence against Jerry Quarry which 'Smokin' Joe' won in seven rounds. By the time Foreman had run his winning streak to 32 wins, 29 by either count-outs or stoppages, he was ranked the number one contender by the World Boxing Association and the World Boxing Council. He clinched the Frazier fight for 22 January 1973 in Kingston, Jamaica.

Let it be said that if anybody ever mentioned putting on a world heavyweight championship fight between two leading Americans in Jamaica, one of the world's top tourist attractions and a land normally associated with long, white beaches, high mountains and lush countryside they would have been laughed out of town, city and even country. But Lucien Chen, a hugely successful businessman and advisor to the Jamaican government, said he would put together a consortium, lodge guarantees of $850,000 for Frazier and $375,000 for Foreman in a Canadian bank and put it all together.

The fight was billed the 'Sunshine Showdown' and took place at the Kingston Stadium, a venue normally used for football and cycling. Both boxers were unbeaten, Frazier with 29 wins and Foreman 37. Both were former Olympic champions and both were hard hitters. Foreman entered the ring as a 3/1 underdog. This was how George remembered the fight, 'I was determined to make the most of my big chance, my golden opportunity, a once in a lifetime gamble. Frazier came in fast and threw a looping left hook, the punch that had sent Ali sprawling on his back in their first fight. But I took it on the arm.

'I found I could reach Frazier with long left jabs and in the second round I started to bring my big right uppercut into play. Boom! I connected solidly with his chin and he went to the canvas. I read later that Howard Cossell made the memorable call in his ABC television broadcast, "Down goes Frazier! Down goes Frazier! Down goes Frazier!" He got up, very unsteady as you can imagine and I knocked him down a third time before the end of the round.

'I was now within striking distance of my goal, the heavyweight championship of the world. A right to the jaw in the second round put him down for the fourth time. I glanced at Frazier's corner and indicated that his second should throw in the towel as their man was finished but there was no response. Another right and he was down for the fifth time and again he climbed to his feet. You would have to give Frazier full credit for gameness. I fired another big right and this one lifted him off his feet before he hit the canvas. Referee Arthur Merchant finally intervened. It was all over, with the round having gone 1.35.'

Referee Mercante would later defend his decision not to intervene sooner when Frazier looked to have no chance of victory, 'Tradition calls for giving the champion every chance, a point I honoured although never at the expense of the fighter's personal safety. Even after the fifth knockdown Frazier was still lucid, still ready to fight, still throwing punches back, or at least trying to. At moments like this, every referee walks a tightrope. In a split second a referee must rely on his own judgement. I decided to let it continue, although I felt Frazier's fate was sealed. After Foreman put him down for the sixth time I waved my arms and embraced Joe. It was all over.'

After losing his title to Ali in October 1974, little was heard of Foreman except for his participation in an unusual exhibition bout of 12 total rounds against five different opponents in Toronto in April 1975. Boxing fans figured that he had retired. In 1976, however, he announced a comeback with the avowed intention of winning back his title, which was still in the hands of Ali. His first opponent was the hard-hitting Ron Lyle at Caesars Palace casino in Las Vegas in January. In the fourth round Lyle knocked Foreman down with a fast left-right combination but he got up before Lyle floored him for the second time. George pummelled his rival with a furious attack in the fifth and knocked him out. *Ring* magazine would name it Fight of the Year.

'I wanted to keep active and keep on track for another heavyweight championship fight,' he said. 'I felt I could win back the title if I'd get another shot. I'd made mistakes, big mistakes, against Ali and I knew I wouldn't make them again. There was an offer of a rematch with the former champion Joe Frazier and I figured I'd take it. The match was set for the Nassau Coliseum in Uniondale, New York on 15 June 1976 and a crowd of over 10,000 turned out. Jerry Perenchio, the promoter, offered me a million bucks plus a percentage of the closed circuit and I told him, "Okay, but I'm not fighting Frazier for the money."

'I had heard it on good authority that Ali was planning to retire in three months after fighting Ken Norton and my team figured that if I beat Frazier convincingly he would postpone retirement because the public would demand that he fight me to prove the first victory wasn't a fluke. Ali was a proud man and he wouldn't risk speculation that he was afraid to meet a rejuvenated George Foreman. No way.'

Because of the one-sided victory for Foreman in the first fight three years earlier and the fact that Frazier had taken a shellacking from Ali, the one Ali dubbed the 'Thrilla in Manila' three years earlier, few expected Frazier to win. Joe at this point had 32 wins and three losses while George was on 41 victories and one loss. Surprisingly the return fight was fairly competitive for its duration, with many surprised at Frazier's good form. His quick head movements make Foreman miss with his heaviest punches.

Frazier was wearing a contact lens for his vision but it was knocked loose in one of the early rounds. After being unable to mount a significant offence, however, Frazier was dropped in the fifth round from a flurry of punches. Referee Harold Valan gave him a count of four but he took the regulation eight seconds. Foreman dropped him again immediately after with another combination and this time he stayed down until eight.

'When Frazier got up he was on shaky legs and I knew the end was near. His eyes were glassy and he had a deep cut on his forehead. Leaning on the mat, his trainer Eddie Futch tried to attract the referee's attention. Before I could deliver what I knew would be the final blow, the referee saw Futch and waved his arms about to signal the end. That was his last fight. Afterwards he announced he was through with boxing, although like the experience of so many ex-champions, his retirement didn't stick. Five years later he made a comeback but for just one fight, which ended in a draw. He never fought again.'

Foreman had shown he was ready to take on Ali again but Muhammad was not showing any great urge for a return fight. Jerry Perenchio, who had promoted the second Foreman–Frazier fight, approached Ali with what he called 'a substantial offer' but to no avail. Perenchio gradually drifted out of boxing after that. Don King, who had made his name with the Ali–Foreman fight in 1974, also contacted Ali but there was no response to his offers. Foreman won his next three fights to remain as the number one contender for the title but came unstuck against the skilful, shifty Jimmy Young in San Juan, Puerto Rico and dropped the decision after 12 rounds.

Foreman claims he had a meeting with 'Jesus Christ himself' while lying exhausted on the rubbing table in his dressing room after the fight. 'He was talking to me, telling me to carry on and don't give up on any account,' George recalled. 'He told me to always come to him and that he was there for me always. That was the moment my life changed, forever. Up to then I had been floundering back into a life of sin and I was given the sense and the strength to save myself. I decided at that moment to devote the rest of my life to the word of the Lord and I have since used my God-given gifts as a boxer to help spread my belief. The answers for all of us are right there in the good ol' Bible.'

On Foreman's return to Houston, he opened the Church of the Lord Jesus Christ in a poor section of the city and became a minister and a devout family man, with ten children, calling them after himself, George I, George II, George III and so on. He also started the George Foreman Youth Centre for underprivileged children. After nearly a decade out of the ring, however, the lure of the fight game became too much and he announced a comeback at the age of 38 in 1987, claiming to be motivated by his church running dry of funds.

At first his talk of a return, widely reported in the media, was treated as something of a joke and the gregarious George had the grace to laugh along. He joked about his age, weight and love of cheeseburgers, and made himself a darling of the media and became attractive to fans in a way that he never was as champion. Gone was the surly George of the past. This was the new George with the big smile.

'I made sure, though, that I worked out regularly in the gym and kept myself in good shape,' Foreman recollected. 'I felt I still had it to get back on top and all I needed was the chance to prove it. If I failed, then at least I had the satisfaction of trying and nobody could condemn me for that. Also, and very importantly, I had God in my corner and that meant everything to me.'

After ten years out of the ring to the very month, more than 30lb heavier than in his championship days and at the advanced age of 38, Foreman made his comeback on 9 March 1987, stopping one Steve Zouski in four rounds in Sacramento, California. His shaven head gave him a menacing appearance that was totally against the image he had fashioned outside the ring as a preacher spreading the word of God. To the amazement of his critics, Foreman won his next 23 fights before dropping a decision to Evander Holyfield in a world heavyweight title challenge on 19 April 1991.

'The verdict was close but unanimous but I still felt I should have gotten it,' he recalled. 'I often had him in trouble with hard rights and sharp left jabs. I staggered him in the 12th round and I thought he was going down but he grabbed me and held on. I didn't manage to get another clean shot at him before the bell rang and Holyfield was announced as the winner. I felt I had let down everybody, my family, my church, my fans and I asked Jesse Jackson in my corner what would I say to the press in the dressing room. He told me to tell them that we didn't retreat and we kept our dignity. I did that and I felt happy. I'd done my best and kept my dignity. What more can you do?'

After three more wins, Foreman came unstuck again when he was outpointed by Tommy Morrison on 7 June 1993. George was in a state of semi-retirement for the next year, keeping busy with boxing commentaries for the Home Box Office entertainment network, known as HBO, when an offer came for him to fight the competent Michael Moorer in a heavyweight championship fight. Moorer had taken the title from Evander Holyfield to become the first southpaw to win the title and was confident he would outbox, outfight and outlast 'the ancient warrior'. After all, he was a mere 27 and Foreman had just passed his 45th birthday.

They came together at the MGM Grand Garden on 5 November 1994 before a crowd of 12,120. Foreman shocked Moorer, not to mention the fans, reporters and millions watching on television by sensationally knocking out the champion in the tenth round after being well behind on points in one of the biggest upsets in modern ring history. Wearing the same trunks he had worn when losing the title to Ali 20 years before, Foreman landed a looping right to Moorer's jaw and the champion hit the floor on his back with arms outstretched in the classic eagle pose.

Moorer pushed himself up on all fours and tried to lift himself up to beat referee Joe Cortez's count but he couldn't make it. It was all over after two minutes and three seconds of round ten and George Foreman was once again champion of the world. Thus, at 45 he became the oldest man ever to win the heavyweight title, beating the previous record held by Jersey Joe Walcott who was 37 when he knocked out Ezzard Charles in 1951.

'The win over Moorer was the greatest achievement of my career,' Foreman remembered. 'I've had great thrills, the first time I won the title, against Joe Frazier in 1973, and winning the gold medal in the Olympics of 1968 but nothing could ever match the win over Moorer. I know the scorecards had me behind on points going into that tenth round but I was always confident I would catch him. I saw the opening I had been waiting for in the tenth and fired a left jab followed straight away with a short right from the hip.

'He went down but I knew even before the count that he wasn't going to get up. Eight, nine, ten and it was all over. I knelt in my corner and thanked Jesus for giving me the strength, the courage and the will to do it. He had never let me down and he didn't this time either. There was mayhem in the ring, and out in the auditorium everybody seemed joyous, happy. That was good. They felt good. I felt good. It was the greatest moment of my life.'

'This was a triumph for the 6ft 4in grandfather from Houston, for all men and women of his generation, for promoter Bob Arum and for all those involved in the big Texan's miraculous comeback,' wrote Claude Abrams at ringside for *Boxing News*. Describing the knockout, he recorded, 'The arena erupted with the shock finish. My jaw dropped open, my eyes fixed in disbelief as the champion barely moved and the referee counted. Moorer made an attempt to rise but when Cortez spread his arms, Moorer was still on his knees.'

Shortly after the Moorer bout, Foreman began talking about a potential superfight against Mike Tyson, who had been the youngest ever world heavyweight champion. The World Boxing Association, however, demanded that George face his number one challenger, the ageing Tony Tucker. When Foreman ignored the WBA, they stripped him of the title. George shrugged his broad shoulders and carried on with his career. The Tyson fight never materialised. Foreman won three more fights but after losing a controversial decision to Shannon Briggs on 22 November 1997 he retired for good, at the age of 48.

Foreman nevertheless planned to have 'definitely and conclusively one last fight', against former champion Larry Holmes at the Houston Astrodome in 1999. It would be billed as the 'Birthday Bash' with George set to make $10m and Holmes $4m. Nothing ever came of it. In February 2004 Foreman was reportedly training for one more comeback fight to demonstrate that the age of 55, like 40, is not a 'death sentence'. But like the proposed Tyson fight, it never happened. Having severed his relationship with HBO to pursue other opportunities, Foreman and the sport of boxing finally went their separate ways.

'I've no regrets,' he said. 'I had a good run and made good money. I had two terms as heavyweight champion of the world and won a gold medal in the Olympics. I have a loving family and God is still in my corner. I ask you, Thomas, what more could any man ask for?'

3

Rocky Marciano

Suzy Q and the little man with the bowler hat

I T was a typical day at Stillman's Gym on the West Side of Manhattan's Eighth Avenue between 54th and 55th Streets. The place was crowded as usual with boxers and managers and trainers and hangers-on and just ordinary fans wanting to watch the fighters going through their paces. Lou Stillman had opened the permanently smoke-filled gym back in the 1920s and everybody going back to Jack Dempsey and Benny Leonard trained there.

It was now late September 1948 and prominent at Stillman's on this day was little Charlie Goldman, the trainer. Charlie was born in Poland and moved to New York where he settled in the tough Red Hook district of Brooklyn. Charlie reckoned he had more than 400 fights as a bantamweight before he packed it in and became a coach. He stood just 5ft 1in and had two broken hands and a nose that obviously had taken too many punches. He had trained four world champions and hundreds of others.

'How are you making out with that fighter from Brockton, Charlie?' he was asked by a boxing writer. 'Oh, he's had a few fights but he's just a beginner,' Charlie said, adjusting the familiar bowler hat he always wore, often in the ring. 'I often have him at the CYO Gym in 17th Street but I prefer him at Stillman's here because he gets better spars. Mind you, he looks so crude that people often laugh and tell me to my face that I'm out of my mind to be looking after him.' Goldman reflected for a moment, thinking about Rocky. 'You know, he scares me too,' he said finally. 'I mean, he does so many things wrong, but I'm scared to change him much because, trying to give him something else, I might take away what he's got.'

Goldman never did take away what the newcomer had. Carefully he moulded him into the only boxer to retire as heavyweight champion of the world without ever losing, or even boxing a draw. Rocco Francis Marchegiano, the son of a poor immigrant Italian shoemaker and his wife who settled in Brockton, Massachusetts, swept through all his 49 fights, winning 43 either by count-outs or merciful referees intervening, and became Rocky Marciano, the most formidable heavyweight of his era and one of the greatest of all time.

The 'Brockton Blockbuster', as he came to be known, was impossible to discourage. The harder he was hit, and he was hit often, the more he would storm back with his wade-in swarming style and land with harder blows.

Ferdie Pacheco, the revered 'Fight Doctor' long associated with Muhammad Ali and regarded as one of boxing's most distinguished analysts, recalled, 'Rocky was one of those people who didn't really care how much he got hit, so jabbing him was easy. He was probably the greatest example of a guy who is a battering ram and is willing to get in and take any kind of punishment to deliver his own. And what a killing puncher.

'I believe Rocky owed his strength not to his father who was small and almost puny but to his mother, a formidable lady. Rocky developed from a chubby toddler into the toughest kid on the block. The message on the streets of Brockton was, "Don't get into a fight with the Marchegiano kid or you'll come out second best." That's how it was.'

I had the good fortune in May 1966 to interview Marciano in George Raft's Colony Club in London where the retired champion was a guest of the Hollywood star. It was the day before Ali was due to defend his heavyweight title in a return fight with the local hope Henry Cooper, which Muhammad would win on a stoppage in six rounds. 'You needn't ask me if I'm planning a comeback and taking on Ali after being in retirement for over ten years,' Rocky joked. 'All the fighting is well behind me now, Thomas.'

Did he always want to be a boxer? 'To be honest I was very disappointed that I never became a professional baseball player,' he said. 'I loved baseball and still do. I idolised many of the great players. The nearest I got was to attract the attention of a Chicago Cubs scout and actually got a try-out with one of their nursery clubs in the city. But I never made it, largely because I had thrown my right arm out of joint.

'Still, it hurt my pride so such that I had to admit defeat to my folks back home but there you are. That's life. But I think failure only made me more determined to be good at some other sport, to make something of myself, particularly for my folks who were so good to me all the way.

'My dad was invalided out of the US Army during the First World War after being gassed in the trenches, and because of his poor health he was not able to hold down a job. I wanted to be in a position one day to have enough money so that he could retire and he and momma could live in a nice house, with no financial worries. Luckily I was able to do that when I got into the big money in boxing.

'I think that pride and determination were perhaps the two things which did more than anything else to bring me to the top of the boxing world and keep me there. I was always determined. If one of my opponents chopped me in half, both halves would get up fighting.'

Rocky recalled that he took his first steps into boxing when he was about nine years of age. His uncle John rigged up a punchbag in the cellar of the Marciano home. 'I enjoyed punching the bag. I remember about that time that I once went home crying because I'd been popped on the nose by another kid,' he said. 'After that, momma used to send one of my sisters with me when I went to the store but after a few weeks on the punchbag I found I could hit hard and the other kids would leave me alone.'

Rocky was inducted into the US Army when he was 20 and spent eight months in Britain. It was in a bar in the Welsh city of Swansea in 1944 that he threw his first punch in anger. He overheard a big Australian soldier making insulting remarks about the US. Eyewitnesses claimed that Rocky's fists were just a blur as they powered into the unfortunate soldier, sending him backwards over a table which crumbled under his weight. He was out to the world. It was to become a common sight, but under slightly more controlled circumstances.

'I had a few amateur fights in the army and when I came out I went on to win top honours in a New England Golden Gloves tournament,' he remembered. 'Deep down, though, I had the notion to become a professional and I was determined to give it a try. I was digging ditches for the local council at the time for 90 cents an hour.

'A buddy from my army days, Allie Colombo, was a boxing trainer in Brockton and he wrote a letter to Charlie Goldman who trained fighters at the CYO gym and Stillman's in New York City. Allie told Goldman he would like Charlie to train him. Charlie wrote back and said I should come to New York and he would see what I'd got.'

Goldman recalled, 'Boy, Rocky was crude. He would need a helluva lot of tutoring, and at 25 he was a bit old to be starting out on a boxing career. Boxing is a young man's game. Most great fighters started in their teens. I also thought his reach of 68 inches, outstretched from fingertip to fingertip, was abnormally short for a heavyweight. But I saw some potential in him even so and I took him under my care. Colombo also said in his letter that he wanted Al Weill to manage him. Weill was a French immigrant and at the time was matchmaker for Madison Square Garden.

'Weill was a very influential guy and had managed three world champions and other top guys. I arranged for Weill to have a look at Rocky, and while Weill told me later that he was not too impressed with him, he reckoned Rocky's raw power could be channelled into a good fighter, maybe even a world champion.'

Marciano remembered, 'Charlie was very patient with me. He would tell boxing writers later that there was no point in trying to turn me into a fancy boxer, with my lack of balance and short arms. He would work on my strong point, which was power. He got me to shorten my punches to get the maximum benefits from them.

'Here's something many people don't know, a bit of a scoop if you like. Charlie said I also threw a lot of punches off balance so he used to tie my legs together with a piece of string about 18 inches long and got me to punch. He said too that I exposed the sides of my body too much so he made me keep my arms together with a newspaper under one arm and then the other arm to make sure I kept my elbows in close. Goldman later called my right hand my Suzy Q and the newspapermen picked up on it. I kinda liked it myself. It gave me a sort of identity.'

Rocky made his professional debut on 17 March 1947, St Patrick's Day, with a third-round knockout win over Lee Epperson in Holyoke, Massachusetts. With Goldman and Colombo in charge of his training, and Weill looking after the business as manager and matchmaker, Marciano made steady progress. In his first 20 fights, only one went the scheduled distance when the Canadian Dom Mogard was still on his feet at the end of the tenth round on 23 May 1949.

Marciano went another 18 fights without defeat, with only four lasting the full ten-round distance before his biggest test to date, a bout with the talented New York contender also of Italian origin, Roland LaStarza, in Madison Square Garden on 24 March 1950. A much more skilful boxer than Rocky and with a longer reach, LaStarza, a college graduate, survived the ten rounds only to lose a controversial split decision in front of a crowd of 13,658 who paid $53,723, the second-largest gate of the year at the New York venue. Both thought they had won, but many observers felt LaStarza was too cautious and that Marciano deserved it on his aggression.

One judge had Marciano winning five rounds to four with one even and the other judge had similar markings for LaStarza. Referee Jack Watson had it level at 5-5 but gave it to Marciano on the count-back system later used in amateur boxing. 'LaStarza claimed he was robbed, I guess like most boxers who lose split decisions,' said Rocky. 'Okay, it was close but I did most of the punching. I knew I had to keep the pressure on him all the time as he was a good boxer who kept on the move. It was my most important win to date and my team felt there and then that I could go on to win the heavyweight title.'

LaStarza remembered, 'It was the closest split decision there ever was. But for those points I could have gone on to become heavyweight champion of the world instead of Marciano. I punched him around in the last two rounds and I felt that if I had started that way earlier I could have knocked him out.

'I would be lying if I said that Marciano wasn't one of my toughest fights but what's the good of lying? He knocked me down, sure, in the fourth round and I didn't know anything at all about the punch until I felt myself on the canvas and the referee was shouting "five". But I got up and went all the way with him but there you are, I lost, unfairly I felt.'

Rocky was disappointed in his own performance but Goldman said later, 'I knew Rocky was going to be a champion by the way he handled LaStarza, a clever boxer. It was close but all the effective punching came from Rocky.'

The fight that convinced Marciano's team that they had a future heavyweight champion of the world on their hands was when Rocky defeated the formidable contender Rex Layne, a big country boy from Utah who had outpunched most of his opponents by sheer power. They met at Madison Square Garden on 12 July 1951. With an eight-inch reach advantage, Layne had lost only one of his 36 fights, a decision he subsequently reversed. Word around boxing circles was that the winner would get an early shot at Ezzard Charles's world heavyweight title once the 'Cincinnati Flash' had defended his title against old foe Jersey Joe Walcott in Pittsburgh scheduled for six days later.

Marciano was a 9/5 underdog against Layne but Weill and Goldman felt their man could pull off a shock win. A few days before the fight Rocky was accused of being anti-social because he declined to shake hands with Layne at a press conference. 'Looking back now, it wasn't because I was anti-social or indulging in bad manners, of course not, but I felt it was time enough to touch gloves with him in the ring and that would be soon enough for me,' he remembered. 'I had been introduced to opponents like that before and every time they told me their hard-luck stories – about their lack of money, about a family sickness, that sort of thing. I'm sure that went close to affecting me in the ring, although it never did, thankfully.

'So if I appeared to be rude before the Layne fight, all I was doing was making sure that nobody sold me a line of sob talk. If my opponent wanted to say something to me, then he could do so when the referee called us together just before the bell. When boxing is your business, you have to be that way because I'm a peace-loving guy but in the end you have to be quite ruthless about the men you have to face in the ring.'

Layne had the best of the early rounds but in the sixth Rocky, fighting out of a deep crouch taught to him by Goldman, unleashed a sledgehammer right 'that severed Layne's front teeth off at the gums', according to one of Rex's handlers. Layne crumbled and pitched forward like a slaughtered steer on to his knees, his right arm braced stiffly against the floor. Then he collapsed and lay motionless, his head resting on the canvas as he was counted out. It was the first knockout Layne had suffered in his career.

'Yes, it was a good win, particularly nobody outside my camp thought I could pull it off,' Marciano recalled. 'Mark Conn, the referee, later told me that my finishing punch was the best executed one he had seen for a long time. That was encouraging. Weill right away started talking to Jim Norris of the promotional organisation, the International Boxing Club, known as the IBC, about a challenge to Ezzard Charles for the world heavyweight title but six days after the Layne fight, Charles surprisingly lost his title when he was knocked out in the seventh round by the veteran contender Jersey Joe Walcott. Joe was 37 and the oldest man to win the crown.'

A return fight clause meant that Jersey Joe was committed to honour it, even though it would be nearly a full year before it would take place. Meanwhile, the former great, Joe Louis, was on a successful comeback in a bid to become the first man in history to recapture the world heavyweight title, a feat that had eluded legendary figures like Gentleman Jim Corbett, Bob Fitzsimmons, James J. Jeffries and Jack Dempsey.

The old 'Brown Bomber' was still a formidable contender and had won all his eight fights, including an impressive sixth round knockout over crafty, tough Lee Savold. Louis was now nearing a championship fight and Marciano stood in the way. They met in Madison Square Garden on 26 October 1951, and Marciano entered the ring with 37 consecutive wins, all but five without the aid of referees' or judges' scorecards. In the past, Louis had defended his world heavyweight title an unprecedented 25 times in 11 years and had won 72 of his 74 fights. While Louis certainly had the edge on experience, on Marciano's side was youth, an important factor. Rocky was 28, Joe 37.

'I can tell you now Thomas that I never wanted to fight Louis,' said Rocky. 'I told this to Weill and Goldman several times but they kept saying that a win would take me nearer a fight for the heavyweight title. I remember saying to Goldman in the gym after the Louis fight was announced, "Charlie, this is the last guy on earth I want to fight. For God's sake, he's been my idol for as long as I can remember."

'Charlie replied, "It's okay Rocky, that's boxing. Sometimes you have to fight the guys you admire. Remember when Sugar Ray Robinson was on the way up? He had to fight his idol Henry Armstrong, the only man to hold three world titles at the same time, a legend in boxing. But Ray fought him and beat him. Sometimes you gotta do what you don't like doing but you do it. Joe understands." I just nodded but I still didn't like it.'

From the outset it was boxer Louis against slugger Marciano. The 'Brown Bomber' against the 'Brockton Blockbuster'.

Louis was scoring with his stinging left jabs and Rocky's nose bled like a tap. After four rounds Joe was ahead on points as he simply couldn't miss the lumbering younger man. In the fifth the course of the fight took a dramatic turn. Rocky connected with a looping right which hurt Louis and he backed away. In the sixth Louis's energy and fire seemed to be ebbing away like a tide going out and Marciano kept the pressure on his aged foe, banging away relentlessly with hooks and swings and uppercuts.

In the eighth a terrific left hook put Louis on the canvas for a count of seven. The big crowd were now on their feet. As soon as he rose Rocky was in again, and crashed a devastating right to the chin. Louis fell over backwards through the ropes and sprawled awkwardly on to the apron of the ring, with his legs remaining under the ropes. Referee Ruby Goldstein remembered, 'I stopped the count at three or four, I can't remember which, but there was no need to count him out. He was unconscious before he crashed on to the apron. Rocky was too young, too tough and he hit too hard.'

Marciano recalled, 'Yes, the win helped me get the title fight with Walcott, who had retained his title against Charles in the return fight, but I felt sad that I had to beat the man I had always worshipped. I hated doing it. Joe Louis was such a decent guy and always brought credit to the sport. Remember what that great sportswriter Jimmy Cannon once said about Louis being a credit to his race, the human race. I would go along with that, wholeheartedly.'

When this writer discussed the Marciano fight with Louis in later years, he said, 'Rocky was the new "great white hope". He had a tough reputation and I wasn't anxious to fight him either. But the promoter Jim Norris smelled money, as promoters do. He knew a money-maker when he saw it, and I still owed the US government $1m and maybe $100,000 a year in interest on unpaid taxes. So, although I didn't want to fight Marciano I couldn't turn down the guaranteed $300,000 for one fight. Anyhow while I figured he was strong, sure, but he fought like a street brawler. I figured I could outbox him anytime.'

'When I climbed into the ring I felt confident. I even felt more confident when I knew I had won three rounds out of the first five. I was right. He was a street brawler. He couldn't touch me when it came to boxing. Everything was fine until the seventh round. My age gave me away. All of a sudden my legs gave out. They had to lift me off the stool for the bell in the eighth. Marciano knocked me down once with a left hook. I managed to get up, then he caught me with another left that put me up against the ropes and followed with a looping right hand. But I just couldn't get out of the way.

'He hit me on the neck and I fell through the ropes. That's the last time I got hit in the ring. I made up my mind it would be my last fight. I remember somebody asked me if I thought Marciano was a harder hitter than Max Schmeling, who knocked me out in 1936. I said, "This kid knocked me out, what, with two punches. Schmeling knocked me out with, oh, it must have been 100."'

Marciano remembered, 'The fight that clinched the Walcott title shot was when I knocked out one of the top contenders Harry "Kid" Matthews in the second round on 28 July 1952. Matthews was a slick boxer with an impressive record and his manager was "Dumb Dan" Morgan. Dan was one of boxing's most colourful managers. He was known as "Dumb Dan" because he talked too much. He always had an opinion or an anecdote on any fight or any fighter. He was going on about Matthews being sidetracked and being denied a heavyweight title fight. I don't think he was but managers are like that, naturally looking out for their own boxer and getting the best deals. When I knocked out Matthews, there wasn't another bleep out of Dumb Dan.'

A crowd of 40,379 fans paid $50,645 at the sprawling Municipal Stadium in Philadelphia on 23 September 1952 to see the Walcott–Marciano clash. Shaped like a horseshoe, the venue was originally known as the Sesquicentennial Stadium where Jack Dempsey lost his heavyweight title in a big upset to Gene Tunney before a crowd of 120,757 on 23 September 1926. The Walcott–Marciano fight turned out to be a real thriller. It would most certainly have been held in the Yankee Stadium or the Polo Grounds, the traditional ballparks in New York where most of the big championship fights were staged but Felix Bocchiccio, Walcott's manager, did not have a licence in the Big Apple because of his alleged underworld connections.

'Around that time, too, Al Weill ran into trouble with the top brass,' said Marciano. 'As well as being matchmaker for the IBC, he was also of course my manager. It seems the people at Madison Square Garden were apparently not happy about Weill's dual role and instructed the IBC to terminate his contract with them. It made no difference to me, except that he was now my full-time manager, which was fine.

'Yes, the Walcott fight. Don't let anybody tell you that Jersey Joe was not a good fighter. Anything but. He was a great fighter, and as cute as a fox. He had me down in the opening round with a fast left hook, a similar punch to the one he knocked out Ezzard Charles with. I wasn't hurt, though. More surprised than anything. Charlie Goldman was telling me to stay down because he wanted me to take advantage of an eight or nine count so as I could clear my head.

'However, I was so annoyed at being put on the canvas so early in the fight, and for the first time in my life too, that I jumped up at three and the referee Charlie Daggert wiped my gloves. I knew there and then that if Walcott had thrown his best punch and I had gotten up, he couldn't put me down for keeps. I knew then that I was going to win.'

Jersey Joe's sharper boxing kept him in front after the first five rounds, sniping and scoring. 'Marciano was still bringing the fight to Walcott, taking the punishment in order to press the attack,' wrote Rocky's biographer Everett M. Skehan. 'It was the only way he knew. But Walcott was taller, heavier and had a reach advantage. He was a superior boxer who knew how to get the most out of every move, and he was using Rocky's style as a springboard for some very sharp counter-punching.'

This was master v pupil – Marciano missing and Walcott scoring. In close Jersey Joe was able to tie up the challenger like a Christmas parcel but 'The Rock' was always dangerous.

He was continuing to take the fight to the champion, always seeking an opportunity to land his big right hand, his Suzy Q. In the sixth, with Marciano still coming forward in a crouch, their heads collided, with Walcott emerging from a clinch with his left eyebrow cut and Marciano with a deep gash on his forehead, near his receding hairline.

'When I got back to my corner I told my handlers that there was something in my eyes and that they were burning and I couldn't see,' Rocky recalled. 'Allie Colombo felt it must have been some kind of medication used on Walcott's face and shoulders that caused the problem but my corner didn't know what to do about it. Allie and Charlie just kept trying to wash the stuff out of my eyes but my eyes seemed to be getting worse all the time.

'My manager Al Weill was now running alongside the ring apron. "Check the other guy's gloves," he was screaming. "There's something illegal on them." But the Pennsylvanian boxing commissioner John "Ox" DaGrossa told him to sit down or he would throw him out of the stadium. Some friend was Da Grossa.

'Looking back, it seems like Walcott did have some stuff between his neck and shoulders where I rested my head when we got in close but if there was any kind of skulduggery, I wouldn't say Walcott had anything to do with it. He was too good a champion to resort to anything like that. He was a deeply religious guy. Somebody in his corner must have been trying some tricks.

'My eyes were still smarting up to the ninth round and I was still way behind on points and Walcott seemed to be heading for certain victory. But I still felt I could get to him eventually. By the end of the 12th round, all three officials had him well ahead. Referee Taggert, in the days when the third man in the ring had a casting vote, had it 7-4 in Walcott's favour, with one round even. Judge Tomasco marked it 7-5 and judge Clayton 8-4. I'll admit it hadn't looked good for me from the start but as I say, I felt deep down I would finally catch him and bring him down. Jersey Joe was a cagey old bird, knew all the tricks and manoeuvres. He had hit me with some good shots but fortunately I was in good shape.

'Going out for the 13th round, Goldman shouted in my ear, "Kid, this is not looking good. You've got to get out there and knock him out now as soon as you can. If it goes the distance, he'll get it and will keep his title. You'll have blown it, the title you've always dreamed of." I was lucky. I finally saw the opening I had been looking for all night. We were near the ropes and I landed a good right hook, my Suzy Q, on his jaw and he went down and out.

'The stadium went really crazy after that. Everybody was cheering and shouting. It had been a great fight and boxing had a new heavyweight champion of the world. Back in the dressing room, it was jammed with family, friends, newspapermen, everybody. My dad was weeping unashamedly. There were questions from all sides from the boxing writers. Was Walcott the toughest opponent I ever faced? Was I ever hurt? Did I really think I could finally catch him? And so on and so on. It was all a great feeling though. I was champion of the world, the number one heavyweight.'

Peter Wilson, writing in the *Daily Mirror*, saw the fight like this, 'The borrowed time that Jersey Joe Walcott has been living on for an un-admitted number of years ran out just 44 seconds after the start of the 13th round of the old man's defence of the world heavyweight title against smashing, dashing, crashing Rocky Marciano. It ran out like sand from an hourglass which has been smashed by a hammer. It ran out after the hardest single punch I have seen one man land on another since Joe Louis won the same title from game Jim Braddock 15 years ago.'

Describing the 13th round, Wilson wrote, 'Walcott was fighting in spurts but they were effective. Then, like the car you never see on a dark road, came that tremendous right, the finishing blow. It left Walcott looking down his own spine with eyes that could not see. He crumpled forward, clutching for a rope. Rocky started a left hook which grazed the champion's – the ex-champion's – head as he crumbled but the Rock held it back. It wasn't needed. Style, skill, pacing, gameness and good punching, all had availed to nothing. Youth and strength are invaluable. Add to them the ability to punch and take a punch, season with guts, and you've got a new heavyweight champion.'

Eddie Borden in *Boxing and Wrestling* wrote, 'The fight was a magnificent, unparalleled performance of sustained courage and spine-tingling drama. They can forget the sensational battles of Jack Dempsey, Joe Louis and other immortals. Marciano can stand favourable comparison with any of the recognised leaders of the past. For all his apparent crudeness and open-for-attack stance, he is not too easy to hit solidly. He has a stubborn aggressiveness which asserts itself, even after getting hit some solid blows. As for Walcott, considerably past his peak, he exemplified and embodied everything a world champion stands for – skilful, crafty, dexterous and dangerous.'

Several years later I had an opportunity to interview Walcott and asked him about the fight. 'You know, I really thought I had him during the closing rounds but I guess I may have gotten a little careless but that's boxing,' he said. 'It would be a lie to say I wasn't disappointed. Of course I was. I had just lost the biggest title in boxing, the heavyweight championship of the world.

'I was sure I could beat him. I had trained like never before to win a fight. I was in the best condition of my career, mentally and physically but Rocky was just a better fighter that night. A nice guy too. Rocky was a great champion, sure he was. One of the best, take it from me. The only consolation I took from the fight, apart from the good purse of course, was that I had been beaten by an American and that the title had stayed in the US.'

Marciano and Walcott would meet in a return fight in Chicago eight months later and this time Rocky knocked out the former champion after two minutes and 25 seconds of the first round, one of the quickest heavyweight championship fights of all time.

'There was a lot of controversy about the finish of that return fight,' said Marciano. 'Many people said that Walcott took a dive because, as was claimed, if he couldn't beat me in 13 tough rounds the first time, it was unlikely he could do it in a second fight. I never agreed with any stories that he dumped it. He said that he just misjudged the count. Fair enough but the fight was on the level. I hit him with a good left hook and followed through with what I felt was an even better right uppercut and he went down. That was it. Indeed, I thought the finishing punch in that second fight was better than the one that knocked him out in the first fight.'

If the Walcott return match was controversial, there was an even bigger commotion over Marciano's title defence against the British and Commonwealth champion Don Cockell at the Kezar Stadium on the outskirts of San Francisco on 16 May 1955. Nobody gave Cockell, based in the south London suburb of Battersea and a pig farmer when he wasn't punching noses, any sort of a realistic chance and he entered the ring as a 10/1 underdog. American writers dismissed his moderate record and sneered at his bulk.

Arthur Daley of the *New York Times* told his readers that 'the British challenger bestirs memories of the fat boy in Charles Dickens' *Pickwick Papers*.' Others referred to Cockell in a variety of uncomplimentary nicknames such as 'the Battersea Butterball', 'the Grandular Globe', 'Dumpling Don' and simply 'Fatso'. British writers, angered by the characterisations of their boxer, called the treatment of Cockell 'disgraceful', one describing the whole thing as 'a big sneer campaign that must be the most devilish attack ever directed at a British champion'.

'Why did I take on Cockell?' Marciano asked rhetorically. 'To be honest, I was running out of challengers. I'd beaten all the legitimate contenders since taking the title from Walcott and in the return fight I knocked him out again. I'd stopped Roland LaStarza in 11 rounds and followed that up by outpointing Ezzard Charles and then knocking him out in eight rounds. There was nobody else around at the time. Anyway, we thought it only fair that we gave a non-American a title shot, and as Cockell was the British and Commonwealth champion, nobody could say that we were ignoring the foreigners.

'I must say Cockell was a resilient fighter who came to fight. It was a gruelling fight and he kept coming in. He sure was game but I was always on top. I got to him in the third round and landed a good left hook to the jaw that buckled his knees but he stayed on his feet. One of my left hooks landed low in the fifth round and the crowd booed. I raised my right glove in acknowledgement that it was unintentional and an accident. These things happen in the heat of battle but I was never an intentional dirty fighter, as some of the writers wrote after the fight.

'In the eighth I knocked him through the ropes with a hard right and he fell back on the apron of the ring. In the ninth I had him down twice before the referee Frankie Brown stepped in and called it off. It wasn't one of my best fights and I wasn't as sharp as I should have been. But I have to pay tribute to Cockell's courage. Don was one hell of a game guy, that's for sure.

'He was in there all the time trying to win, even if the odds were very much against him. He was no horizontal heavyweight like so many British guys in the past. I kept hitting him with my best shots and he had nothing to be ashamed of. I just couldn't keep him down. He had a lot of guts and was much better than anybody ever said he was. Don Cockell was certainly an underrated import and never let anybody tell you otherwise.'

If Marciano was not fully satisfied with his win, and his failure to score a clean knockout, he was hardly expecting the pasting he got from the boxing writers. *Time* magazine described Rocky as being 'as clumsy as any champion since the big Italian, Primo Carnera in the 1930s'. The *New York Times*, under Arthur Daley's by-line, said, 'Marciano is the best amateur ever to win the world professional championship.' Joe Williams in the *New York World Telegram and Sun* wrote, 'Marciano violated practically every rule in the book. He hit after the bell, used his elbows and head at close quarters, several times punching below the belt and hit Cockell once when he was down.'

Marciano felt the criticism of his tactics was unjustified, 'I never set out to deliberately foul an opponent. It was just my natural style, the way I had always fought and nobody ever complained before. In fairness, Cockell did his share of rough stuff too, though no writer ever mentioned that. But I recall some high-ranking official of the British Boxing Board of Control saying in an interview after the fight that any violation of the rules I committed was unintentional and that went for Cockell too. Remember, he was fighting for the heavyweight championship of the world, the most important title in boxing, and he could hardly expect a joyride, could he?'

Marciano's last fight was the sixth defence of his title he had won in 1952. This was his meeting with one of the all-time greats Archie Moore at the Yankee Stadium, New York on 23 September 1955. Moore held the world light-heavyweight title at the time but he often fluctuated between the 175lb class and the heavyweight division. The fight drew a crowd of 61,574, the largest by far ever to see a Marciano contest. Rocky's purse was another high, $328,374, plus $140,000 from closed circuit television in theatres. The fight would also gross $2,248,117, second at the time only to the 1927 Dempsey–Tunney return bout.

Moore more or less clinched the Marciano fight with a points win in May 1955 over the big Cuban, Nino Valdez, a highly rated contender, in Las Vegas when it was just a little dusty town in the Nevada desert and long before it became the glitzy entertainment capital of the world. However, it was Moore's third-round knockout three months earlier of the world middleweight champion Carl Bobo Olson, who had designs on the heavyweight title, that finally sealed the Marciano fight.

'I had decided before the fight that this was to be my final one,' said Rocky. 'I had been a boxer for eight years and was undefeated heavyweight champion of the world. I had achieved my goal, and had nothing to prove once I'd beaten Moore, which I felt capable of. Also, I had been away from my wife Barbara and young daughter Mary Anne for long periods in training camps and now I wanted to spend more time at home with them. I had put a bit of money aside so I hadn't any financial worries. I think I was making the right decision. Taking on a tough one like Moore for my last fight? Yes, it was a real challenge but I wanted to prove that I'd beaten all the top contenders. I can tell you that Archie was a remarkable fighter.'

That he was. Even today, some 60 years later, he is rated by most experts as the best light-heavyweight champion in boxing history. In a poll of experts conducted by the British magazine *Boxing News* in 2013, Moore, known as the 'Old Mongoose' and 'Ancient Archie', was the only 175-pounder in its list of the top ten boxers of all time. From St Louis, Missouri, Moore boxed all over America in the early days, even travelling to Australia where he won all his seven fights and South America, where he had seven wins and a draw. Archie was shamefully forced to hang around until he was 36 and in his 16th year of boxing before he got a long-deserved shot at the world light-heavyweight title, outpointing Joey Maxim in 1952 and staying at the top for ten years.

Moore was his own publicity agent when he campaigned for the Marciano fight. 'I reasoned that being the leading contender for the title was not enough,' he remembered. 'I needed to promote myself and the fight so I issued a wanted poster for Rocky, just like the ones you see in the movies. I had Marciano on the poster dressed up like a convict and underneath were the words "Reward for anybody who can get Rocky Marciano into the ring with me. Notify Sheriff Archie Moore." That started the ball rolling.

'I wrote to all the sports editors with newsletters demanding a chance at Marciano – and it worked. The men in the grey suits who sat in on boxing commissions began to take notice of this guy causing all the noise, and I finally got the title fight. It shows you what a bit of perseverance will do.'

The fight started fast, with both men exchanging hooks, crosses and uppercuts in close but it was Moore who was scoring much better. His shots were more accurate. The first round clearly went to Archie as he walked jauntily back to his corner with the assurance that this could be an easy fight. Shortly after the second round got under way, Moore followed a light left hook to the jaw with a whiplash right and Rocky went to the floor, for only the second time in his career.

'The referee Harry Kessler was counting, one, two, three and I jumped up at four,' Marciano recalled. 'This was going to be a tough one, make no mistake, but I was in prime condition and I wasn't too worried. Archie didn't get a second shot at my chin and I figured I would soon get on top. I kept on the attack in the third, fourth and fifth rounds and though I took some good shots from Archie, I felt I was getting through to him. I landed a good right in the sixth that put him down. He jumped up at four I remember but towards the end of the round I connected with a hard left-right combination and he went down again.

'This time he took an eight count and I thought he looked a bit shaky when he got to his feet. But I have to give him full credit for fighting back with good left hooks, right crosses and uppercuts. The ringside physician Dr Vincent Nardiello seemed to be concerned about Moore's condition and he climbed into the ring to check him out. One of Moore's eyes was closed tight but he let him go on. I heard later that Archie told him on no account did he want the fight stopped, and as this was a championship fight, he would have to be knocked out if he was going to lose at all.

'I put him down again in the eighth round from a looping right and he was still on the canvas when the bell rang at six. Maybe if it had happened a few seconds earlier he could have been counted out. We'll never know for certain. I finally put him down again in the ninth round for the full count.'

Marciano's biographer Everett M. Skehan graphically described the dramatic finish like this, 'Early in the ninth Marciano drove the battered and weary challenger into the ropes. He threw a wild volley of punches, the cumulative effect of which overpowered his exhausted opponent. Moore sank grudgingly to the canvas. He sat bleary-eyed near his own corner while the referee counted. Clutching the ropes, he attempted to rise. Then he slumped back down and was counted out.'

In a packed dressing room Rocky told the gathering of reporters that this was his last fight but the next day he was quoted as saying that he might in fact stay on as there was growing pressure on him to go for the round 50 wins. Over the next few months there were rumours and counter-rumours over his future until finally in April 1956 he announced officially that it was all over. He dabbled in business interests, had a brief career as an actor and took part in a fantasy computerised fight with Muhammad Ali, winning on a knockout in 13 rounds. 'It was kinda nice, y'know, putting the great Ali down for the full count,' he joked.

On 30 August 1969, the eve of his 46th birthday, Marciano was in Chicago looking over an amateur prospect he had hoped to sign up for a pro career. He was scheduled to fly home to Fort Lauderdale, Florida, when he got a call from Frank Farrell, an insurance executive friend, to give a speech in Des Moines, Iowa. Rocky postponed the trip home and boarded a small private plane, a Cessna 172.

It was night-time and bad weather had set in, making visibility poor. The pilot, Glenn Belz, had only 231 total hours of flying time, no more than 35 of them at night, and when the plane began to lose power he tried to set down at a small airfield outside of Newton, Iowa. Instead it hit a lone tree in a cornfield two miles short of the runway. Marciano, Belz and Farrell were killed instantly, with Rocky's body pinned beneath the wreckage.

Marciano's tragic death made headlines around the world and elicited a flood of tributes from former opponents. Joe Louis, beaten in eight rounds by Rocky in 1951, said when told, 'This is the saddest news I've ever heard. He was a man all youth looked up to and was a close and personal friend of mine. Terrible, terrible news.' Marciano was inducted into the International Boxing Hall of Fame in Canastota, New York, in 1990.

4

Ken Buchanan

Joe Louis poster started it all

THE Scottish carpenter who carved out a brilliant career that took him to the world lightweight title and a place in the International Boxing Hall of Fame in Canastota, New York, and the World Boxing Hall of Fame in Riverside, California was Ken Buchanan. A classy boxer with lightning reflexes, Buchanan is up there with the likes of great British 135-pounders who invaded US shores such as the skilful Freddie Welsh and the whirlwind that was Jackie 'Kid' Berg.

Regarded by many as the best British lightweight of all time, oddly enough he was never given the credit he deserved in his homeland and was more respected in the US and South America where he proved an immensely popular attraction. Indeed, he became so disillusioned with the boxing public in Britain that at the age of 24 he handed back to the British Boxing Board of Control his Lonsdale belt, awarded to boxers for keeps who win a British title and defend it successfully twice.

'America always accepted me with open arms and I was always grateful for that,' he said in an extensive interview with this writer in Dublin in 2001. 'New York was particularly good to me, and I boxed there several times. Naturally Madison Square

Garden was my favourite venue. I used to say that you hadn't really made it in boxing unless you fought at the Garden, the Mecca of boxing. All the greats have boxed there – Sugar Ray Robinson, John L. Sullivan, Harry Greb, Gene Tunney, Willie Pep, Sandy Saddler, Joe Louis, Benny Leonard, Ike Williams, Jimmy McLarnin – and that's just a few off the top of my head.

'Not too many boxers have that opportunity, certainly from Europe, but I always considered myself privileged to have climbed through the ropes there. It was always a great thrill. The action may have moved away from New York today to places like Las Vegas and Atlantic City but for me, the Garden was, and still is, the number one. From a boxer's point of view, once you've boxed in the Garden, you can die in peace.'

Born in Edinburgh on 28 June 1945, Buchanan wanted to be a boxer since he was eight years of age. 'I remember it was the Christmas of 1953 and my dad Tommy and I were out walking when he suddenly noticed a poster outside the local cinema, the Palace Picture House,' he recalled. 'It was a poster advertising a boxing film called *The Joe Louis Story*, about the former world heavyweight champion who had retired about two years earlier. My dad remembered him so we went in. Louis was played by the boxer Coley Wallace. Little did I realise then that the film would determine my future.

'I was fascinated by the whole thing. The close-ups, not only of Louis but other boxers in the gym and in the ring, and the action sequences. The whole thing enthralled me, and I said to my father coming out that I wanted nothing else than to be a boxer. There was something about the whole thing I loved, and the honesty and the true heroism of the boxers appealed to me. Not only being a boxer but a world champion no less. I reckoned that there was no point in going into the sport unless I wanted to be champion of the world, and that was the driving force behind my decision.

'My dad said he would do something about it and promised me he would get me enrolled in a local boxing club. Mind you, he didn't do it right away but I kept reminding him, or pestering him might be a better way to put it. I could visualise myself winning a cup and the whole school cheering me on. I couldn't wait to climb into a ring and the sooner the better. Dad eventually got me enrolled in the Sparta Amateur Boxing Club in Edinburgh and when he told me I jumped for joy. I couldn't be happier. I was on my way.'

After a very successful amateur career Buchanan turned professional on 20 September 1965 with an impressive win in two rounds. He won the British title in his 24th fight with a knockout over Maurice Cullen in 11 rounds. Now in the world ratings, he was matched with the Spaniard, Miguel Velazquez, in Madrid in January 1970 but lost the 15-round decision after being on the canvas in the ninth.

For Buchanan, it was merely a setback and made him all the more determined to fulfil the promise he had made to his father all those years earlier to be a world champion. 'Yes, it was a slip but I knew there would be a world title shot out there for me sooner or later and I would be ready for it,' he remembered.

The opportunity came sooner than expected. Ismael Laguna, the silky Panamanian, was due to fight former champion Sugar Ramos in San Juan, Puerto Rico. When the Cuban pulled out, a quick substitute was needed and Laguna's manager Cain Young sought an opponent he felt his man could beat without too much difficulty. Buchanan's manager Eddie Thomas suggested his boxer and as far as Young was concerned, the Scot was perfect, even if he was the leading contender.

The 15-round match for the undisputed world lightweight title was scheduled for 26 September 1970 at the open-air Hiram Bithorn Stadium in San Juan. 'Being the number one did not automatically mean you would get a title shot,' recalled Buchanan. 'Unfortunately it doesn't always work like that in boxing, with all the wheeling and dealing that goes on behind the scenes. But now I had the big chance and I intended to take it with both hands. I was ready for the greatest challenge of my career.'

Tall for a lightweight at 5ft 9in, Laguna, known as 'The Tiger', was one of the best world champions of the 1960s. One of ten children, he was a smooth, skilful boxer with a strong left jab and a solid punch in both gloves. Growing up, he idolised the boxers who trained at the local gym and would spend his time there after school. The boxers, for their part, took a liking to Laguna and taught him the rudiments of the noble art, how to score effectively at long and short range and at the same time keep one's guard up.

Laguna won the world lightweight title with a majority decision over Carlos Ortiz of Puerto Rico in Panama City in April 1965 but lost it back to Ortiz in San Juan seven months later, again over 15 rounds. Their third match, in New York in August 1967, also ended in a decision for Ortiz. Three years later Laguna regained his old title with a stoppage in nine rounds over Sugar Ramos in Los Angeles. After one successful defence, Laguna was ready to take on the challenge of Buchanan.

'When I arrived in San Juan, I was hit by the compressing heat,' he said. 'Somebody said it was 100 degrees. I knew it was going to be a problem, bringing on breathing difficulties, but I was ready. Few gave me much of a chance, including the British commentator and writer Reg Gutteridge. He went on record as saying that Laguna was an outstanding champion and coupled with the fact that I was boxing away from home, plus the intense heat, he tipped Laguna to win. It was a view shared by most people. Laguna entered the ring a 5/2 favourite.'

Buchanan put up the fight of his life. He went on the attack from the start, though after three rounds in the hot sun, the effect of the heat was sapping his strength. But he kept going and after eight rounds there was not a lot between them. Laguna, who was used to these conditions, seemed to gain extra strength from then on, using his expert combinations to good effect against Buchanan's aggression. Buchanan staggered the Panamanian in the 12th and the result seemed to hinge on the last three rounds.

'I was dead beat going out for the 13th but I had to give it all I had. Laguna seemed as strong as ever but somehow I summoned enough strength to go on the attack and my corner told me I finished the stronger at the final bell. Believe you me,

Thomas, I was never more happy to hear a last bell than in that fight. I didn't have much left but I still felt I had enough to take the decision and the title. It went to a split decision, with the referee Waldemar Schmidt giving it to Laguna and the two judges casting their vote for me. I was lightweight champion of the world.

'The newspaper reports next day in San Juan said that I was now the first British boxer to win a world title abroad since the great Ted Kid Lewis was welterweight champion half a century earlier. I was very pleased to learn that. Lewis, a Londoner, was one of the most talented Britons who took on the best of American fighters and was very popular with US fans because of his whirlwind, all-action style.'

The rejoicing did not last long, however. In taking on Laguna, Buchanan had defied the wishes of the British Boxing Board of Control which, as a member of the World Boxing Council, had not recognised the fight on the grounds that Laguna had not defended his title against the man it considered the number one contender, Sugar Ramos, a former rival. They subsequently withdrew recognition from Laguna on the flimsiest grounds. This era saw the beginning of political in-fighting with newly created organisations springing up all over the place which continues to be a sore spot on world boxing to this day and continues to cause confusion. They would become known as 'the alphabet boys', or collectively as 'alphabet soup'.

The Buchanan–Laguna fight, though, was recognised by the World Boxing Association as well as the New York State Athletic Commission and *Ring* magazine. Nevertheless, whatever way the WBC and Britain wanted to look at the situation, Buchanan was the *real* champion, having defeated the linear title-holder. Also, there was that unwritten law that titles are won in the ring not in commissions' offices. On Buchanan's arrival back home, nobody could convince the British Board that Buchanan was a world champion.

The title fight received scant coverage in the British press, and on arrival home by plane to Edinburgh, the expected crowd turned out to be just six. Four of those were his wife Carol, his son Mark and his parents-in-law. To complicate matters even further, Buchanan had boxed Laguna without asking permission from the British authorities to box abroad and he was told he would not only be disciplined but banned from boxing in his native land.

'We protested but to no avail,' remembered Buchanan. 'I was quite clearly a prophet without honour in his native land. Ten weeks after I won the title, I made up my mind to continue my career in the US, where I felt I would be more appreciated. Jack Solomons, the London promoter, had arranged with Harry Markson, the president of Madison Square Garden, for me to box at the famous New York venue and set the date for 7 December 1970.

'The Garden, the dream venue. I can't say how thrilled I was to appear there. I was matched with the unbeaten Canadian welterweight Donato Paduano in a non-title fight. He was 10lb heavier at the weigh-in but I wasn't too worried. I felt I could handle him. On the plus side, he was a few inches shorter and wasn't regarded as a big puncher. The main reason I agreed to the fight was that it was to be on the undercard of Muhammad Ali's fight with the South American, Oscar Bonavena. Ali was one of my idols along with Joe Louis and the fact that I was appearing on the same bill as "The Greatest" was a real thrill, believe me.

'I used my skill to outbox Paduano and when the opportunity came, I moved in and landed solid blows. I won on all three scorecards and the crowd gave me a standing ovation. I was happy to have made a good impression on New York fans, and even more so, to have had a successful debut at my dream venue. I must tell you this too. Before the fight, Angelo Dundee, Ali's trainer, came in the dressing room and asked if he could use the room. I thought he was kidding and just laughed but it was true. Ali hadn't been allocated a room. Next thing Dundee brings Ali in. What a thrill.

'Sharing a dressing room with the man many consider the greatest heavyweight of all time, indeed the greatest at any weight. We had a great bit of banter. He said, "I'm top of the bill tonight. When you are top of the bill and I'm on the undercard, the favour can be returned." I said, "Sure, I'd be only too happy to do so." So there you go. What a night. Boxing in the great Madison Square Garden for the first time, sharing a dressing room with Muhammad Ali, and topped off by a clear win. It didn't get better than this.'

Buchanan was a big favourite at Madison Square Garden from then on, and the fans always gave him a warm reception. In 1971, the Scot began to enjoy his status as one of the best world champions around. The first defence of his title was scheduled against Cuba's Sugar Ramos, whose place he had taken to defeat Laguna, but three days before the fight Ramos pulled out again. Ruben Navarro, the fifth-rated lightweight, was called in and they met in Navarro's native Los Angeles on 12 February 1971.

The 10,360 fans were preparing to celebrate a local victory when Buchanan was dropped in the first round but the champion fought back and was well on top after 15 rounds. The three judges all gave it to him by a wide margin. Britain's Harry Gibbs had it 9-2 with four rounds even, and the two Americans, Arthur Mercante and Lee Grossman, had identical scores of 9-4 with two even. The win earned Buchanan recognition as undisputed champion, and even the British Board went along with it. When he signed to defend his title in a return with Ismael Laguna, the World Boxing Council withdrew recognition as Pedro Carrasco, the talented Spaniard, was their official number one contender, but the British Board stood by Buchanan.

The rematch was scheduled for Madison Square Garden, Buchanan's favourite arena, for 13 September 1971 and a crowd of 13,211 passed through the turnstiles to witness their adopted hero defend his championship. It would be a nice change to box in the relative cool of the Garden, having experienced the searing heart of Puerto Rico the previous September. Buchanan had been made a slight favourite in the betting but his training preparations were hampered when he was cut across the bridge of his nose – an injury administered not by a sparring partner by own his son Mark, with a metal toy.

This was how Buchanan remembered the fight, 'Laguna was always trying to crowd me but I would stick with my boxing and attempt to keep him off balance. I hurt him with a right cross in the second round and he backed away. He knew there and then that he was going to be in for a rough night. In that second round I felt my right eye closing after he landed a right and by the end of the third it was swollen right up. My manager Eddie Thomas ran the edge of a razor blade across the lump under the eye and the blood seeped out. It meant that after a round or two, the swelling would come down a bit and then it would close tight.

'I could live with that. After all, when you are in there with your world title on the line, it's no picnic. Laguna was now more determined than ever to win back his title but I was ready for anything he came up with. My dad was also in my corner and he kept telling me to keep pushing Laguna back with every chance I got and I did that. I had him back-pedalling. I was glad to hear the last bell but I knew I had done enough to win. I was right. I got the unanimous decision and I was still lightweight champion of the world. It was a great feeling. Nothing like it.'

When the Buchanan party returned home, they received news that Madison Square Garden wanted him back for a title defence against Roberto Duran, who was reportedly determined to bring the world title back to Panama 'where it belongs'. The fight would be worth $125,000 to Buchanan, considerably more than he got for the Laguna return bout. The World Boxing Council however was demanding that Buchanan defend against Pedro Carrasco. There would be less money so he opted for Duran, which meant he was forced to relinquish the WBC belt. The Duran defence would get official recognition from the World Boxing Association, the New York State Athletic Commission and the British Boxing Board of Control. That was more than good enough for Buchanan.

The match was set for Madison Square Garden on 26 June 1972. It was to be a tough test for Buchanan as Duran was a natural-born fighter and did not need much tuition. In any event, he discarded any semblance of scientific boxing. He was a brawling, street-fighting slugger who overwhelmed opponents with his immense strength, grim determination, strength-sapping body punching and strong right-hand blows. By all accounts, a real tough hombre. Duran boasted a record of 27 wins, one loss and no draws as against Buchanan's 43-1-0 tally.

Sam Toperoff, the Brooklyn writer and TV producer, probably summed up Duran best when he wrote, 'There were no other fighters around quite like him in the 1970s. He was a throwback in more ways than one, a mysterious, dark figure from some tropical mythic past. His dark eyes glowed, perhaps with the same fire of the Mexican father he never remembered, enigmatically, with a vestige of the Indian blood he also surely possessed. In victory, Duran was never gracious. A sneer was his typical reaction to success in the ring. He had little inclination or the time to develop an honest respect for an opponent.'

Recalled Buchanan, 'Two weeks before the fight we signed contracts at Les Champs restaurant in midtown Manhattan and it was the first time we came together. The Garden publicist John Condon tried to play up Duran's tough past by saying that street-fighting in Panama was as popular as baseball in the US. Duran, speaking through an interpreter, confidently predicted he would knock me out within nine rounds, and added that he thought Ismael Laguna was a better boxer than I was. I responded that while he was entitled to boast and make all kinds of predictions, I preferred to do my talking in the ring.

'I said I thought there were more deserving contenders around than Duran but the Garden offered me $125,000 and I took it. I was offered $150,000 by a Panamanian promoter but I turned him down. I had been treated so well in the past by the Garden people and I felt an allegiance to them. You have to stand by what you believe is best.'

A near-capacity crowd of 18,821 paid $223,901, a new indoor record for a world lightweight title fight. Buchanan was a 13/5 favourite but seconds into the fight he felt the full force of the challenger's raw power when a right cross sent him stumbling, and which referee Johnny LoBianco ruled a knockdown. From then on Duran swarmed in with uppercuts, hooks and swings and the Scot needed all his guile to stay out of trouble. That was the pattern of the fight, with Duran piling up the points and Buchanan looking worse for wear by the minute.

In the fading seconds of the 13th round, and with the big crowd yelling and on their feet, Duran landed a low right hand that travelled upwards from about knee high and struck the Scot squarely on his protective cup. Buchanan grabbed his groin, his face contorted in pain, before keeling over like a crippled liner and sinking to the canvas. Referee LoBianco had not seen the low blow but the fight was temporarily halted while officials tended to the distressed champion. After about 15 seconds he was able to rise and was taken to his corner. LoBianco went over, had a look at Buchanan, and waved his arms wide. It was all over. Roberto Duran was the new champion. At the time of the finish, the Panamanian was ahead by 9-2-1, 8-3-1 and 9-3.

'I told the referee I was all right except for a slight pain between my legs and wanted to go on but he insisted in stopping the fight,' remembered Buchanan. 'It was robbery. The whole place was booing. They couldn't believe it was all over because of a foul blow and that I should have been the winner. My dad went to the commission offices the next day and tried to get the chairman Ed Dooley to change the result but he said that they couldn't believe a fighter wearing a protector could be hurt. In any event, they said a fight could not be won on a low blow, a rule they brought in back in the late 1920s or early 1930s, some time like that. It was after the British heavyweight Phil Scot claimed fouls in two fights in Madison Square Garden.

'But I do feel that the current powers-that-be in the commission offices should have another look at the Duran fight, even after all these years, see the low blow and award the fight to me. It would only be right and proper, I think. Even the referee admitted later after seeing a re-run of the fight that he should have disqualified Duran there and then but he had made his decision on the spur of the moment like any normal referee but couldn't change it. Forty years on, I still don't know why he couldn't.'

There was little sympathy for Buchanan. Bert Sugar, writing in *Boxing Illustrated* and who would soon edit and own *Ring* magazine, said, 'Referee LoBianco got a lot of flack, most from Buchanan's followers, but the Briton was going nowhere. He was a very slick fighter but he was no match for Duran. In the 13th round Buchanan got all the fight kicked out of him, and I don't think LoBianco saw the punch that ended the round.'

Dave Anderson reported in the *New York Times*: 'Duran dominated the tempo throughout with a flailing assault that virtually erased the Scot's artistic left jab to the delight of the Panamanian's loyalists. From the start Duran was in command, roughing up Buchanan constantly, nullifying the Scot's skills. No longer could Buchanan minimise Duran's credentials that the Panamanian had never defeated a world-ranked lightweight. Duran defeated Buchanan decisively.

'As to the controversial finish, Buchanan wore a protective cup under his trunks. It's possible that the Scot crumbled because of both a punch and a knee. But whatever the reason, it didn't alter his failure to thwart the perpetual punches of the 21-year-old Panamanian, the second-youngest lightweight champion in history. Al Singer was 20 when he won the title in 1930 with a first-round knockout of Sammy Mandell at the Yankee Stadium.'

Boxing News, in an uncredited report, said, 'It was a violent battle. The Panamanian's relentless attacks continually ruffled the more stylish Buchanan. Ken's lance-like left jab could not contain a powerful slugging opponent who never stopped coming forward. Sheer power won the fight for Duran. He was after Buchanan from the start, slugging and slashing at him. Buchanan scored with effective counters from time to time but could never fully cope with Duran's head-down, brawling tactics. Despite Buchanan's protests at the controversial finish, the aggressive Duran was clearly in front on points at the time.'

There was talk of a return match but it never happened – 'much to my regret', lamented Buchanan. He had three more fights in New York but was never the same force. The Scot won European and British title fights but another world title fight eluded him. In his retirement years he boxed in unlicensed bouts before hanging up the gloves for good. Buchanan wrote two successful autobiographies and is regarded today as one of the finest boxers ever produced on this side of the Atlantic. Nobody can ever dispute that.

5

Joe Louis
Truth behind the hate fight

THEY called him the 'Brown Bomber' and the name stuck. A powerful, accurate puncher and a much more skilful boxer than he was ever given credit for, Joe Louis held the heavyweight championship of the world, boxing's most prestigious title, for a record 11 years and 252 days. He defended his crown 25 times, also a record, often giving the challengers a second shot if there was any doubt about the result the first time.

In 1970 when he was on a promotional tour of Britain and Ireland promoted by the County Kerry strongman Butty Sugrue, who boasted he could lift a full beer barrel over his head and often did, I had the opportunity of meeting Louis in Dublin and discussing his long career before, during and after he was champion. It was a fascinating experience.

Two of Louis's most famous and often-discussed fights were his clashes with the German Max Schmeling. The first one, on 19 June 1936, one year before Louis won the title, ended in a sensational upset when Joe was knocked out in 12 rounds by the veteran considered past his peak. The second, on 22 June 1938, a year after Louis became champion, was all over after two minutes and four seconds of round one when referee Arthur Donovan intervened to save the German further unnecessary punishment.

'Let me say if I may that much was made in the press about hatred creeping into those fights, particularly the second one at a time when war clouds were gathering over Europe and Nazi stormtroopers were flexing their muscles and terrorising Jews in Germany and neighbouring countries,' said Louis. 'Mike Jacobs, known affectionately as "Uncle Mike", promoted both fights as he had me under contract. For the first fight he built up the publicity by exploiting the "good American of the free world" and the "bad German of the oppressive nation". It was much the same for the second fight.

'Far too much was made of the America v Germany issue, particularly for the second fight. Then again I guess it was to boost the gates, publicity drummed up by the promoter. I never hated Schmeling. He was always a good friend of mine, both before and after, long after the fights but Mike Jacobs as well as the newspapers drummed up the hate angle. So there you are.

'I had won all my 27 fights, 23 either by count-outs or stoppages, and considered a sure bet to beat the reigning champion James J. Braddock. Schmeling was Adolf Hitler's favourite sportsman, but he had a somewhat spotty record. Since losing his title on a close decision to Jack Sharkey in 1932, he was stopped in ten rounds by Max Baer, a future champion, a year later.'

With his black hair and heavy eyebrows, and the air of an uhlan – a Germany cavalryman armed with a lance – American sportswriters referred to him as the 'Black Uhlan'. He was considered well past his prime, as well as being eight years older than the 22-year-old Louis, a telling factor the longer the fight went.

Louis entered the ring at the Yankee Stadium as a prohibitive 10/1 favourite and a crowd of 45,000 passed through the turnstiles. The fight was originally set for the previous day but heavy rain caused a postponement for 24 hours. Promoter Jacobs had hoped for a bigger gate but reckoned many fans feared a second delay and stayed away. In any event, it did not look to be much of a match, considering the odds and their respective records.

'In my corner Chappie Blackburn, my trainer, told me not to go for the knockout too early and that I was to keep jabbing so as Schemling couldn't get his big right in,' recalled Louis. 'That was Max's favourite punch and he had won most of his fights with it. "For God's sake, keep your left arm high," warned Chappie. I nodded. I knew what to do.

'The first round went much as predicted. I was jabbing all the time, moving around, watching that famous right hand of his. At the bell Schmeling went to his corner and his right eye was closed. In the second round I did what Chappie told me not to do, drop my left hand. But I wanted to try a good left hook. Suddenly Schmeling saw the opening, fired his right hand, got me on the chin and I saw stars. I was shaken and I went back to my jabbing for the rest of the round.

'Chappie admonished me in the corner and told me to just keep jabbing for this round and leave it at that. I did this but in the fourth I couldn't resist firing a left hook when I saw an opening but Schmeling countered with his right to the chin and I was down, for the first time in my career. I jumped up at two but I was still dizzy and I guess I never fully recovered from then on. Schmeling finished me off in the 12th round with more right hands and referee Arthur Donovan counted me out. It was all over.

'I suppose I *was* a bit overconfident going into that fight, though I don't want to use this as an excuse. But I was learning how to play golf at the time and Chappie said that golf was fine but that I wouldn't want to lose my edge. I didn't because I trained regularly at my training camp at Pompton Lakes in New Jersey. I was also seeing a lot of the ice-skating star Sonja Henie, even though I had a regular girlfriend at the time, Marva Trotter.

'But as I say, these weren't excuses, even though many people put them forward as such. I just lost to a better man. There would be a next time, Mike Jacobs told me and there was. I ran up a good few wins and Jacobs matched me with the champion James J. Braddock in Chicago in June 1937, a full year after my loss to Schemling. I knocked out Braddock in eight rounds. Mike kept his promise and got me a return fight with Max in June 1938.'

Before the first Schmeling fight Louis had defeated two former world heavyweight champions, the big Italian Primo Carnera and the playboy puncher with the deadly right hand, Max Baer. Carnera was a much better fighter than he is generally given credit for. At 6ft 5.75in and weighing 270lb he moved well and had a strong left jab but he allowed himself to be manipulated by underworld figures who controlled his career. A former circus strongman in his native Italy, he was launched by businessman Leon See, and when See took him to America to campaign for a world heavyweight title fight, gangsters moved in, negotiated deals with See and finished up looking after his career.

There has always been deep suspicions about Carnera's world title win over Jack Sharkey on 29 June 1933 when the Boston fighter was floored by a Carnera right uppercut that many said missed the target. After two successful defences, big Primo lost the title exactly a year later when he was knocked out in 11 rounds by Max Baer in a fight in which Carnera was knocked down 12 times. Once when both tumbled to the canvas, practical joker Baer roared, 'Last man up's a sissy.'

Baer had the making of a great champion if only he had taken himself seriously. From Omaha, Nebraska, and later basing himself in Livermore, California, he started off promisingly by winning 22 of his first 24 fights. In 1930, his second year in the ring, he was charged with manslaughter after an opponent, Frankie Campbell, died as a result of being knocked out in the fifth round in San Francisco. Baer was subsequently cleared of criminal charges but was suspended from Californian rings for a year.

Max seemed to pull his punches after that until the retired champion Jack Dempsey took an interest in his career and advised him to shorten his punches. In 1932 Baer knocked

Ernie Schaaf unconscious in the tenth and final round in Chicago just before the bell rang after what had been a fairly even bout. Six months later Shaaf died following a knockout in 13 rounds against Carnera but his defeat was attributed in part to the beating administered by Baer.

Louis took on Carnera at the Yankee Stadium on 25 June 1935 before a crowd of 60,000. 'The win over Carnera was the biggest of my career up to then,' he said. 'Carnera had already lost the title but a win would enhance my career no end. When I climbed into the ring at the ballpark and saw the massive crowd, I was awestruck. Chappie Blackburn told me in the corner to jab and feel him out and that I wasn't to leave myself open on any account.

'Chappie always knew what was best for me and I never failed to follow his instructions, well, rarely anyhow.

'I found after the first round that Carnera couldn't really punch, despite his size, although he had a fairly decent left jab. As the rounds went by I felt I was able to slip his jabs and move inside his hooks and uppercuts. In the fourth or fifth round, I can't remember which, Chappie told me to take no risks. "Your chance will come. Pace yourself and everything will be all right."

'I was beginning to get under his guard around then and going out for the sixth Chappie told me to "go for him in this round". I hit him with a sharp right hook to the jaw and Carnera pitched forward on his knees, then on his face. This was it. He was up at four. I moved in, threw more punches, ending with an overhand right, again to the jaw, that dropped him for the second time. I fired a left and a right and he went down for the third time. When he got up, he put his left hand on the ropes as if to steady himself but the referee Arthur Donovan moved in fast and waved his arms. It was all over.

'Harry Balogh, the famous announcer, or MC as they call them nowadays, brought me to the centre of the ring and proclaimed me the winner. I just want to say, however, that Carnera was the gamest guy I ever knew. He took his punishment unflinchingly and never wanted to quit. I'm sure he would have wanted to go on but he'd had enough. A really game guy was Primo.

'After my win over Carnera people started talking about a title fight with Jimmy Braddock, who had just won the title from Max Baer in a stunning upset. I think Baer was a 15/1 favourite as Braddock was considered washed up. But there you go. That's boxing.'

Louis's managers John Roxborough and Julian Black felt their charge was ready now for the big ones and matched him with Baer scheduled for the Yankee Stadium on 24 September 1935. 'I reckoned that a win over Baer would really enhance my prestige as Baer was still a formidable contender, despite having lost the title to Braddock on a decision just three months earlier,' recalled Louis. 'I had another matter on my mind. Right after the fight I was getting married to my girlfriend Marva Trotter. I wanted to win for Marva too.

'Marva was at ringside and that pleased me. Jack Dempsey was in Baer's corner and I knew Jack had given him some good pointers on how to handle me. I found Baer easier to hit than I had imagined. Baer looked very scared, I thought. I jabbed him in the first round to sound him out until I could find the openings. Baer landed two good rights in the second round but they didn't hurt. I was confident I could take him. In the third I put him down with a right hand and he took a count of nine. Another right and a left hook and he went down again, this time for four when the bell sounded.

'In the fourth I put him down again with a left hook to the jaw and a right to the head and he took the final count on one knee. He later sat on the canvas, his legs folded under him, and waved to the crowd.

'I don't think he really quit, as was claimed at the time. I reckon he simply felt he had taken enough and just couldn't find the energy to get up.

'Some writer said after the fight that I had thrown something like 254 punches and only missed once. I don't know how true that was. All I knew was that I'd had a good win and it was my best fight. Baer said after the fight that I was lucky to win and that he had an off-night. I was disappointed he took it that way.'

Schmeling's stunning win over Louis should have gotten the German a title fight with new champion Braddock but boxing is never fair. It wasn't then and it's not today – and unlikely ever will be. Because politics plays such a big part in the sport, deserving contenders are sidetracked for one reason or another. In the early years of the 20th century, great black heavyweights like Sam Langford, Joe Jeanette, Sam McVey, Harry Wills and others were shamefully given the runaround although that had to do with the notorious colour bar more than any other factors.

Negotiations involving the New York State Athletic Commission, Madison Square Garden, promoter Mike Jacobs and the managers of Louis and Braddock all got in the way of a Braddock–Schmeling fight, directly or indirectly. Jacobs had signed Braddock to defend against Schmeling at Madison Square Garden on 3 June 1937 and the German turned up for the weigh-in in his boxing kit to show that he had honoured his part of the contract.

There was an underlying fear however that if Schmeling won the title, he could take it back to Germany and it might stay there in an era when America claimed it somehow 'owned' the championship. Jacobs was finally 'persuaded' by anti-Nazi political groups in New York to change his mind, cancelled the Braddock–Schmeling contract and signed Braddock to defend against Louis on 22 June, 1937, not in New York but at Comiskey Park, Chicago, a baseball ground and home of the Chicago White Sox.

Braddock came off the dole queues in Hoboken, New Jersey, to reach the pinnacle of boxing's heights, against all the odds. The original 'Cinderella Man' because his story read like a fairytale, Braddock had Irish blood and always wore a shamrock on his trunks. One of seven children, he was still a child when his parents moved the family from New York City to Hoboken. He learned his boxing in a local gym where the former heavyweight great Joe Jeanette, also known as Jenette, was coach.

'Braddock was a really nice guy, a gentleman,' said Louis. 'He made slow if steady progress, and while possessing a solid right hand punch, he proved that there was no real substitute for hard work, dedication and a stubborn nature. However, the boxing writers went for me to win and take his title. Before we get into the actual Braddock fight, there is something you should know, and it's very often misinterpreted. There were stories that if I won, I would have to hand over ten per cent of my purse monies to Braddock for the next ten years.

'Braddock's manager, the canny Joe Gould, allegedly said that if this did not happen, he would not sign for the fight. Yes, Braddock got his ten per cent but not out of my purses. The money came from promoter Mike Jacobs's gate receipts, which is a different story and the only true one. I learned later that Jacobs got tired of this arrangement and simply stopped making the payments. However, I also learned that Gould took Jacobs to court and Jacobs gave Gould a lump sum, which Gould was apparently happy with.

'Braddock and Gould did well out of the fight in any event. Besides the ten per cent issue, Gould was offered a guarantee by Jacobs of $500,000 or half of the gate as well as the revenues from the gate. Gould opted for the $500,000. As to the fight itself, Braddock surprised me near the end of the first round when he dropped me with a surprise right hand but I jumped up right away and went into the attack to show I wasn't hurt.

'I didn't give him a chance to nail me after that but he was stubborn. I landed some good shots to his head and body and he stood up to them but I figured I'd bring down his defences eventually. It happened about a minute into the eighth round. I shot a hard left hook to the body, followed by another left hook, again to the body and followed up with a right cross to the head and he went down for the full count. It was all over and I was heavyweight champion of the world. It was a great feeling.

'People all over were celebrating the win. In Chicago they stayed up all night shouting and running through the streets. They had bonfires on street corners. It was the same in New York. In Harlem, thousands marched up and down the avenues all night long. There was talk of me defending the title against the Welshman, Tommy Farr but I really wanted to meet Schmeling again and get a chance to turn the tables.

'Jacobs had his way, however, as promoters do and he got me the Farr fight first, in August 1937, which I won on points over 15 rounds. Farr was a tough opponent with a peculiar style, ducking and swaying a lot. No matter what I hit him with, he stayed on his feet. He took a punch better than anybody I knew. At the finish Farr thought he had won but I got the decision, and everybody else seemed to agree with it. Now the way was clear for the return fight with Schmeling.'

The eagerly-awaited match was held on 22 June 1938. It was billed as a grudge fight and a crowd of 70,043 passed through the turnstiles at the Yankee Stadium. Schmeling had received a telegram from Adolf Hitler wishing him luck and there were also goodwill messages from high-ranking Nazi figures such as the propaganda minister Joseph Goebbels and foreign minister Joachim von Ribbentrop.

In the run-up to the fight President Roosevelt had invited Louis to the White House and told him that all America wanted him to win and that a victory would also be a triumph for America. Looking back 30 years later with this writer, Louis said he did not see it like that at all.

'The fight was steeped in politics from the time it was signed,' he said. 'In reality Schmeling was my friend and I was his. But I guess we had a job to do. My job was to beat him, and his job was to beat me and may the better man win. But the papers turned it into a propaganda war, as they do. Anything for a good angle, and what better way to picture the fight at the time than to play up the "good American" against the "bad German", just as Mike Jacobs had said. It worked I guess, with a massive crowd turning up.'

Louis won when referee Arthur Donovan intervened after two minutes and four seconds of the first round to save Schmeling further unnecessary punishment, or as Nat Fleischer reported in *Ring* magazine, 'To prevent Max being killed.' Fleischer wrote, 'At the bell Louis tore into Schmeling with rights and lefts and bore the German to the ropes. These drives were no long swings. The punches were barely eight inches and they took all the fight out of him. They paralysed him.'

Perhaps the most descriptive report of the fight was despatched by Bob Considine, a syndicated columnist with the William Randolph Hearst newspaper chain. 'It was a shocking thing – that knockout,' said Considine. 'Short, sharp, merciless, complete. Louis was like this: He was a big, lean copper spring, tightened and retightened through weeks of training until he was one pregnant package of coiled venom.

'Schmeling hit that spring with a whistling right hand punch in the first minute of the fight – and the spring, tormented with tension, suddenly burst with one brazen spang of activity. Hard brown arms, propelling two unerring fists, blurred beneath the hot white candelabra of the ring lights. And Schmeling was in the path of them, a man caught and mangled in the whirring claws of a mad and feverish machine.'

Louis remembered, 'We were now even, with one win apiece, and that's the way I like to look back on it. But I must repeat. There was no hatred between us. We were sportsmen. We had a job to do and that was it. It was either him or me. Yes, I came out of my corner fast but on Chappie's instructions. He wanted me to get it over as quickly as possible. Schmeling was a danger always and as I say I had a job to do and I did it. As I've told you, the papers made a big thing out of the "hate" angle but it wasn't true.

'It wasn't until after the war when I saw Schmeling again in America and we hugged each other like old friends. We kept in touch after that and when I celebrated my 56th birthday in Las Vegas, Max was a special guest. I wanted it that way. There is a lot of wheeling and dealing in boxing, and there is no denying that, but in the end, the boxers themselves are the best of friends, good sportsmen. In the ring you are out to do your best to win. Outside it, it's different. Schmeling and I will always be good friends.'

What was Louis's quickest win as champion? 'I beat five challengers in the first round – Schmeling, John Henry Lewis, Jack Roper, Buddy Baer and Tami Mauriello but I'm not sure which was the quickest,' he said. 'I know I beat Schmeling in 2.04. I couldn't forget that one. You say Mauriello was second, in 2.09. Yes, I guess that would be about right.

'We met at the Yankee Stadium in September 1946, three months after I beat Billy Conn in the return fight. Mauriello was a New Yorker, and as his name suggested, had Italian blood. He was a hard puncher particularly with his right and I knew I had to be wary of him. There was a crowd of nearly 40,000 in the ballpark. Sure enough, he came out fast and fired his big right hand to the head and knocked me into the ropes.

'I covered up to get my bearings and Mauriello came in to press home his advantage. I got through with a left hook and he went down. When he regained his feet at the count of five, I dropped him with another left hook that draped him over the top rope. He'd had enough and the referee Arthur Donovan counted him out.'

Louis was floored on several occasions during his career but he always got up to win, except in the first Schmeling fight and his comeback bout with Rocky Marciano. One of the heavyweights who put him on the canvas was Tony 'Two Ton' Galento, the 'Beer Barrel Palooka'. A rotund, balding, shaggy-chested saloon owner from Orange, New Jersey, Galento was an odd character to say the least. Just before a fight in 1932, he had eaten 50 hot dogs just a win a $10 bet. His handlers had to slit the waistband of his trunks to get them on. Galento then waddled out and knocked out his opponent.

When he signed for the Louis fight, scheduled for the Yankee Stadium on 28 June 1939, Galento had a banner spread across his bar with the words, 'I'll moider da bum.' Tony really believed it too. When approached by one writer who reminded him that he would be entering the ring a heavy underdog and at 5ft 9in he would be dwarfed by the champion, Galento replied, 'I said Louis was a bum, and that's what he is, a bum. I have the most powerful left hook in the business and he's not going to avoid that. I'm as tough as steel too so anything he can throw at me I can take.'

'The crowd came to close on 40,000 which wasn't bad,' recalled Louis. 'I wasn't going to take Galento lightly because I was aware of his knockout punch in that right hand of his. He was a street slugger, a brawler and they're always the ones to watch out for. He staggered me with the left hook in the first round so I had to be careful. Going out for the second round Chappie Blackburn told me he was very strong and not to go for the knockout. Just box him and soften him up. But I wanted to finish him. I landed a hard left hook and he went down but got back up in time.

'In the third I felt I was getting to him but he got through with his big left hook and I went down. The crowd were shouting. An upset in the making? I jumped up with a count but I had to respect this guy. I went back to my jabbing which were ripping old wounds on Galento's face. In the fourth round Galento went all out for a knockout but he played right into my hands. I mixed it with him, much to Chappie's scared looks in the corner, and had him reeling and rocking with lefts and rights before he went down. Referee Arthur Donovan moved in and it was all over.'

This writer reminded Louis of what Donovan said in later years, 'When Galento knocked Louis down, I could see that Louis was badly hurt, even though he jumped to his feet without a count. If Tony could have landed another left hook, he would have won the title.' Rubbing his chin reflectively, Louis agreed, 'Donovan had a point there. I can tell you that Galento really could wallop. A lot of people were pulling for him. He had a special appeal for a lot of white people. Tony and I remained friends. I used to go to his saloon in New Jersey from time to time and we'd have a good laugh about the things we used to be serious about.'

Billy Conn, the Pittsburgher and world light-heavyweight champion, was another important figure in the ring life of Louis. By early 1941 Louis was starting to run out of opponents and was going through his so-called 'Bum of the Month' campaign when he took on and conquered every available heavyweight around. Short ones, tall ones, fat ones, skinny ones. You name them, Louis fought them. But the handsome Conn was certainly no bum. He was a fast, flashy boxer with a fine left hand, a strong right and one who could mix his punches with the best in the business.

Louis wanted to take on Conn, especially as Billy was claiming that Joe was ducking him but promoter Mike Jacobs was not so sure. 'Uncle Mike' told Louis that Conn was only a light-heavyweight and would be too light for a heavyweight championship fight, especially going in against a powerful hitter like Louis. 'The fight wouldn't draw a nickel,' said Jacobs. When Conn heard this, he argued that he had already taken on and beaten good heavyweight contenders such as Bob Pastor and Lee Savold, knocking out Pastor in 13 rounds.

Jacobs relented, seeing that there was nobody else around, and set the match for 18 June 1941 for the Polo Grounds in New York and a crowd of 54,487 turned out. The fight turned out to be a classic. Louis was behind on points after 12 rounds because of his inability to catch and hold the shifty, speedy challenger. On several occasions Conn opened up with barrages of blows that stunned the heavyweight champion and caused him to hold. In a desperate last stand, Louis finally trapped his tormentor in the 13th when a volley of lefts and rights sent Conn to the canvas and he was counted out by referee Eddie Joseph after two minutes and 58 seconds of the round. It had been a desperately close call.

'Conn was one of the hardest opponents of my entire career,' remembered Louis. 'He was here, there and everywhere, and always sticking out that snappy left jab followed by jarring hooks and uppercuts. I just couldn't pin him down to set him up for a pay-off punch. Every time I went back to my corner as the rounds went by, Chappie was looking more and more worried. Chappie's strategy was that I just had to keep the pressure on him and that Conn would eventually tire out. "He will tire, just wait," he said to me at the end of the tenth, I think. I nodded but hell, his tiredness was taking a long time.

'When I got back to my corner at the end of the 12th, Chappie barked, "You're losing this one unless you go all out, hell-for-leather and get him. You'll have to knock him out or you'll lose the title. You can't leave it for the 14th or 15th round. That's too late. Go for it now." The minute's interval flew by. The bell went for the 13th and I knew this was it. I heard later that Conn was told in his own corner that I was getting tired and that he should get in there, slug it out and put me on the boards and finish me off. That was Conn's big mistake.

'He came out fighting, like a true Irishman I guess, and started slugging toe-to-toe. He shot over a hard left hook but I countered with my own right hand and lo and behold he staggered. This was it. I followed through with a volley of lefts and rights and he slumped to the canvas. I watched as he tried to get up but he just couldn't make it. It was all over but what a close call. If Conn had kept his head, he might have been the new champion. It's nearly 30 years since that fight but I remember it as if it was only yesterday.'

The win over Conn was Louis's 18th successful defence of his title. Mike Jacobs planned to put them together in a rematch but Conn broke his hand not in a training session, as the publicity had it, but in a row with his father-in-law, former Major League baseball player 'Greenfield' Jimmy Smith. As it was, the fight was postponed indefinitely. They would not meet again until after the war when Jacobs matched them in an eagerly awaited return fight in the first heavyweight championship bout since hostilities ended. The venue was the Yankee Stadium on 19 June 1946.

Jacobs had predicted an attendance of 70,000 because of the anticipated interest and the fact that the first fight had ended inconclusively in many people's minds. Altogether the crowd came to 45,265. Even so, the take on the gate was $1,925,564, making it the second-largest receipts in boxing history, topped only by the second Gene Tunney–Jack Dempsey fight in Chicago in 1927 which drew $2,658,660. However, the fight was a disappointment. Conn had lost the speed and dexterity he had displayed in the first contest and Louis was always on top, a furious combination of lefts and rights sending the lacklustre challenger down and out after two minutes and 29 seconds of round eight.

Recalled Louis. 'I opened fast but I knew at that moment that he wasn't right for this fight. I thought he lacked determination. I don't think he was in there to win, just go the distance. That's my view anyhow. Billy may have a different viewpoint. I guess he would. When he went down in the eighth round I knew he wouldn't get up. He didn't.

'I had a new trainer then, Manny Seamon. Poor old Chappie Blackburn died of a heart attack in 1942. His health was never great. Seamon did a great job with me but I'll never forget Chappie. We called each other Chappie by the way. He made me a boxer in the first place and he was with me 'til the end of his life. He was my closest friend. Chappie was tough on me, and I sometimes disagreed with his advice but in the end he was always right. I suppose he is remembered best as my trainer but he was a good fighter in his own right in his early days.

'Look up your record books or your files or get in touch with boxing people in the States and you will discover how good he was. In his day as an active boxer he was fast and had a good left hook. Although Chappie only weighed around 135lb he took on greats like Joe Gans and Sam Langford and Philadelphia Jack O'Brien. Today he would have been world champion but back then when he was boxing, around the turn of the century or so, black men found it hard to get any kind of recognition because of the colour of their skin. A real shame.'

Louis was coming near the end of his career by 1947 and his final two defences were against another veteran, Jersey Joe Walcott. Around then there were no legitimate contenders around, ones seriously considered as being worthy to challenge for boxing's greatest prize. The most likely contender had been the Pennsylvanian ex-miner Joe Baksi, who had recently looked impressive with stoppage wins over the English fighters Bruce Woodcock and Freddie Mills in London. But that summer Baksi put himself out of contention after losing a controversial points decision to a local in Sweden, Olle Tandberg.

Mike Jacobs showed no enthusiasm for matching the ordinary Tandberg with Louis in a title fight. Baksi said he did not want to take on Louis 'at the moment'. Eventually in desperation, the promoter went for the veteran Jersey Joe Walcott but only for an exhibition match with Louis over ten rounds. Jacobs felt that Walcott would not be a big enough attraction in a real fight but the New York State Athletic Commission insisted that any ten-rounder with Louis would have to be for the title so Jacobs somewhat reluctantly agreed to sanction it over 15 rounds.

A capacity crowd exceeding 18,000 came to Madison Square Garden on 5 December 1947 to witness the first black v white heavyweight championship fight since Louis dispatched John Henry Lewis in the first round in 1939. The racial issue was now a thing of memory, albeit bad memory, and happily the newspapers completely ignored it. The fight went the full 15 rounds and Louis was lucky to leave the ring with his title intact.

'I had been hoping to get it over quickly but it didn't work out like that,' said Louis. 'Walcott was a shifty performer. Not with Billy Conn's footwork and dazzling speed but he moved a lot, from side to side, and fired punches from different angles. I couldn't figure him out. I hadn't encountered his style before, surprisingly enough considering my long years in the ring. Or maybe it was me. I guess I was slowing down, and I was.

'I really thought I got to him in the ninth when I staggered him with a short hook but he just shook off the blow and fought back. I'd lost my chance. For the rest of the fight Walcott fought in spurts, just doing enough to keep in front, I guess, and mainly went on the retreat. He seemed determined to stay on his feet until the end and snatch the decision. I just couldn't hit him with a single shot to set him up for the knockout. He was just too damn slippery, and fair play to him. That was the strategy planned by his team and it worked.

'At the final bell I tried to leave the ring before the decision was announced. I knew I had lost but what's the point of hammering it home. Manny Seamon, my trainer, held me back and told me I'd have to wait for the official decision.

Harry Balogh, the announcer, grabbed the overhead microphone, pulled it down and announced that one judge Frank Forbes marked his card in my favour, 8-6 and one even. The other judge Marty Monroe had it 9-6 for me and the referee Ruby Goldstein marked it 7-6 for Walcott, with two even.

'I had held on to my title by a desperately narrow margin. I was just lucky. The big crowd booed the decision, a strange sound for me to experience, but they knew too that Walcott was a real winner even if I was still the champion. Bags of letters and telegrams were delivered to the New York State Commission calling for either the commission, the mayor or the governor to reverse the decision and give the title to Walcott by default. I began to feel guilty about calling myself champion. There was only one solution. I had to fight Walcott again to settle things once and for all.'

The return fight was set for 25 June 1948 at the Yankee Stadium and a crowd of 42,267 turned out. It was an exceptionally dull fight for round after round with Louis waiting for the right opening and Walcott shifting and countering. In the tenth, referee Frank Fullam intervened to tell both men that unless they put some action into the fight, he would throw both of them out. Luckily, in the 11th round Louis saw the opening he had been looking for and went for the kill – and there was no better finisher in boxing then than Louis.

This is how Nat Fleischer of *Ring* magazine saw the finish, 'Louis first nailed Walcott with three fast, numbing straight lefts to the head and then drove a crushing right to the jaw. All the fight left the Jerseyite. His legs became rubbery. He caught a right to the body that brought his guard down and then came the hurricane of punches. Walcott tried to hang on but nothing could save him from the fury of Louis' attack. Utterly defenceless, he was spared further punishment only by collapsing in his tracks. He was counted out after 2.56 of the 11th round.'

Louis's recollections of the fight were still clear after over 20 years, 'Few of my fights gave me as much satisfaction as that win over Walcott the second time round. I know it was a dull fight until that 11th round but I had to wait for the right opening. I knew Jersey Joe would sooner or later get a bit overconfident the way Billy Conn did and he would come into my range. He did in the 11th and that was when I saw my opening and fired my best shots.'

Louis was still champion of the world. As he left the ring, he could hear the pleasant thunder of cheers as he had so often heard in the past. He had erased the memory of his bad performance six months earlier. He was still the 'Brown Bomber' to his fans. In the dressing room he announced that this could well be his last fight although he wanted some time to think it over. As it happened, he did not officially retire until five months later. On 1 March 1949 he called a press conference to announce that he had informed the National Boxing Association, known today as the World Boxing Association or the WBA, that he was retiring. His reign had been a magnificent one, 11 years and 25 successful title defences against the best contenders and never once ducking anybody.

Louis was in deep debt by now, however, with the Internal Revenue Service hounding him over unpaid taxes. 'There was no way I could pay the outstanding tax except by climbing back into the ring,' he explained. Predictably, he came back on 27 September 1950 to meet Ezzard Charles at Yankee Stadium. Even though Charles had proven himself to be the best heavyweight in the world with victories over the top contenders, he was recognised only by the National Boxing Association, the NBA. The general feeling was that with Louis making a return to the ring, Charles would really have to defeat the old 'Brown Bomber' to prove himself 'the real champion'.

Charles was born in Lawrenceville, Georgia, but had lived in Cincinnati, Ohio, since early childhood. The NBA, the New

York State Athletic Commission and the other authorities around the world agreed that the winner of a Charles–Louis fight would be recognised as the true and official champion.

Charles may be something of a forgotten man today, which is totally unfair as he is quite clearly one of the all-time greats. Nicknamed the 'Cincinnati Cobra' and the 'Cincinnati Flash', he has been vastly underrated by many historians. Charles compiled an outstanding record in his 19 years in the professional ring and triumphed over some of the best boxers of his day.

Arguably he was better as a middleweight and light-heavyweight than a heavyweight when he often had to concede weight. Ezzard defeated the great Archie Moore three times and had five wins over rock-chinned stylist Joey Maxim. He was criticised for being too cautious as heavyweight champion but he lost only four of his 13 championship fights, two to new champion Rocky Marciano when he was considerably past his best.

'The way I figured it,' recalled Louis, 'championships are won and lost in the ring, not in commissions' offices or boardrooms or courtrooms or anywhere else. That's the way I won my title and before I retired that was the way I wanted to lose it. Charles was undoubtedly the best of the heavyweights around and had won the NBA title but nobody else recognised him, not even *Ring* magazine.

'Moreover, as he was the best I wanted to fight him and prove once and for all whether he had a legitimate claim to the title. Me, I was hoping to make a bit of boxing history by becoming the first heavyweight champion to win back the title, something that nobody else had ever done. Many tried, such as James J. Corbett, Bob Fitzsimmons, Jim Jeffries, Jack Dempsey, Max Schmeling. They all failed. I thought I might have been the one to do it.'

The attendance of 13,562 was much lower than expected as Charles was not a top drawing card and many felt that Louis stood little chance of upsetting the NBA champion, a talented ring technician. Boxing writers like Grantland Rice of the *New*

York Herald Tribune and Arthur Daley of the *New York Times* picked Louis.

The gross gate totalled $205,000 but the signs of the future lay in the most extensive coverage yet of a fight, with the CBS network paying $146,000 including the radio rights. Estimates of the home-front audience amounted to 25 million. A whole new era had arrived in boxing.

The fight proved clear evidence of Louis's decline. He won no more than two or three of the 15 rounds and Charles earned a unanimous decision. On one occasion Louis caught his opponent with some solid punches but he was unable to pursue his advantage with sufficient speed. 'In the tenth there was another rush of hope when Louis's left jab repeatedly rocked Charles,' wrote Arthur Daley, 'but nothing came of it. Sad as it is to have to admit it, Louis is through. The road ahead has to be downhill.

'Perhaps there is something to the ancient but stern admonition, "No cheering in the press box, please." But a guy wouldn't be human if he remained neutral in this fight. The one-time cotton picker from Alabama saved boxing and gave it some nobility, innate decency, integrity and class. No sir, I rooted for Louis, unashamedly.'

Grantland Rice wrote, 'They don't come back is still across the gates of Never Never Land. Joe Louis found that out when Ezzard Charles proved that youth and speed and skill still have the call over age and power. Louis, slow of foot, slow of hand with his reflexes burdened by 36 years, found his nimble opponent far too good.

'I gave Charles 13 rounds and Louis two. Louis took the worst beating he had ever known since the first Max Schmeling fight. He was completely outclassed in every department. Round after round Louis took a terrific physical beating. Both men were willing to fight every second but Charles had all the weapons.'

Louis remembered, 'Charles was a good fighter and don't ever let anybody tell you otherwise but I knew from early in the fight that I didn't have it anymore. I was 36 and Charles was 29. I weighed 218lb and he was 183lb. I figured the extra weight would give me an advantage but it didn't. Charles was a cutting puncher rather than a knockout artiste and he just wore me out.

'I saw the openings but I just couldn't grasp them quick enough. That's what happens when you get old in boxing. I knew from the seventh round on that I couldn't do it. Charles kept piling it on and there was nothing I could really do about it. It wasn't a case of reflexes or anything like that but I just didn't have it. I remembered thinking to myself, "If only I'd fought you in my prime, or even six or seven years earlier. There would have been a different result."

'The thing was that Charles was never a massive puncher, rather a smooth fighter. But every time he landed, and he landed often, his blows were hurting and hurting bad. I remember the mayor of New York, Ray Impelliteri, coming up to my corner, the fifth round I think, and telling Manny Seamon and Marshall Miles that I should keep sticking Charles with the left hand to take the play away from him and keep him off balance. I was trying that but it didn't work.

'Arthur Daley, Grantland Rice and the other sportswriters to a man were right. I didn't have it any more. Some people said maybe I was rusty because the Charles fight was my first in competitive action for over two years and that I should have had a couple of warm-up fights. Maybe, I don't know. All I do know is that Charles beat me fair and square. You know, Ez told me later that he felt bad about beating me. He told me I was his idol and he took no pleasure if whacking me to the body and the head. I know that, but boxing is business after all.'

Louis was Robinson's idol too. 'I felt sad at seeing the end of Joe Louis,' Sugar Ray told this writer. 'It was hard to take. In his dressing room later, blood seeped from cuts above both of his eyes. One of his eyes was swollen shut. I was with him all the way but it was like trying to console an old, blind man. Squinting in pain and embarrassment, he was unable to put on his pants or locate his shoes. I bent down and worked his feet into his shoes and tied the laces. I helped him out of the ballpark.'

In retrospect, it is quite possible that the two-year lay-off did affect Louis's timing. He won his next eight fights, including an impressive win in six rounds in June 1951 over the capable contender Lee Savold, the same number of rounds it would take the new kid on the block Rocky Marciano to beat the Minnesota battler eight months later.

The impressive win over Savold might have been enough to get Louis another chance against Charles. Unfortunately, a month after the Louis–Savold fight, Charles gave Jersey Joe Walcott another title shot and Ezzard, against all the odds, was knocked out in seven rounds. With the world heavyweight title now in his possession after four unsuccessful attempts, Walcott showed no great hurry to risk it against Louis, who had two wins over Jersey Joe, even if one was disputed.

Louis's comeback inevitably ended in defeat when he ran into the juggernaut that was Rocky Marciano on 26 October 1951. The old 'Brown Bomber', at 37, was nine years older than Marciano, who was known as the 'Brockton Blockbuster'. Louis was stopped in the eighth of a scheduled ten-rounder at Madison Square Garden and announced his retirement, this time for keeps.

'I felt very confident going in against Marciano and while he was essentially a brawler, I figured I would be able to outbox him and I did, for three of the first five rounds,' said Louis. 'I found him easy to hit with left jabs. In the sixth I felt he was either getting stronger or I was slowing down. Probably both.

'Rocky knocked me down in the eighth with a kind of long, looping right hook but I got up before the referee Ruby Goldstein could start a count. Rocky, though, would not be denied. He had me down again with a short left hook and I took an eight count this time to clear my head.

'Rocky was after me right away and he knocked me against the ropes and followed through with a right hand which I couldn't avoid. The punch hit me on the back of the neck and I fell backwards through the ropes and on to the ring apron, with my legs still in the ring. I was lucky I didn't fall out of the ring, like Luis Firpo against Jack Dempsey in the 1920s. Goldstein had seen enough and stopped it. Ruby was right. I was going nowhere.

'I had no excuses and I haven't now. Rocky beat me fair and square. Was he a harder puncher than Max Schmeling? Well, it took Max took about 100 punches to knock me out. Marciano did it with a couple. In the dressing room everybody was crying, even Sugar Ray Robinson. The next thing Marciano came into the dressing room and said, "I'm sorry Joe. I'm sorry I had to be the one to do this." Rocky was a good guy, a real gentleman. Boxing needed people like Rocky Marciano.'

Red Smith wrote in the *New York Herald Tribune*, 'An old man's dream ended. A young man's vision of the future opened wide. Young men have visions, old men have dreams. But the place for old men is beside the fire.'

Louis never boxed again. President Kennedy would wipe out his tax bill but he still needed walking-around money. He made personal appearances, endorsed cigarettes even though he never smoked in his life, became a wrestler, a referee in boxing and wrestling matches and finally a greeter in Caesars Palace casino in Las Vegas. Louis never left the town and died there, wheelchair-bound, on 12 April 1981, a month short of his 67th birthday. He was inducted into the International Boxing Hall of Fame in Canastota, New York in 1990.

6

Mike Tyson

'Something wicked this way comes' – Macbeth

THERE is a distinct possibility that boxing history will not be kind to Mike Tyson. It can be said with more than a grain of truth that he wasted the potential to be the greatest of modern world heavyweight champions. He was billed variously as the 'Baddest Man on the Planet' and 'Iron Mike' and while he has to be up there with the best, he always had the air of a man whose built-in self-destruct mechanism was constantly ticking away.

In his turbulent private life, Tyson was accused of raping beauty parade contestant Desiree Washington and assaulting two elderly motorists, for which he served time in prison; lodging a $100m lawsuit against promoter Don King alleging financial irregularities; owing the Internal Revenue Service over $18m; had a gun put to his head by his one-time trainer Teddy Atlas who claimed Tyson was paying unwelcome attention to an underage girl; and several other anti-social incidents.

At a press conferences, he told Lennox Lewis, 'I'm coming for you, man. I want your heart and I want to eat your children,' even though the Briton had no offspring.

After defeating Jesse Ferguson, he said, 'I tried to catch him on the tip of his nose because I wanted to push the bone into the brain.' Before he fought the author's fellow-countryman Kevin McBride, he said, 'I'll gut this guy like a fish.' All these utterances did not exactly go down well with boxing scribes or anybody else. Then, of course, he famously twice bit the ears of Evander Holyfield resulting in immediate disqualification and worldwide shame.

But at his best, Tyson looked unbeatable, and was until he lost his title in a stunning upset against James 'Buster' Douglas in 1990. Before that he struck fear into the best men of his time by capturing the imagination of sports fans around the world when he burst on to the scene in the mid-to-late 1980s with thunder in his gloves and fire in his eyes. Three of his one-round victories in heavyweight championship fights – against Michael Spinks in 91 seconds, Carl Williams in 93 seconds and Bruce Seldon in 109 seconds – are in the top 12 fastest of all time. Indeed, during his 20-year career, he had nine wins in under 60 seconds.

Despite his shortcomings, it can never be forgotten that Tyson became the youngest ever world heavyweight champion at 20 years and one week short of four months when he blasted Trevor Berbick inside two rounds with a stunning left hook in November 1986. He had beaten the record set up first by Floyd Patterson who was champion at 21 years and ten months in 1956, and Muhammad Ali, then known as Cassius Clay, who won the title at 22 years and one month in 1964. Tyson is ranked at number 16 in *Ring* magazine's list of the 100 greatest punchers of all time. Many believe he was the last great heavyweight champion.

With his powerful physique and unsmiling face, Tyson looked menacing, always entering the ring in old-fashioned black shorts and boots without socks, several cultures away from the glitzy gowns and colourful ringwear which were fashionable at the time. Mike had been brought up on old fight films owned by his management team of Bill Cayton and Jim Jacobs, and was struck by the ordinary ring attire of greats like Jack Dempsey, Jack Johnson, Benny Leonard and others.

This writer came face to face with Tyson when he visited Dublin for a question-and-answer session in 2010. Afterwards we chatted in the company of my late wife Betty who could truthfully boast later that she was the first, and possibly the only, Irish lady to get a warm kiss on the cheek from Mike Tyson no less.

'Much of the stuff written about me is exaggerated by writers,' he said in that high-pitched voice and unmistakable lisp. 'It makes a big story so they write it. A lot of it is true but not all of it, I can assure you. I've changed my life around. Anybody can change their life around if they want to. If I did it, anybody can do it. I went through it all – cars, women, money, everything and today I think I've come out of it all a better person. Today my life centres around my wife, taking care of our kids, paying my bills, doing the important things in life. I also read a lot, mainly books dealing with history.'

It would be up to psychologists to probe what snapped in Tyson's mind over the years but there is little doubt that he had a troubled childhood. His life seemed to be one long fight almost from the day he was born, the youngest of five children, on 30 June 1966 in Brooklyn, New York. His father Jimmy, originally from Jamaica, would leave the family home soon after and the rearing of the children was left to Mike's mother Lorna May in the tough Bedford-Stuyvesant district of Brooklyn.

'We later moved to Brownsville when I was ten and she died six years later and I was left in the care of Bobby Stewart, a counsellor, and former boxer Cus D'Amato, a trainer and manager, and Cus would become my legal guardian. Sadly my mother only saw me as a wild kid running the streets, coming home with new clothes that she knew only too well that I didn't pay for. I never got a chance to talk to her or know about her before she died of cancer. It had no effect on my later life but it's still a crushing thought, emotionally and personally.

'As I say, I was constantly in trouble and finished up being committed to the Tryon School for Boys, a correctional institution in upstate New York. There, I was left in the care of Bobby Stewart, a counsellor and former boxer, who began teaching me to box. Stewart later introduced me to D'Amato, a native New Yorker from the Bronx. D'Amato was famous in boxing circles as a trainer and manager, and had guided Floyd Patterson to the heavyweight championship of the world and Jose Torres to the light-heavyweight title. He also trained the future middleweight champion of the world Rocky Graziano as an amateur.'

When Tyson was released from Tryon, D'Amato suggested the lad move in with him and his long-time companion Camille Ewald, a Ukrainian, into his 14-room home in the Catskills region of upper New York overlooking the Hudson River. Cus ran a gym over the local police station, hoping to find another champion. One day he received a call from Stewart asking him to look over a promising kid named Mike Tyson. D'Amato liked what he saw and the veteran boxing man would soon become Mike's legal guardian in place of his late mother.

'Like most amateurs I wanted to represent my country in the Olympics.' recalled Tyson. 'They were held in Los Angeles in 1984. I won the Junior Olympics in Denver, Colorado but I lost out in the Olympic trials on a bad decision against Henry Tillman and he won the gold medal. I was terribly disillusioned with the amateurs and anyway Cus figured I was ready for the professionals at that stage. I made my debut on 6 March 1985 in Albany, New York and stopped Hector Mercedes in the first round. It was a very encouraging start.'

Along with Bill Cayton, an advertising executive, and Jim Jacobs, a wealthy former handball player, D'Amato set out a programme of two fights a month for the promising heavyweight with the hammer punch, with the aim of qualifying for a world championship chance. Sadly, Cus did not live to see his boxer's true potential and subsequent domination of the heavyweight division realised. On 4 November 1985, three days after Tyson's 11th fight, he died of pneumonia.

Mike was now looked after by his management team of Cayton and Jacobs and he seemed in good hands. Both were keen boxing fans with Tyson's interests at heart. They had formed a company named Big Fights Inc. that bought up old fight films, retaining rights to the material, and showed them on television. Theirs was an unrivalled collection of boxing lore and Tyson looked at the films regularly with both advisors, picking up tips as well as noting their old-fashioned ring garb.

Tyson soon filled out to a powerful 220lb. D'Amato had taught him the classic bobbing and weaving movements that are a necessary part of a stocky heavyweight's movements in order to present opponents who had longer reaches with a difficult target. 'Cus was a hard taskmaster, and there is no doubt about that, but he taught me all I knew,' recalled Tyson.

'He advised me to hold my hands high in the peek-a-boo style and slip and weave out of your opponent's range before closing in to deliver my own punches. Cus would tell writers, "Mike's trademark combination is a right hook to the body followed by a right uppercut to the chin, and few boxers will remain upright if caught by this combination." True, it worked in the ring. Many experts speculate that D'Amato's death was the genesis of many of the troubles Tyson was to experience as his life and career progressed.

One of Tyson's most important wins on his way to the title was his victory over Mitch 'Blood' Green, a former New York gang leader and said to be the inspiration for the movie *The Warriors* that centred on gang warfare in the Big Apple. They met on 20 May 1986 at Madison Square Garden. 'It was a real thrill to box at the Garden, the Mecca of boxing, for the first time,' Tyson remembered. 'All the greats had fought there, Joe Louis, Sugar Ray Robinson, Gene Tunney, Harry Greb, Muhammad Ali, Willie Pep, Sandy Saddler and on and on. I had been watching them in action at the Garden on our fight films.

'Green was a big guy, 6ft 5in and weighing 219lb. He had won four consecutive New York Golden Gloves titles as an amateur and he had been going around saying, "I'll knock out Tyson. He's a pretender to the throne." Right up to the day of the contest he was complaining about getting a raw deal

CLOSE ENCOUNTERS WITH THE GLOVES OFF

from his promoter Don King and was demanding release from his contract with King's son Karl. He was moaning that I was getting $200,000 and he was only getting $30,000.

'I wasn't concerned with all that complaining. My job was to get in there and win and that was the important thing as I saw it. I knew I was going to beat him as soon as we entered the ring and there were no more vibes from him. The fight went the full ten rounds and that was fine with me. You can't knock every opponent out. I won every round and that was the message I was putting across. Going the full distance for only the second time in my career was fun. I didn't want to sound egotistical but I found him real easy. I think I would have knocked him out if he hadn't held on so tightly.'

Before the end of the year Tyson would get his big chance at the world heavyweight championship. He climbed into the ring at the Hilton Hotel, Las Vegas on 22 November 1986 which happened to be the anniversary of President Kennedy's assassination in 1963. But few in the desert city of pleasure and gambling were thinking of the president. They were trying to figure a way to make money from the prohibitive odds of 4/1 which the gamblers were quoting on Trevor Berbick, the new young sensation from Canada by way of Port Anthony, Jamaica.

A deeply religious man known as the 'Preacher', Berbick had an on-off relationship with Don King and was said to have knocked on the promoter's hotel room door in Las Vegas at 6.30am brandishing a Bible and wearing a large crucifix. 'The Lord is on your side,' he exclaimed when a shocked King opened the door. 'Only with thine eyes shalt thou behold and see the reward of the wicked.'

Berbick had caused one of the biggest upsets of the decade in March 1986 when he won the WBC version of the heavyweight title by outpointing Pinklon Thomas. It was his second bid for the championship, having being outpointed by Larry Holmes in 1981. That was the year Berbick outscored Muhammad Ali, a fight that convinced the old champion that he should hang up his gloves for good.

It was Berbick who now stood between Tyson and history, as Mike was attempting to become the youngest ever heavyweight champion of the world – at 20 years and just four months. But Berbick did not stand for very long. This is how Mike saw the fight, 'When we came face to face in the centre of the ring, I saw fear in his eyes and I knew I could go for an early knockout. I started fast with hard shots from both hands and I felt confident I would get him. He was strong but I never thought he was as strong as I was. He wasn't doing much moving, just more or less standing in front of me. At the start of the second round I landed a hard right and he went down. He took a standing count.

'I hit him with hard lefts and rights and he was hanging on desperately. I shook him off and dropped him for the second time with a left hook to the head. He rose but staggered across the ring and fell again, his left ankle folding under him. When he got up, Mills Lane, the referee, waved him off. It was all over and I was heavyweight champion of the world, the youngest in the division in all history.

'I remember saying to my cornermen, "This victory is for my great guardian Cus D'Amato." I wouldn't have done it without Cus. He made me the champ. I won the belt for him. I could imagine him looking down in the company of many great fighters and saying, "That's my man down there. I always knew he would win the title some day." He was right. Cus would have been delighted no end with my victory. Sure, he would have been critical here and there but he always wanted me to give my best performance and do things right.'

Challengers now were lining up to take on the new champion, each confident of defeating him. After all, boxing's biggest prize was on offer. Four months after winning the championship Tyson took on the challenge of James 'Bonecrusher' Smith. Again, the big fight was set for the Hilton Hotel on 7 March 1987 and it was for Tyson's World Boxing Council belt and Smith's World Boxing Association title. It would be the first step by Tyson's management team towards their man unifying the heavyweight championship.

Smith, from Magnolia, North Carolina, was the first college graduate to win a version of the title, having obtained a degree in business administration in Raleigh, North Carolina. During a spell in the US Army from 1976 to 1978 he earned his 'Bonecrusher' nickname. 'I crushed a few bones, broke a few noses, fractured a few ribs,' he would tell reporters.

After that Smith worked as a prison guard and counsellor, married a teacher, raised two children and toyed with boxing. Eventually in 1981, at the age of 23, he decided to go full-time into the sport and inside five years he had won the WBA title. When he and Tyson came face to face in the centre of the ring for the pre-fight instructions, Smith's considerable advantages in height, reach and weight were very obvious. He stood 6ft 4in and at 224lb he outweighed Tyson by 14lb.

The betting boys, however, were unimpressed and Tyson was installed as 8/1 favourite. There were takers at these odds even in the gamblers' paradise of Las Vegas, and most of the betting money changed hands on the naming of the round in which punters thought Mike would win. Few dollars were laid on the fight going the distance.

Tyson, still only 20, came to make war but the 33-year-old Smith, after tasting a vicious right hook in the opening seconds, decided he did not relish any more of those or he would be staring up at the ring lights for ten seconds or more. From then on, he fought a negative survival campaign. He grabbed and held whenever Tyson got close, like a drowning man hanging on to a lifebelt. The fight soon developed a boring pattern of Tyson throwing a punch, Smith holding, Tyson throwing another blow and Smith smothering again and so on.

Neither did the 'Bonecrusher' ever try to work his way out of a clinch, simply clinging on and waiting for the patient referee Mills Lane to prise them apart. Smith hardly threw much more than 30 shots in the entire fight. Smith's safety-first spoiling tactics certainly did not win him any friends in the crowd, with the boos getting louder as it wore on to the point that there were even chants of 'fight, fight' towards the end. Tyson won quite clearly, on scores of 120-106 and two markings of 119-107. It was his 29th win in a row and only the third time he had been forced to go the full distance.

'Yes, I was very, very disappointed the way the fight turned out,' he recalled. 'Smith was in there to stay the course and he simply did not want to fight, much to the frustration of myself and the crowd who had paid good money, with people paying $1,000 for a ringside seat. I agree that he was strong but he just wouldn't fight. He held me so tightly that I could never get set. Don't forget that he was fighting for the world heavyweight championship and what does he do? He holds on tightly like a limpet.

'That's no way to act in such an important fight, is it? I firmly believe, and it would be the view I'm sure of every boxer, indeed any sportsman or sportswoman anywhere in the world, that it's your duty to entertain the public. You've got to give them good value to the best of your ability, and I can't say that "Bonecrusher" Smith gave them that service.'

The show must go on, nevertheless. Tyson and his team had set their sights on unifying the championship and the only one left was the International Boxing Federation belt. Michael Spinks, a former Olympic middleweight champion and one of two fighting brothers from St Louis, Missouri, held that title but after agreeing to defend against Tyson, he decided to opt out in favour of an easier defence, against the New Yorker of Irish extraction Gerry Cooney, which earned him $5m.

The IBF stripped Spinks of the title, declared the championship vacant and sanctioned a fight between Tony Tucker, the number one contender, and James 'Buster' Douglas on 30 May 1987. Tucker came from behind to win on a stoppage in ten rounds, leaving the way clear for a unification bout with Tyson, who was fresh off an impressive win in six rounds over Pinklon Thomas. The unification match was set for the Hilton Hotel in Las Vegas for 1 August that year.

The flamboyant promoter Don King billed the fight as 'Glory hallelujah' and told the media, 'Not since the days of Muhammad Ali has there been one king of the throne, one champion of the world to respect and admire as the greatest heavyweight on God's earth. Now we have cleaned up the mess of all these champions, just like we promised we would, and after this fight we will have just one to whom we shall bow the knee. Glory hallelujah!'

Tucker originally came from Grand Rapids, Michigan, the town that produced the immortal world middleweight champion Stanley Ketchel, the 'Michigan Assassin', and modern great Floyd Mayweather Junior. Basing himself later in Houston, Texas, Tucker spent a long spell in Emanuel Steward's famous Kronk Gym in Detroit where he learned his boxing skills. An impressive 6ft 5in and coming in at 222lb, Tucker had all the equipment to make a big name for himself in boxing but lacked the killer instinct, a quality Tyson had in abundance.

There was the promise of shocks to come when Tyson staggered his opponent with a mean left uppercut in the opening minute but from then on, 'Iron Mike' was in control without really reverting to his most brutal style. Tucker was not helped by breaking his right hand in the second round and boxed on the defensive for the remainder of the fight. Constantly on the attack without putting Tucker on the boards, Tyson won the votes of all three judges after 12 rounds.

'Tony Tucker gave me the hardest fight of my career,' remembered Tyson. 'I was in real pain at the end of the first round. It was nothing to do with Tony's punching although he did shake me up pretty bad in the opening minute. The pain was caused when he trod on my right foot, and broke my toenail. My right foot was throbbing throughout the fight.

'He kept moving all the time but around the halfway stage I felt I had him because he was slowing down. My punches were getting to him. I will say that he took some good punches to the head and body but he fought back, as tired as he was. He got a bit cocky towards the end and went into an Ali shuffle but I didn't mind that too much. He was probably showing that he still had a chance to win the fight and I understood that. I knew I had the decision at the end. I was now universally recognised as world heavyweight champion and that was a good feeling.'

The fight which the boxing world now wanted to see was Tyson v Michael Spinks, the number one contender, but Spinks seemed in no hurry to take on the champion. Tyson, in any event, decided to meet other opponents and add to his finances. Tyrell Biggs, who won the super-heavyweight gold medal in the Los Angeles Olympics of 1984, was blown away in seven rounds and Larry Holmes, the former world heavyweight champion, was finished in the fourth, both fights taking place in Atlantic City. Tony Tubbs, a former WBA heavyweight champion, lasted only as far as two minutes and 54 seconds into the second round in Tokyo.

The date for the Spinks fight was finally set for 27 June 1988 and the Convention Center in Atlantic City was packed on fight night. It was the seventh defence Tyson was making since winning the WBC version of the title in November 1986. If anybody, Spinks was the man most likely to upset him, helped by the personal problems Tyson said he was experiencing.

The challenger was, after all, unbeaten in 31 professional fights and an impressive amateur career that saw him win the 1976 Olympic gold medal in Montreal. He had been the undisputed world light-heavyweight champion and had gone on to hold the IBF version of the heavyweight title, twice getting 15-round decisions over Larry Holmes. Spinks also had the added incentive of following his brother Leon, another ex-Olympic gold medallist, who had also won the world heavyweight title.

The theories about Tyson's business and domestic diffic-ulties, the former brought on by the death of his co-manager and the latter by his troubled marriage, had also tempted some gamblers to go for Spinks. Then, too, Mike still fretted over his late, great mentor Cus D'Amato.

As it happened, Spinks had no chance. Tyson, entering the ring without robe or socks, moved straight into the challenger from the bell and connected with a right to the head. Spinks had no option but to hold. Tyson pushed him away, backed his opponent against the ropes and landed a smashing left uppercut followed by a powerful left hook to the body and

Spinks sank to his knees. He was up at two, took the mandatory standing count, and threw a right cross, more in hope than anything else, but Tyson moved inside it and dropped the ex-Olympian with a heavy right to the jaw for the full count. It was all over in 91 seconds, the fourth-fastest knockout in the history of the heavyweight championship.

'I always felt I could beat Spinks from the moment the fight was signed,' Tyson recalled. 'True, I had a lot of personal problems at the time but I just had to forget about them and get on with the business in hand. My trainer Kevin Rooney told me in the corner as I waited for the pre-fight instructions that he bet his share of the purse I would knock Spinks out in the first round. From the first bell I knew he couldn't hurt me and he didn't. The papers quoted me after the fight as saying, "I can beat any man in the world because I'm still the greatest." Yes, I think I said that.'

By now Tyson's private life was no longer private, and was spiralling out of control, unravelling like a ball of wool. Jim Jacobs, Tyson's co-manager, was stricken with leukaemia and died quite suddenly, leaving Tyson emotionally adrift. Mike's wife Robin Givens, most famous for her role as a glamorous pupil in the TV sitcom *Head of the Class* and who Tyson had married in secret, resented that Jacobs's widow continued to share a one-third interest in Tyson's earnings and along with Givens's manipulative mother, started to take a strong interest in Mike's finances.

To add to this, Givens's sister revealed that he was abusing his wife a mere five months into the marriage. Don King, never far from controversy, was also part of the muddled scenario. The promoter had a big interest in most of the heavyweights of the day and had begun a campaign to 'Take Over Tyson'. Meanwhile, Tyson got involved in a 4am street fight with a former opponent, Mitch Green, in Harlem, New York, and fractured his hand, as well as knocking himself out after crashing his BMW into a tree.

If that were not enough, he smashed up his mansion after a row with his wife and hurled a TV set and furniture into the street after telling Robin and her mother to 'get out of my life'. In Moscow where Robin was filming, he smashed a TV camera and chased his wife and her mother through the hotel lobby.

If that weren't all, he signed an exclusive contract with Don King in defiance of his manager Bill Cayton; sacked his long-time trainer Kevin Rooney because the coach supported Cayton, who sued for $10m; was accused by two women of sexual harassment; and flew to the Dominican Republic in Don King's private plane to finalise his divorce after a marriage that had lasted one year and eight days.

'After all the distractions, I just wanted to get on with my boxing career,' he said. 'I wanted to take on the best heavyweights in the world and prove that I was the number one man, just like Ali and Marciano and Louis and the other champions over the years in boxing history. They ducked nobody and if somebody gave them trouble, they took them on a second time. That's the mark of a real champion and that's the way I wanted it to be for me.'

In the midst of all the mayhem, Tyson still managed to squeeze in two title fights, against Frank Bruno, an idol in his native Britain, and Carl 'The Truth' Williams, a New Yorker who boasted, 'I'm the man to end Tyson's reign. Just wait and see.' Bruno was dispatched in five rounds in February 1989 after Mike was staggered by a big right uppercut in the first round. Five months later Williams was in trouble from the first serious attack when Tyson dropped him in the opening round and as referee Randy Neumann stared into the boxer's glassy eyes, he had no option but to stop it – after 93 seconds.

Tyson planned to retire after the Williams fight, having cleaned up the heavyweight division of all legitimate challengers. He also wanted to sort out his mudded private life. Don King, who was by now Mike's manager as well as his promoter, was planning an easy defence of the title and selected a virtual 'no-hoper', James 'Buster' Douglas. 'This will be another one-rounder,' forecast the confident King. 'But the fight was considered such an outrageous mismatch that he couldn't get TV coverage in any American venue and was forced to take it out of the country, with Japan prepared to put it on.

Douglas was very much the journeyman fighter, and about as dependable as a ladder with several rungs loose. But he laughed off suggestions that he would be the fall guy in what would be his big chance. When somebody showed him a copy of the *Los Angeles Times* with the headline 'Tyson in the mood for Buster's last stand' he laughed, 'This will be Tyson's last stand.' But when Tyson entered the ring in Tokyo's domed Korakuen Stadium on the cold afternoon of 11 February 1990, Mike was a prohibitive 42/1 favourite, the greatest odds in boxing history.

Shock of shocks. It did not work out quite like that. This is how Earl Gustkey of the *Los Angeles Times* saw the fight, 'For Iron Mike Tyson, unbeaten in 37 fights and thought to be on the way to Rocky Marciano's career heavyweight record of 49-0, the unthinkable happened. Before a crowd of about 30,000, Douglas won nearly every round, closed Tyson's left eye and knocked him out in the tenth round. Tyson had nearly pulled it off near the end of the eighth round. He dropped Buster with a hard right uppercut, and whether or not Douglas beat the count was the subject of heated debate afterward. Videotape showed Douglas was down for 13 seconds. Tyson's manager/promoter Don King filed a protest but to no avail.

'The final scene played out in the tenth round was almost impossible to believe. Tyson was hit with a tremendous right uppercut to the chin near Douglas's corner. He reeled backwards and Douglas was on him instantly. Tyson was defenceless as Douglas smashed him with a right and left, another right, and finally a long sweeping left hook that put Tyson on his back. As he hit the blue canvas, his mouthpiece popped into the air. He groped for it and stuffed it into his mouth backward. As the Mexican referee Octavio Meyron counted him out, Tyson's face was slack and his mouth open. His glazed eyes were aimed towards the stadium's centre field fence.'

For days after the fight King was still protesting over the long count, citing the famous Jack Dempsey–Gene Tunney incident in 1927 when Tunney was on the boards in the seventh round for 14 seconds. To support his claim that Tyson was robbed, King got the backing of the WBC president Jose Sulaiman and the WBA chief executive officer Gilbert Mendoza but the full tide of public opinion was against them and he backed down reluctantly.

'I don't want to make excuses for being knocked out by Douglas as it's over and done with now but I wasn't properly prepared for that fight, physically or mentally,' Tyson remembered. 'I was way overweight and I didn't consider Douglas was a serious challenger for my title. I didn't even watch his fights on video. I had easily beaten all the guys who had knocked him out so why should he pose a threat to me? Anyway I was having a good time in Tokyo. I don't remember the referee counting me out. When I got back to my corner I asked one of my guys, "What happened?" I was told, "You've just being counted out, Mike. It's all over." It was.'

There were immediate ramifications of the sensational upset. Before the Douglas fight, Don King had scheduled Tyson to defend his title four months later against the number one contender Evander Holyfield in Atlantic City. The impresario Donald Trump was bankrolling the match, with Tyson getting between $22m and $25m in what was being projected as the richest fight of all time. This was now gone. Also ended was Tyson's seven-fight $24m contract with the HBO television network which had two fights remaining.

The planned return fight never took place. Douglas lost his title eight months later when he was knocked out in three rounds from a right to the jaw by Holyfield. A title fight between the new champion and Tyson was arranged for the autumn of 1991 but Tyson got himself arrested in July for the rape of 18-year-old Desiree Washington, Miss Black Rhode Island, in an Indianapolis hotel room. He was found guilty in March 1992 and sentenced to six years in prison followed by four years of probation. He served three years.

After being four years out of the ring, Tyson made his comeback and after four early wins including regaining the

WBC belt, he qualified for the long-awaited title fight with Holyfield. The match was set for the MGM Grand Garden, Las Vegas on 9 November 1996 for the WBA title, Tyson having forfeited the WBC belt for failure to defend it against Lennox Lewis. But another shock loomed for Tyson as he was stopped in ten rounds in a fight he never looked like winning.

'Tyson was the allegedly invincible 10/1 favourite,' wrote George Kimble of the *Boston Herald*. 'At the opening bell, Holyfield charged to the centre of the ring, took a glancing rapier thrust from Tyson's right and moments later rocked Tyson with a decent left hook of his own, setting a pattern that would endure for much of the night. As the fight wore on, it was Tyson who became increasingly weary. Time and again Holyfield would wade into battle, dodging Tyson's lethal but increasingly wild punches to deliver picturesque left hooks and short right hands.

'Having taken command of the fight, Holyfield nailed Tyson with a short right in the tenth that sent him staggering backwards halfway across the ring. Holyfield was unable to finish the job then only because the bell intervened. Holyfield pressed his advantage in the penultimate round, and was pounding Tyson about the ring when referee Mitch Halpern intervened with 27 seconds of the round gone, setting off wild pandemonium among the 16,325 customers at the Garden and millions more watching on television around the world.'

Tyson recalled, 'What can I say? People lose, everybody loses in fights, in life and that's how it is. After the first round I don't remember much of the fight as I was in a daze. I don't want to make any excuses. I didn't then and I won't now. He headbutted me but I probably did the same thing to him, too. I can't remember. Do you know that after the fight was over, I was so dazed that I asked my cornermen, "What round did I knock out Holyfield in?" It was crazy.'

Tyson and Holyfield met in a return fight seven months later, again at the MGM Grand Garden. Tyson felt he could regain the title, telling a media conference a few days before the fight, 'I made mistakes last time and I assure everybody that I'm in better shape this time, much better shape. I'll regain the title.' Alongside him on the raised platform, Holyfield declared, 'Everybody can have a bad day, and Mike had his bad day last time. He's getting a chance to prove who is the best heavyweight in the world, as I believe we're the two best.'

This time Tyson was disqualified at the end of three rounds for chewing off a hunk of the WBA champion's right ear and biting his left ear to end their rematch in a fast and fraudulent fashion. Early in the second round Tyson came straight ahead just as Holyfield, bending low from the waist, rose to embrace him. There was a clash of heads and Tyson emerged with a cut that spurted blood. After trailing by three points in the third, Tyson chomped on Holyfield's ears and referee Mills Lane, a district attorney and court judge in his other lives, intervened. 'One bite is bad enough but two bites – that's it,' Lane declared later.

Ron Borges of *Boxing '97* magazine reported, 'The fight started in much the same way as the first one. Holyfield was stronger in mind and spirit, pushing Tyson backwards, tying him up, refusing to back down, smothering his opponent's power shots and rattling his head with a strong right hand that appeared to buckle Tyson's back leg. Tyson trailed for two rounds before the fight was stopped in the third because a coward broke the rules rather than face the very real possibility of taking another beating and ending up on his back or doubled over in a corner, as happened to him in their first encounter.'

Dave Anderson of the *New York Times* wrote, 'When Tyson was butted, his bitterness and anger exploded. But head butts in clinches are part of boxing. The true gladiators have fought harder with blood streaming down their faces, either from a punch or a butt – Sugar Ray Robinson, Rocky Marciano, Marvin Hagler, Carmen Basilio. Instead of fighting, Tyson bit Holyfield's ears harder.'

Ken Jones of *The Independent* reported, 'There can be no escape for Mike Tyson now. His ill-starred career is in jeopardy, his behaviour so savagely bizarre that all sympathy for him has gone. Who but that squalid crew of associates and hangers on can defend him now? The truth is that the bully has been found out. He was only at his best when the going was good.'

Tyson remembered, 'It was the worst night of my professional career, and I did something I had never done before, and never did again. I can't say exactly why I acted like that, other than saying that when Holyfield butted me, and he did it several times, in the first fight as well, I thought I might lose because of the cut over my left eye, caused by a butt. I snapped and reacted and paid the price for it. The fight had started well. I was confident and I was moving well but those butts, in all three rounds, changed the course of the fight. There you go. I'm happy to say he and I are the best of friends today. He is a class brother.'

Tyson was fined $3m and banned from boxing for a year. He announced a comeback but his best days were behind him. On 8 June 2002 he was knocked out by Lennox Lewis in eight rounds. On 22 February 2003, in a bizarre mismatch, he managed to dispose of Clifford Etienne in 49 seconds. Out of the ring for nearly 18 months, he returned only to be flattened in four rounds by Danny Williams on 30 July 2004. Finally, 11 months later and approaching his 39th birthday, he retired after six poor rounds against the moderate Irishman, Kevin McBride, and promptly hung up his gloves – for keeps this time.

Tyson may have finished with boxing, but boxing was not finished with Tyson. In the spring of 2012 he performed his one-man show *Mike Tyson – Undisputed Truth* for a week at the MGM Grand, Las Vegas. In the summer it transferred to New York for a two-week run at the Longacre Theatre on Broadway. Written by his wife Kiki, Mike narrated his rollercoaster life and times, inside and outside the ring, with anecdotes about his opponents, promoter Don King and how he once found his former wife Robin Givens in a compromising position with the Hollywood star Brad Pitt. The show later toured Europe.

'Life's good today and I'm a happy man, despite all the ups and downs,' said the one-time 'baddest man on the planet' who has certainly mellowed with age now that he is heading into his 50s. 'I've had an extraordinary life – everything's happened to Mike Tyson. That's what life is all about. But I don't know what I would do without my family. We all know that life is temporary. I'm going to grow old and die tomorrow or ten years from now or 40 years if I'm lucky. But when you are with your family, it makes you feel that you will last forever.

'The future of boxing? A lot of people have pronounced the death of the sport but I don't see it that way at all. It's a bit quiet now but it will come back. It's been around for almost 200 years, legally that is, and it's not going to die. Wait until we get the next great heavyweight and we will want to see him again and again. That's how it goes in boxing. There is a great champion, then there's a lull, and another great champion comes along and so on. Just wait and see.'

7

Jack Dempsey

The Mauler and the Jazz Age

ON the blistering hot afternoon of 4 July 1919 in Toledo, Ohio, a crowd close to 19,000 passed through the gates at a specially constructed open-air arena to see Jack Dempsey challenge big Jess Willard for the heavyweight championship of the world. The temperature was just beyond 100 degrees and the discomfiture was such that most of the fans sat in their shirt sleeves, with the women in light clothes in a special enclosure organised by the actress Ethel Barrymore.

Promoter Tex Rickard had reason to be satisfied. With Dempsey he had the biggest attraction in the game, a two-fisted slugger with the utmost belief in himself and a man he was sure would win the title and go on to become one of boxing's all-time greats. Rickard was right on both counts. Dempsey would break box-office records right through the Roaring 20s, the Jazz Age, as a massive draw and the most popular boxer of his generation.

By modern standards Willard would not be considered a particularly big heavyweight, standing 6ft 6.5in tall and weighing around 230lb. But by the standards of his time he was a colossus, and was known as the 'Pottawatomie Giant', after the town in Kansas where he was born on 29 December

Old pals act with, from left, Sugar Ray Robinson, Floyd Patterson and Archie Moore

Sugar Ray Robinson, right, and Carmen Basilio shared two classic fights, with a points win for each

'Come and get me because I'm ready,' says George Foreman

The author takes it on the chin from George Foreman

Muhammad Ali regains the title by knocking out George Foreman in eight rounds

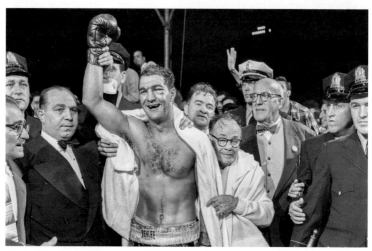

Rocky Marciano is the new world heavyweight champion following his knockout win in 13 rounds against Jersey Joe Walcott

Rocky Marciano misses with a powerful right on the way to knocking out Ezzard Charles in the eighth round

Rocky Marciano hammers Ronald LaStarza on the ropes in the 11th round

The author chats with Rocky Marciano, right, and Hollywood star George Raft

Ken Buchanan grimaces as he sinks to the floor against Roberto Duran in round 14

A neat right uppercut to the author's chin from Ken Buchanan

Joe Louis's greatest win, over Max Schmeling in the first round

Joe Louis sizes up Billy Conn in their first fight

Joe Louis lifts Tami Mauriello off his feet with a left hook in the opening round just before the finish

Joe Louis shows the author his famous right fist

Mike Tyson finishes off Trevor Berbick in the opening round

Referee Dave Barry counts over Gene Tunney in the famous Long Count fight with Jack Dempsey

The author joins Georges Carpentier, left, and Jack Dempsey at an awards dinner

Sugar Ray Leonard on the attack against Marvin Hagler

The author and his son Colin meet Sugar Ray Leonard

Earnie Shavers and the author at an awards dinner

Earnie Shavers is on record as the hardest puncher in ring history

Talking turkey as Joe Frazier chats with the author

George Foreman smashes Joe Frazier to defeat in two rounds

Trailing on points, Joe Louis finally catches up with Billy Conn in their first fight

Freddie Mills samples Billy Conn's left hook

'Careful what you write about me' says Muhammad Ali to the author alongside Billy Conn, with Ali's mentor Angelo Dundee in the background

Evander Holyfield, left, mixes it with Mike Tyson in an early round of their first fight

All smiles from Evander Holyfield and the author

The underrated Ezzard Charles, who was world heavyweight champion and uncrowned light-heavyweight king

Jersey Joe Walcott floors Ezzard Charles for the full count in the seventh round of their third fight

James J Braddock holds the bag for Jersey Joe Walcott as veteran manager 'Dumb' Dan Morgan looks on

A section of the large crowd who witnessed the Jack Dempsey–Carpentier fight

Georges Carpentier watches the crouching Jack Dempsey's next move in the opening round

Georges Carpentier, left, on the way to a win over George Cook in four rounds.

1881. It was on the edge of a Native American reservation and Jess rode wild horses in his teens. He saw his first boxing match when he drove a six-horse team into a small town in Oklahoma. Fascinated by the sport, he decided to give boxing a try and had his first fight at the late age of 29.

Willard went on to win the heavyweight title by knocking out a faded Jack Johnson in 26 rounds in Havana, Cuba in April 1915. But against the tigerish Dempsey he stood little chance. It was all over in three rounds when Jess tottered to his corner and sat down heavily, his jaw broken, his cheekbone fractured and his great white body a mass of bruises. 'I guess I'm beaten,' he gasped in a mass understatement to his seconds as the towel sailed into the ring. After one of the most one-sided fights in ring history, Dempsey had become the eighth man to win the title since James J. Corbett knocked out John L. Sullivan in the first world heavyweight championship fight fought with gloves in 1892.

When Dempsey came to London in 1973 for a testimonial dinner in his honour organised by the Anglo-American Sporting Club, I had the opportunity of interviewing him. One of the questions I put to the old champion was, 'What was it like to be the best heavyweight in the world at 24?'

'It was a great feeling,' he said in between signing menus for fans. 'I'd never experienced anything quite like it. To realise that you were the champ, the number one, was a terrific feeling. You know, I thought I had won in the first round. When Willard went down for the fourth time in that opening round, the referee Ollie Pecord counted him out and raised my right hand. The whole arena had gone crazy, with everybody shouting. My manager Jack Kearns, known as "Doc", had grabbed me and pulled me down the steps and yelled, "Let's get out of here. I'll see you in the dressing room."

'I went down the ring steps and had to push my way through the crowd who were milling around. Then I heard Kearns's voice behind me. "The fight's still on," he shouted. The bell saved him and nobody heard it. It seems the bell rang at the count of eight. Let's do it all over again.

'I boxed him in the second round because I wanted to try and conserve my energy but Kearns was yelling that I should finish him off. I went all out in the third and hit him with everything I could think of – hooks, uppercuts, jabs, you name it, I fired it. I knew I hadn't got much more to go and then at the interval the towel came fluttering in and it was all over. I was the new champion.

'Kearns surprised me in the dressing room when he said that he had made a bet of $10,000 against $100,000 that I would win in the first round. He lost that one and the $10,000 was deducted from my $19,000 purse money. I was angry about him making bets without telling me but that was Kearns, probably the original hustler. He was an underhanded guy but he had gotten me the championship fight and I guess that was all that mattered.'

Kearns indeed was a hustler but he was good for Dempsey. There is no doubt about that whatsoever. In 1896 at the age of 14 and with a great zest for life, Kearns joined the Yukon gold rush by stowing away on a freighter. He did not strike it rich and returned home to the state of Washington where he worked as a farmhand. A natural-born drifter, he finished up as a boxer in Montana and later opened a boxing club there. Moving to New York he saw the young Jack Dempsey fight in a small club and persuaded the kid to join up with him. The rest is history.

'There are a lot of stories as to how he was called "Doc" but certainly not because he was a medical man or anything like that.

'He was a bit of a rogue but he showed me how to dress and conduct myself in public, that sort of thing,' remembered Dempsey. 'More importantly he got me the fights that mattered on the way to the championship, turning me into the leading contender.

'We split up several years later after I won the title when he objected to me marrying the actress Estelle Taylor. It wasn't that he disliked Estelle. On the contrary, he did like her, a real beauty. But I was devoted to Estelle and I guess "Doc" resented his loss of control over me. I got my nose straightened as I was interested in making Hollywood movies.

'Nor was I happy with our financial arrangements. Harsh words were exchanged and we parted. That was it, the end of our six-year partnership. I linked up with a new manager by the name of Gene Normile and I guess you never heard of him. Few have today. Mainly, though, the promoter Tex Rickard organised my career and I left it to him.'

Dempsey recalled that Kearns concerned himself with managing other boxers including world welterweight and middleweight champion Mickey Walker and many years later the two world light-heavyweight champions Joey Maxim and Archie Moore. He also spent five years as a matchmaker with the promotional organisation, the International Boxing Club, in the 1950s.

Nothing much was heard of Kearns until 1964 when he made the sensational allegations that under his explicit instructions Dempsey's gloves were 'loaded' in the Willard championship fight. That is to say they were treated with either a hardening substance or alternatively one of the gloves was hiding a heavy piece of iron to increase the force of the blows.

Kearns maintained that he sneaked a container of Plaster of Paris in place of talcum power into the dressing room, and that when Dempsey wet his taped hands, the substance hardened and that his man 'had hands essentially covered in cement'. Kearns said he had too much riding on Dempsey to risk a defeat. Kearns made the claim in a *Sports Illustrated* excerpt from his autobiography in 1964 which was published posthumously as 'Doc' died a year earlier. 'The claim was ridiculous, absolutely ridiculous,' said Dempsey, continuing his reminiscences. 'Nobody believed Kearns.

'Eddie Eagan, the chairman of the New York State Athletic Commission, possessed a film of the fight with Willard and one of the things it showed before the fight started was having my taped hands examined in the ring and the gloves put on – and watched closely by Willard and his people. It was all done in the open, nothing in secret.

'*Boxing Illustrated* magazine later tested the idea and found that the plaster would crack the first time you hit somebody, leaving you with broken plaster in your glove. At best, this would make punching your opponent extremely painful and at worst, would break your hand. Even the makers of Plaster of Paris said their product could not possibly be used in the manner Kearns described.

'The second argument about hiding a piece of iron in my glove was too preposterous to even think about it. Would I have been able to drop a piece of iron without anybody noticing it? Very, very unlikely. In any event, the film of the fight often showed me pushing Willard away with open hands.

'My attorney instructed me to sue *Sports Illustrated*, which I did. I was determined to prove that the cover and the inside story were both libellous, had damaged my reputation and name as well as causing me untold distress and loss of income. Old "Doc" Kearns, a rascal to the end.

'People used to say that every asset I possessed as a boxer was developed in me by "Doc" Kearns. Okay, he got me started in the game but he didn't do everything. When I was at the height of my career I was often amused to read how he tied my right hand behind my back in training sessions and got me to use my left hand to develop it. I guess that was all in the imagination of press agents. The truth of the matter is that I've always been naturally left-handed. Even in the early days I used my left more than my right.

'Kearns also claimed he taught me body-punching. Not quite true. John Lester Johnson, a black boxer I fought in 1916, three years before I won the title, was my teacher. The tough battle ended in a draw and I learned a lot from Johnson. I had always thought that the only effective punch in boxing was a left hook to the chin but I soon learned that was all wrong. A good body blow is worth twice a punch to the chin and I learned that from Johnson. I perfected the body shot and it's what won most of my fights for me.

'I found it always paved the way for a shot to the chin. Let me say that Johnson hurt me badly, and I figured that if he could do as much damage to me with body punches, why couldn't I do the same to my opponents? There and then I became convinced that the best way to success in boxing was body punching and to this day nobody can convince me otherwise. In my following fights I employed that style and it worked.

'As a youngster I was rather frail but I developed my body when working on a farm. My parents were anything but rich and as soon as I was old enough to lift a bucket, I was sent out to work on a farm. I worked from dawn to dusk and I worked hard, building up the muscles in my arms, shoulders, back, my whole body. Later I worked in a copper mine, serving as a general utility man. I did the jobs nobody else wanted to do, hauling, lifting, swinging a pick, and all this many feet underground.

'My job in the copper mine got me into boxing, but there was no thought in my mind than that I wanted to be a boxer. There were some tough guys in the mine and they used to play jokes on me and forced me into fights. I had a lot of professional fights in my career but a lot more down the mine. Some of the guys were impressed by my natural fighting abilities and suggested I get a manager or an agent and become a boxer. When I left the mine I gave the boxing a bit of thought, and felt I might give it a try. Anyhow, I had nothing to lose.

'New York was an important fight town in those days and that's where I headed to start my boxing career and met "Doc" Kearns. To cut a long story short, I reckon I had about 11 managers over the years from beginning to end but it was "Doc", for all his faults, who was the most important one. He got me the title fight with Willard which started it all.'

Dempsey reigned as world champion for seven years. His first major win in a championship fight, and his third defence of the title, was over the talented Georges Carpentier, the 'Idol of France', in New Jersey on 2 July 1921. Carpentier was flattened in four rounds in what was (a) boxing's first million-dollar gate, (b) attended by a record crowd of 80,183 and (c) the first time a championship fight was broadcast.

The Frenchman had won the world light-heavyweight championship nine months earlier by knocking out Battling Levinsky in four rounds and issued a bold challenge to Dempsey for the heavyweight championship. He backed up his claim by pointing out that he was European heavyweight champion and was therefore entitled to go for the world title.

'When I climbed into the ring at Boyle's Thirty Acres arena and looked out over the massive crowd, I was flabbergasted,' said Dempsey. 'There were people everywhere. The sports writer Arthur Brisbane said it was like a big saucer of honey filled with flies. I'd never seen anything quite like it. The first round was quiet as I wanted to feel him out. I knew he had a big right hand and I was wary of that.

'I felt it in the second round when he caught me high on my left cheekbone, just here. There was a good chance that if he had caught me on the chin that he would have knocked me down and a fair chance that he would have knocked me out. There is a photograph somewhere, look it up, of me wincing at the impact of the punch. Yes, it was a good shot but it wasn't in the right place, luckily for me. As the round wore on, he shot a few more rights but I slipped them.

'I learned later that Carpentier had broken his hand with that first right hand punch in the second round and yes, I remember he was mainly using his left in the third round. But I felt I was getting on top. I was roughing him up with hooks to the head and body and I knew I had him beaten. He had lost a lot of his fire and I felt it was only a matter of time now before I'd knock him out.

'In the fourth I nailed him with a good left hook and he went down for nine. He got up groggy and I moved in fast. Another left and he was down again, and while he was falling I got him with a right. It was all over.

'The timekeeper told me that 57 seconds of round four had elapsed. At the finish I rushed over to help him back on his feet. I feel I must pay tribute to Carpentier's courage, however. He stood up to all my best shots. A real game guy, and one of the greats.'

Dempsey took a two-year break from the ring after the Carpentier fight. On the advice of his manager he invested in a few businesses and contented himself by boxing a few exhibitions to keep in reasonable shape. The promoter Tex Rickard advised him to box a little less as too much exposure would not do Jack's image or his reputation any good. Dempsey also took a long holiday in Europe with a party that included the syndicated sportswriter Damon Runyon who had nicknamed him the 'Manassa Mauler' after the Colorado town where Dempsey was born.

After being out of competitive action for a full two years Dempsey returned to the ring on 4 July 1923 to defend his title against Tom Gibbons in Shelby, Montana after receiving an offer from a haphazard conglomerate of local businessmen who knew nothing about boxing, never mind promoting a world heavyweight championship fight. They ruined the town. It was the only Dempsey title fight not promoted by Rickard – and it showed.

Dempsey called it 'the most fouled-up promotion of my boxing career'. After paying Jack and Kearns $100,000 on signing the contract and guaranteeing them a similar amount 30 days before the fight, the promoters ran short of money and turned to the banks and local businesses to help them out. They too went bust.

'It was incredible,' recalled Dempsey. 'The local promoters were putting on a big fight and they had no money. They were amateurs in every sense of the word. "Doc" and I agreed to go ahead with the fight anyway and forget about the rest of the money. During the prelims, guys lassoed the fences, pulled them down and got in for free. There was no organisation whatsoever. I won on points against a tricky opponent and after the fight "Doc" and I got out of town as quickly and as quietly as we could. I don't know what would have happened if we had hung around until the promoters started remembering that we were the only ones who made any money on the fight. Poor old Gibbons himself didn't get a cent. I heard later though that it got him seven or eight weeks on the vaudeville circuit.'

Putting the Shelby fiasco firmly behind him Dempsey returned to the ring two months later, this time for his regular promoter Tex Rickard, to meet Argentina's Luis Firpo at the Polo Grounds in New York on 14 September 1923. Rickard knew that this one would be a massive draw and he was proved right. It was boxing's second million-dollar gate with a crowd of 85,000 packing the famous ballpark.

Rickard had a colourful life. Born in Missouri, he left school at the age of nine and, while still a youngster, worked cattle drives from Texas to Montana. At 21 he became a town marshal in Henrietta, Texas and also tried his hand at cattle ranching in Brazil. In 1894, at the age of 23, he went to Alaska and discovered gold but later claimed that he sold his claim for too low a price.

Rickard drifted into boxing as a matchmaker in New York before turning to promoting and staging several world title fights. He was introduced to Dempsey by 'Doc' Kearns and a lucrative partnership was born. When Rickard heard that Firpo had challenged Dempsey, he agreed to match the pair. The Argentinian had a fairly impressive record with several big names among his victims and more than anything else he had a knockout punch in his right hand.

'To be honest, Thomas, I didn't think an awful lot of Firpo from the moment I signed to fight him,' Dempsey remembered. 'I felt he was just a wild hitter who hoped to land the big one on somebody's chin and that would be it. I reckoned I could take his best shots and hit back with my own, harder and more accurate. He would outweigh me by about 40lb. But Rickard, the promoter, warned me to take no chances. Firpo's a hitter, Tex said, and one lucky punch and my prized title would be sailing down to South America.

'I started fast, jabbing with the left to sound him out. Then I missed with the follow-through right. Firpo suddenly moved in and lashed out with his famous right hand which landed on my cheekbone. I think if I hadn't been going away at the time the punch would have knocked me cold. I was dazed for a few seconds but managed to find Firpo's jaw with a left hook and

Firpo hit the canvas. I knocked him down seven times in that first round. But he kept getting up. I stepped over him a couple of times. I didn't know what I was doing.

'Suddenly, out of the blue, he fired a left and then a right that sent me flying through the ropes and on to a reporter's typewriter at ringside. I've honestly no recollection of what happened next but I was told later that a few reporters pushed me back into the ring. We exchanged blows near the ropes and then the bell rang.

'When I got back to my corner, Kearns told me later that I asked him what round I was knocked out in. "You weren't knocked out, you son-of-a-bitch," he barked. "Now get out there and finish off this guy before you are really knocked out." My head had cleared by now and I left my corner fast. I landed a left hook under his chin and followed with a quick right cross. He swayed like a ship in a storm and crashed down, his arms outstretched above his head. Referee Johnny Gallagher counted him out. Everybody went wild. I was still world champion but whew! It was close.'

I asked Dempsey to tell me about his two famous fights with Gene Tunney, the ex-marine who moved in society circles, could recite Shakespeare and was a close friend of literary giants like George Bernard Shaw, Ernest Hemingway and F. Scott Fitzgerald. Tunney was a very skilful boxer from New York and set out in life to achieve three ambitions – win the world heavyweight title from Jack Dempsey, retire as undefeated champion and marry into society. He would achieve all three.

It was Tunney who inflicted the first championship defeat on Dempsey when he outpointed the champion on a rain-swept evening in Philadelphia on 23 September 1926, and repeated the win a year later in Chicago in what became known as 'The Battle of the Long Count'.

'Let me say first off that I was beaten fair and square in both fights, even the second one when I knocked Gene down and he was on the boards for 14 seconds, four over the regulated time,' said Dempsey. 'I have no excuses over both defeats. The first fight broke all records. It had the largest attendance, 120,757, and the gate receipts had never been as high, $1,895,733. The betting boys had me favourite as I remember it.

'Tunney was a good scientific boxer with a hard punch, despite what you may have read about him having no dig. He walked right out of his corner in the first round and landed a good straight right to the face. A couple of inches lower and the punch would have knocked me down. My punching was off target for most of the fight, probably because I had been out of the ring for three years, although I don't want that to seem like an excuse. It was just a fact.

'I was definitely slower, or maybe Tunney was faster. I found myself blaming the wet ring but it didn't seem to bother Gene's footwork. When I would finally get a good footing, he would be gone. He glided around the ring like he was on skates in an ice rink. He was constantly on the move and whenever I went looking for him, he would stick that left jab into my face, keeping me off balance, piling up the points.

'There seemed nothing I could do, though I tried. The handlers in my corner were going hysterical, sensing that I was going to lose. One of my trainers, "Jerry the Greek", shoved smelling salts under my nose and fanned me between rounds but it didn't seem to make any difference. He kept telling me, "Get this guy out of there and let's go home." But there was nothing I could do. Isn't there a saying about the spirit being willing and the flesh being weak?

'I thought I got to him in the third and fourth rounds because he slowed down but I just couldn't follow through like in the past. Also, if I went in, he would have had the strength to hit back and break up my attack and that might have been a little risky. I had to get him with a good shot from long range but I didn't think that was ever going to happen. All I did know was that if I was going to get beaten, and that seemed likely, then I would finish on my feet. He wasn't going to knock me out.

'When the bell rang at the end of the tenth round I knew I was the loser. It's a sad thing to hear the guy with the microphone yell into it, "The winner and new heavyweight champion of the world…" when you are the old one. I walked over to Tunney's corner, put my arm around him and said, "Gene, congratulations, you're a great champion. Lots of luck to you."

'I started back for my own corner and to leave the ring. Then something happened that had never happened to me before. The people were cheering for me, calling out my name in a way that I had never heard before. I never realised how much I hungered for a sound like that and now here it was – on the night I lost my title. There were often a lot of boos when I had climbed into the ring in the past. Many felt I should have done service in the armed forces during World War I and they resented me for that. But now they were cheering for me. It was a very warm feeling indeed.

'In the dressing room, newspapermen crowded the place, clamouring for an interview. Flashbulbs popped all over. It was bedlam. When I got back to my hotel room, my wife Estelle was waiting for me. "What happened, Ginsberg?" was the first thing she said, using her pet name for me. "Honey, I just forgot to duck," I said and we hugged and hugged. It was very emotional.

'In any event, I was no longer champion but Tex Rickard knew the prospect of a return fight when he saw one. It all added up. My alibi was that I had been out of the ring for three years and had a lot of aggravations with one thing or another. A return match would settle things once and for all, and find out who was the real heavyweight champion of the world.'

It seemed a natural but Rickard wanted to make sure Dempsey was the legitimate and number one contender for Tunney. With that in mind he matched Dempsey with Jack Sharkey, a New Yorker-cum Bostonian of Lithuanian parentage who had proved himself in the top rank, even though he was of a temperamental nature with many of his punches often straying below the belt. They were paired in New York on 21 July 1927 with the winner going in against Tunney for the title, and a crowd of 75,000 passed through the turnstiles at the Yankee Stadium.

'I felt good going in against Sharkey and I figured I could handle him. I also had a new manager. Rickard had suggested that Gene Normile was not the right one for me and said I should switch to Leo P. Flynn, a well-known manager who had a large stable of fighters and had all the right connections.

'Flynn gave me good advice. He told me Sharkey was a better fighter than Tunney and that I was to get that into my head. But he did say one other thing. He told me that Sharkey couldn't take it in the body and that's where I was to aim. When I got in, he said, keep punching to the body until his hands drop and then let that right hand go, then the left and I'd knock him out.

'Sharkey was indeed a good fighter, as good as I'd seen. For the first five rounds I couldn't get to his body, as Flynn had suggested. He was always moving. The last thing an ex-champion, indeed any boxer, loses is his punch but his legs go first. When the old pins go, you're in trouble, believe me. By the sixth I was getting tired and Sharkey was still there. My return with Tunney was looking decidedly bleak and I heard later that Rickard, the promoter, was looking very worried.'

This is how Nat Fleischer described the seventh round in his *Ring* magazine report from ringside, 'Dempsey came out of his corner in a crouching position. He avoided several jabs and then rushed in and landed a left and right, both with telling effect. The first punch seemed to land on Sharkey's leg and the second one just below the belt. Sharkey turned his head and complained to the referee Jack O'Sullivan who refused to heed him, dropping his guard.

'Dempsey, not waiting for the referee to intervene, shot up a short left hook to the jaw and Sharkey fell on his face in apparent pain. He tried to rise but could not and the fight was over.'

Dempsey's recollections of the seventh round were, 'I hit him with one of the last good punches of my life. I put everything I could throw into it. I couldn't miss. His chin was sticking out there, unprotected and I just let go with that left hook to the chin. Opinions we divided as to whether I had fouled him or not. Some thought I had gone below the belt while others insisted he simply wore his trunks high.

'In any event I was convinced I had won the fight fair and square and that Sharkey should never have dropped his hands to his sides. My left hook to the jaw was the blow that ended the fight, not the ones to the stomach. Sharkey had no business saying anything to the referee. That's up to his cornermen. He said later he wasn't looking. Hell, why wasn't he looking? In the ring, you must protect yourself at all times and he didn't. Sharkey made the mistake himself. I didn't.'

Dempsey's knockout victory, however controversial, opened the way for his return with Tunney in what would be boxing's fourth million-dollar gate. In fact, total receipts at Soldier Field in Chicago came to $2,658,660 and the attendance was 104,943. Rickard wanted to hold the fight over until 1928, a year after the Sharkey match, to allow time for plenty of publicity but he was talked out of it by the millionaire boxing commissioner George Goetz who was planning a long holiday in Africa in 1928 and would have missed the fight had it been held then.

'Rickard set the date for 27 September 1927 which was all right by me,' recalled Dempsey. 'A lot has been written about that fight and exact details of the early rounds are a bit hazy today but I do recall that I was falling behind on points as the rounds progressed. Still, I was grimly determined to win back the heavyweight championship, my championship.

'Nobody had ever done if before. James J. Corbett had tried and failed. So had Bob Fitzsimmons and Jim Jeffries. I was reminded about the old boxing adage – they never come back. But I gave myself a real chance of victory, despite my legs and despite being two years older than Tunney.

'I was only 32, not really old for a boxer if you think about it. Jersey Joe Walcott won the heavyweight championship at 37 when he knocked out Ezzard Charles in 1951. There are a lot of guys around today well over 32 and still contenders. Check your record book and you'll find it's true.

'I don't remember the exact round-by-round details of the fight and again the record book or old newspaper files will fill you in. But I know I was behind on points after six rounds. Tunney was smart, like he was in the first fight. Always moving and jabbing, moving and jabbing. I couldn't seem to get a good shot at him, no matter what I did. My corner told me to wait for the right opportunity but you can't wait forever. After all, this was a championship fight. I needed to hit him solidly if I was going to have any kind of a chance. I'd lose if it went the full distance.

'My chance came in the seventh – in a corner. I hurt him with a pretty good right hook and he staggered for a moment, his knees sagging. I followed up with an equally good left hook and he started to go. The big crowd were yelling like mad by this stage. I followed through with six or seven more punches and Tunney slumped to the canvas. I had been dreaming of this moment for the past year and now it had finally come. I felt I was about to make ring history – the first heavyweight champion to win back his crown.

'I admit I lost my head. Dave Barry, the referee, rushed over and shouted, "Go to your corner, Dempsey, now." I said I was staying right there and wasn't moving. I completely forget about the rule that said that a man scoring a knockdown should immediately retire to a neutral corner. I wondered to myself what was a neutral corner. When you're fighting, at least the way I used to fight, all corners look alike.

'Thomas, it's hard to stop what you are doing, standing over a guy and waiting for him to get up, and start figuring out which corner is farthest away from where it's all happening. The rule also said that if there was a knockdown, the referee was supposed to take the guy who threw the punch to a neutral corner, then come back and pick up the count in unison with the count of the knockdown timekeeper.

'Barry didn't do that. Instead he finally pushed me to a neutral corner and then went back to Tunney who was still on the canvas. But instead of picking up the count from the timekeeper, let's say "nine, ten and out", he started from one so he broke the rules too. Tunney got up at about seven or eight. I'll never really know whether he could have gotten up before ten. Gene later told me he could have. Maybe so but I personally believed, and still believe, that he could not have. Who can say?

'When he finally got up, he back-pedalled around the ring, keeping well out of my reach and I couldn't get another clean shot at him. By the eighth round Tunney was himself again. I beckoned to him to 'come in and fight' but he wasn't having any. Wise man. People forget that Tunney knocked me down in the ninth and the referee pushed him to a neutral corner and this time picked up the count from the timekeeper, which he should have done in that seventh round. At the last bell I congratulated Gene and said, "You're a good guy." He was.

'Everything happens for the best. I was then 32 and I felt a lot older. It was time to quit and leave the game for younger men. You can't go on forever but a lot of boxers think they can but they can't. Get out in time. It's a tough game and a lot of guys stay in there too long with serious consequences.'

Another integral part of Dempsey's career centred around the formidable contender Harry Wills. The fight never took place, though it was through no fault of Dempsey's. Often described as one of the greatest heavyweights to have never fought for a world title, he was from New Orleans and was known as the 'Black Panther'. Wills was hampered through his career because of the colour of his skin, a victim of the notorious colour bar which hampered so many boxers in the early years of the 20th century.

Wills worked on the docks before turning to boxing in 1910 to earn some extra money and inside four years he had developed good boxing skills and speed in the ring. Like many black boxers of his day, he found it hard to get fights with white heavyweights because matchmakers and promoters did not want to get involved in the thorny racial issue.

Wills demonstrated his prowess against white heavyweights when knocking out contender Fred Fulton in the third round in 1920. He issued a challenge to the new heavyweight champion Dempsey for a title fight, and while Dempsey was willing to take on Wills, promoter Tex Rickard was reluctant to stage a mixed-race championship fight because he feared a repeat of the race riots that broke out all across America and scandalised the nation after Jack Johnson took the title from James J. Jeffries in Reno, Nevada on 4 July 1910. Tex also feared a Dempsey–Wills fight might well be boycotted.

'I was perfectly prepared to take on Wills but Rickard was totally against it,' said Dempsey. 'It may not be generally known that we actually signed for the fight in 1922 in the presence of all interested parties including Rickard, Wills, his manager and officials of the New York State Athletic Commission although no date or venue had been named. The commission later issued a statement saying that I would have to face Wills or forfeit the title.

'As I say I was fully prepared to fight Wills any time, any place, but the signing of the contracts turned out to be all bluff. Rickard later insisted he would not promote a black v white title fight, and when another promoter offered to stage the fight, Rickard said he himself was my promoter and nobody else could step in so the fight never happened. The controversy went on for years and Wills never got his deserved title shot. That's the way it was with black contenders in those days.

'In 1926, Rickard announced I would defend my title against Gene Tunney in September. By then Wills would have been past his prime and he was beaten by Jack Sharkey just after I fought Tunney. After being well in front, Wills fouled Sharkey in the 13th round and was disqualified. Harry was really out of the picture now. A great pity about him. He was a good one.'

In his retirement years Dempsey kept busy. He made several movies, boxed exhibitions, officiated at boxing and wrestling matches, made personal appearances and promoted boxing shows. He also served as a commander in the US Coast Guard and owned a popular restaurant on Broadway. He died on 31 May 1983, three weeks short of his 88th birthday, and was inducted into the International Boxing Hall of Fame in Canastota, New York in 1990.

8

Sugar Ray Leonard
Golden Boy of the 1980s

HANDSOME and clean-cut, with a dazzling smile and supreme boxing skills, Sugar Ray Leonard was hailed as a star to replace the fading Muhammad Ali in the 1980s. He succeeded with a string of brilliant contests to become one of the greatest boxers of the modern era, even if he upset the establishment by the ease with which he could pick his own lucrative title fights.

After winning a gold medal as a light-welterweight in the 1976 Olympics in Montreal, Leonard's stellar career as a pro took him to world championships in five divisions, over $11m in earnings and fame that spread far beyond boxing. He retired four times but was master of the comeback, setting himself audacious goals and achieving them, adding to his own legend every time.

Leonard had classic fights with greats such as Thomas 'Hitman' Hearns, Marvin Hagler, Roberto Duran and Wilfred Benitez and is generally listed in the top five or six in boxing's all-time greats lists. While he did not have the charisma or the popularity of the original Sugar Ray, Robinson by name, he was not too far off. In a worldwide poll of boxing experts conducted by *Ring* magazine in 2014, Leonard was in sixth place, behind Robinson, not surprisingly at number one, followed by Henry Armstrong, Muhammad Ali, Roberto Duran and Joe Louis.

How did Leonard pick up the Sugar Ray nickname? 'It was when I was an amateur, during the Olympic trials,' Leonard recalled in an interview with this writer during a visit to Dublin in 2006. 'One of the US coaches, Tom "Sarge" Johnson, used to call me "Sugar Man" but not "Sugar Ray". I came up with that myself. I admired the great Sugar Ray Robinson like nobody else. He could do just about anything and is universally recognised as the most complete boxer in ring history. He was a great champion at welterweight and middleweight, as you know.

'Robinson could box, he could fight, he could dance and equally important, he had a solid chin which could absorb the hardest of punches. Look up your files or book and you'll find very, very few boxers ever put him on the floor for a count. He was never knocked out and was only stopped once when the heat got to him against the heavier Joey Maxim in a light-heavyweight title fight. I somehow managed to get a complimentary ticket for a big fight in Las Vegas, and when I saw Robinson in the ringside seats, I went up to him, introduced myself as a boxer in the US Olympic trials and asked him could I use his nickname.

'I remember what he said very clearly. "Yes, I know about you," he replied, "and yes, I would consider it a real honour to use my name and you go ahead but make sure you look after it, Ray. It's kind of special to me, as I'm sure you're aware. But no problem – and good luck." I thought that was very, very generous of him, and he even went up further in my admiration for him, if that was possible. If the great Sugar Ray Robinson was on my side, I knew there and then that I could make the grade.'

Leonard was born on 17 May 1956 in Wilmington, North Carolina, the fifth child and fourth son of Cicero and Gertha Leonard. His mother named their newest arrival after her favourite entertainer Ray Charles. She used to tell her family and friends that little Ray might become a big singing star, just like her idol.

The boy's father, a former US Navy cook, worked at the Coca-Cola factory. When work slackened down at the plant in 1960, Cicero Leonard packed up the family and moved all of them to Washington DC and later to Maryland where they acquired a mortgage on their own home in the Palmer Park district. Ray's three brothers were sports mad and they persuaded him to try his hand at physical activities.

'Roy, Kenny and Roger, along with my dad, suspected me of being a bit of a sissy and said I should come down to the local boys' club and work out,' he remembered. 'I sparred with one of the boys there but I was terrified and decided not to do it again. I tried wrestling and roller-skating but I just didn't feel at home. Competitive sports had little appeal for me. Mind you, I enjoyed exercising and working out on my own but that's as far as it went.'

It is quite likely that the boxing world may never have heard of Ray Leonard if the local authorities had not opened the Palmer Park Recreational Centre, even with very little finance available for proper equipment. However, the centre's director Ollie Dunlap and coach Dave Jacobs approached local traders to offer whatever they could afford, and local junkyards were also scoured for odd and ends, maybe a mirror or two that the kids could practise in front of. By now the young Ray Leonard had become tired of the family jibes about being a sissy and decided to do an about-turn and go back to working out with the other boys. Leonard turned out to be a quick learner in the ring and soon picked up the rudiments of the sport, though he suffered his share of bruises and humiliations. He was also developing physically. When Dunlap and Jacobs began to enter their boxers in local tournaments, Leonard became hooked on the noble art. In 1972 at just 16 and a lightweight, he won a local Golden Gloves title and followed it with a win in an international tournament between the USA and the USSR. He won his bout on a knockout.

More Golden Gloves titles followed as well as National AAU championships so that by the time the Montreal Olympics came around in the summer of 1974, he had won a place on the team following the trials. Leonard breezed through the opposition in Montreal, defeating the Cuban light-welter, Andreas Aldama, in the final.

'After two rounds I felt I had the decision and the gold medal,' he said. 'Only a knockout could save Aldama and I knew he wasn't going to achieve that. He came at me aggressively in the final round but I felt this attack made him all the more vulnerable. When the final bell rang I was announced the winner on a 5-0 score. The US did exceptionally well that year, winning five gold medals as well as a silver and a bronze.

'It was the biggest Olympic haul we ever had. The other four US gold medallists were flyweight Leo Randolph, lightweight Howard Davis and the Spinks brothers, Michael at middleweight and Leon at light-heavy. As you know, as professionals later on, Michael won the world light-heavyweight and heavyweight titles and Leon won the heavyweight championship.'

Leonard knew how to market himself even then, and enchanted Middle America by competing in all his bouts in Montreal by boxing with a photograph of his young son Ray tucked into his boot. With his easygoing charm and good looks, besides his considerable talent, he was the most popular and newsworthy winner in Montreal. When he came home, Leonard was reluctant to cash in on his immense popularity and turn professional. He had seen the way so many boxers had been manipulated by promoters and managers and he vowed he would never join that list.

It was family circumstances that prompted Leonard to box as a professional. His father was ill and could not work and his mother had a heart attack. Plus, he had his girlfriend Juanita and their young son to support. Ray contacted Mike Trainer, a lawyer friend of the family. Trainer got together a number of business friends who between them loaned the boxer $20,000 for four years at eight per cent interest. A company was formed, Sugar Ray Leonard Inc, with Ray the sole proprietor and he took a weekly salary of $475. This was the stuff of fairytales.

'It was a good arrangement, and Mike himself also put in $1,000 of his own money,' remembered Leonard. 'The main thing was none of the investors owned a part of me. I was my own boss. But I needed a manager and a trainer, somebody to arrange my fights and my preparations. We did a lot of research and eventually narrowed the field down to three – Eddie Futch, who guided Joe Frazier following the death of Yancey "Yank" Durham, Gil Clancy, who handled among others Emile Griffith, who was welterweight and middleweight champion of the world, and Angelo Dundee, the man behind the success of Muhammad Ali.

'We finally settled on Dundee. I talked it over with Ali and he and I agreed that Angelo would be the right man. Angelo had been with Ali since 1960 when Ali was known as Cassius Clay. He seemed to have all the right connections. He knew everybody in boxing, the officials, the newspapermen, the TV commentators and presenters. We spoke to Dundee and agreed on a deal – 15 per cent of my earnings. He said he would take me along slowly, match me with the right opponents and gradually build me up. He reckoned it would take about three years before I would get a shot at a title and by then I would be seasoned enough to take on the best.'

Dundee was the most successful boxing man of his time, whether as a manager, trainer, cut-man, dealer or perhaps a combination of all four. When the author was in the company of Ali's team in London in 1966, Angelo filled me in on his own story. Apparently, his real surname was Mirenda, his parents having emigrated to New York in the early years of the 20th century from Calabria in southern Italy. Their eldest son Joe was already with them and four more sons and two daughters arrived later.

Angelo, named after his father, was the sixth child, born in 1921. By then, the surname was Mireno but Joe became a boxer and took the ring name of Joe Dundee after a world welterweight champion of the 1920s. Later on, when another brother Chris went into boxing management in New York, he also took the name of Dundee.

'When I became his assistant, I too became a Dundee,' said Angelo. 'I began working in the corner of boxers who were sent out of town for contests and I learned a lot from fellow cornermen like Ray Arcel, who worked with many greats, and Charlie Goldman, Rocky Marciano's trainer.'

In 1955 Carmen Basilio was the first world champion Dundee trained, and in a long and busy career, Angelo would be associated with a string of world champions including featherweight Sugar Ramos, welterweights Luis Rodriguez and Jose Napoles, junior middleweight Ralph Dupas, light-heavyweight Willie Pastrano and heavyweight Pinklon Thomas. But most famously, he will always be known as Ali's man, and when Sugar Ray Leonard turned professional, Dundee had to be the man in his corner. 'With Angelo as my coach, I knew that he was the best, the very best, in the business,' said Sugar Ray.

Leonard made his professional debut amid nationwide publicity on 5 February 1977 at the Civic Center, Baltimore against Luis 'The Bull' Vega from Ponce, Puerto Rico in a scheduled six-rounder. Sugar Ray had good credentials, as Olympic light-welterweight champion and winner of 145 of his 150 contests.

The fight, which was televised by CBS, drew a crowd of 10,170, a record for the venue. Vega was a tough opponent who had never been off his feet in 22 fights. Leonard won the decision and broke another record. His winning cheque was $40,000, the highest fee at the time for a pro debut. Vega earned just $650. 'I had to pinch myself to realise all this was happening,' he remembered. 'Especially to a one-time sissy like me.'

By the end of 1978, Leonard had won all his 17 fights, including three over ranked opponents. More importantly, he won the North American Boxing Federation welterweight title and was given a world title shot at Caesars Palace, Las Vegas, against one of boxing's all-time greats Wilfred Benitez, the WBC champion and a master of attack and defence.

The youngest of eight children, Benitez was born in New York and brought up on boxing as his father Gregorio, or

'Goyo' as he was known, had boxed as a boy in Puerto Rico and often set up playground matches for his sons in the Bronx, charging passers-by 25 cents to watch. At the age of seven, the family moved back to Puerto Rico where little Wilfred became an amateur boxer. He turned professional at 15 and in March 1976, at 17, he became boxing's youngest-ever world champion when winning the World Boxing Association junior welterweight title. Three years later he won his second world belt, at welterweight.

Benitez's manager Jimmy Jacobs insisted that, as champion, Wilfred was entitled to the greater share of the purse but Leonard's man Mike Trainer disagreed, saying that Sugar Ray was the bigger draw. In the end Leonard got $1.2m and Benitez $1m, the first time two welterweights had taken a million dollars for a fight. There was a second world title fight on the card, with Marvin Hagler challenging Vito Antuofermo for the middleweight championship.

'I knew Benitez was going to a tough opponent and he was,' recalled Leonard. 'Look up his record and you will see. Most of his early fights were held in Puerto Rico but he boxed occasionally in New York, where he was a very popular performer. The referee was the excellent Carlos Padilla and I knew I would get a fair deal from him. Padilla had officiated in the Frazier–Ali fight four years earlier, the "Thrilla in Manila".

'When he brought us together in the centre of the ring for the last-minute instructions, Benitez and I were nose-to-nose for a full 30 seconds. It was a mind game but I was scared senseless. From the start I wanted to show Benitez who was the boss. I thought I won the first two rounds and in the third I dropped him for a standing eight count. I still felt I was missing a lot, though.

'Our heads came together in the sixth round. I was fortunate but Benitez emerged with a deep vertical cut on his forehead. However, it didn't affect his performance because he was still firing good shots to the head and body. I felt in command, though, but I still couldn't find my knockout punch. My corner told me it was anybody's fight after 13 rounds and

Benitez won the 14th, perhaps his best round. But it was still close, too close for comfort, and Angelo told me before going out for the 15th and last round, "You've got to get him now, or he'll get the decision." That was it.

'I was still looking for that opening to finish Benitez and I finally got it, with about a minute to go before the last bell. I dropped him with a good left hook. He took the mandatory eight count and when he got up I went after him, throwing clusters of punches. Suddenly the referee moved between us and signalled it was all over – with just six seconds to go on the clock. Benitez was finished at that time. I was the new WBC welterweight champion of the world at 23, and it felt good.'

Benitez later moved up to light-middleweight and won his third world title to become the fifth boxer to hold championships at three different weights, and the first for 43 years – since Henry Armstrong in 1938. Sadly Benitez's career gradually fizzled out amid management squabbles and soft living. After retiring from the ring, his health went into steady decline and he ended up virtually destitute, relying on hand-outs from his mother.

Things eventually got so bad that in December 1995, his family were forced to petition the Puerto Rican government for financial assistance on his behalf. As a result, the authorities decided to introduce a pension of $600 a month for retired boxers.

'I had planned to retire as undefeated champion after the Benitez fight,' Leonard recalled. 'I had made good money and my family was secure so I asked myself, "Why should I stay on in boxing and maybe get myself permanently injured?" As it was, I was banged up pretty bad in the fight. My face was swollen and there were large welts under my eyes. My right hand also hurt and while I had it x-rayed, nothing was broken. All this was testimony to what a great fighter Benitez was. It was the toughest fight of my career up to then, maybe of all my career.

'While I was in hospital having my x-ray done, my advisor Mike Trainer came to see me. He said I should quit as I had nothing to gain by continuing boxing and that I should definitely hang up my gloves. I said I'd think about it. Over the next few days and weeks I gave my retirement plans a lot of thought and finally came up with a decision. I was going to carry on. I was still in my prime. I was still only 23 and I felt I still had a lot to offer. Besides, there were still lucrative purses out there.'

Meanwhile Leonard married Juanita Wilkinson, a local girl, in January 1980. His management organisation was also refined, with Dundee now on a flat-fee basis rather than a percentage, with Mike Trainer and Janks Morton, who had been with him since his amateur days, retained as his decision-making partners. It was now time to continue his career and an attractive offer came to defend his welterweight championship against Dave 'Boy' Green from Chatteris, Cambridgeshire. It would be a voluntary defence. The date was 31 March 1980 and the venue was the Capital Centre in Landover, Maryland.

A capacity crowd of over 19,000 turned up for what turned out to be a short-lived affair. During the pre-fight instructions, Green glared at Leonard as the world champion produced his own interpretation of the Ali shuffle. From the first bell, there was only one man in it, and it wasn't the challenger.

As Mike Lockley reported in *Boxing News*, 'Green simply had no answer to the rapid combination punches which frequently threaded through his guard. Leonard at times seemed to treat the fight as little more than a public workout as he strutted around the ring, hands low, content to flick out lazy jabs. He had predicted that Green would fall in the first round but showed no inclination to apply pressure until the fourth and final round. But when the American put his punches together, he looked awesome.

'A right uppercut rocked Green in the fourth and a final stunning left hook caught him as he was falling back. Green's head hit the boards with a sickening thud and referee Arthur Mercante signalled the end without bothering with a count. The result was first announced as a technical knockout but was corrected to a clean knockout. The ending, though spectacular, was always on the cards. Green gave it all he had but was handled with consummate ease by a champion who is fast establishing himself as a modern great.'

Leonard remembered, 'Green was a good fighter. He caught me with a couple of good shots to the body and was an awkward kind of guy to deal with. He reminded me of a mini Ken Norton, the guy who beat Muhammad Ali in their first fight and broke his jaw, if you recall. Yes, he was like Norton in the way he bobbed and weaved and rolled with the punches, always looking to work downstairs.

'The left I caught him with in the fourth round was, I think, one of the hardest punches I've ever thrown in my entire career. Some people used to say I couldn't punch and that I was much more of a clever, showy boxer but I think I showed any doubters in the Green fight that I could hit hard where and when necessary. When Green hit the floor and lay still, I kept saying to myself, "Get up, Davy boy! Get up! Get up now!" I didn't want a fatality. Gradually and happily he came to and was placed on a stool near his corner. I was relieved.'

Leonard had several controversial fights in his career, including the two with the great Panamanian, Roberto Duran. Sugar Ray lost the first one but won the second. Duran was a magnificent boxer who, after being unbeaten as lightweight champion of the world from 1972 to 1978, had been campaigning for a couple of years as a welterweight. Defeated only once in 72 bouts over 13 years, the Panamanian was a macho man with no concern for his opponents and even less for the rules.

'What are rules for?' he once remarked. 'Only for breaking.' In that regard, he was a throwback to the legendary Harry Greb, known as the 'Pittsburgh Windmill', who regarded referees as 'guys who make a career out of interfering with fighters' styles and are simply meddlesome beyond belief'.

A fighter, first and foremost, Duran's sole purpose was to destroy his opponent, one way or another, without being too bothered about the methods he used. The Panamanian would have an extraordinarily long and busy career, starting in 1967 and having his final fight 34 years later – in 2001. His wrenching of the world lightweight title from Scotland's Ken Buchanan in June 1972 summed up his whole career – savage and merciless. Roberto would win world titles in four weight classes.

Duran was the undefeated world lightweight champion when he ducked between the ropes on the night of 20 June 1980 as the challenger for Leonard's welterweight title at the Olympic Stadium, Montreal. A crowd of 46,317, the largest ever for a championship fight in Canada at the time, and a close-circuit TV audience of something like 1.5 million in North America, saw a battle that lived up to its expectations. Duran, looking in hard-rock condition, came charging out of his corner at the first bell and never let Leonard, at 24 the younger man by five years, get into his stride.

Sugar Ray was expected to box and move but he surprised everybody by standing his ground and fighting it out. Whenever he changed tactics by grace and movement throughout the fight, Duran's incessant rushing and swarming style nullified any advantage Leonard may have gained. Whenever Sugar Ray got his rhythmic skilful style going, he scored effectively but the Panamanian rarely allowed him much scope with his constant pressure. It was always going to be a close fight over the scheduled 15 rounds, and that is how it turned out.

Leonard Gardner, whose 1963 novel *Fat City* remains among the greatest boxing books ever written, covered the fight for *Inside Sports*. 'Duran, with the experience of 71 bouts against Leonard's 27, was showing Leonard the ropes but Sugar Ray proved to have extraordinary durability and gameness,' he wrote. 'There were times when I doubted he could survive them but in the middle rounds he came back. He fought head to head with Duran, slamming him with hard combinations that had no apparent effect. It became a contest of fighting heart, a slugfest between two men with great speed and punching skills.

'The fight was Duran's, although the judges made it close. One scored ten rounds even. With that kind of judging, there seemed the possibility of a draw, but the voting, after a correction in addition, was unanimous: 145-144, 148-147,

146-144. Duran had taken the title but both men had fought with such fire that the fight would rank with the great ones.'

Leonard recalled, 'To a large degree Duran nullified my skills. I tried to step under his clutch but you had to give him credit for the way he fought and the way he restricted me. There were lots of butts inside and he really dazed me in the second round with an overhand right. I was only able to come through because I was in such perfect shape. I thought I had a way to beat him and I attacked his body but it didn't affect him.

'I did a lot of damage and I scored well in the centre of the ring and on the ropes. I thought the 11th round contained some of the fiercest fighting of my career, with both of us going hell for leather. It was the same in the 12th, 13th, 14th and 15th. At the final bell the judges had their final say and they called it for Duran. Fair enough. You have to respect their decision and I had no excuses, or still haven't.'

There were calls for Leonard to retire but he could never leave boxing with such a close defeat hanging over him. He would regret it for the rest of his life. In any event, he knew he could beat Duran the next time. On 25 November 1980, five months after the first fight, the two greats climbed into the ring at the Superdome in New Orleans. Despite the first loss, Sugar Ray was the favourite at 6/5. This time, however, he did not have Jake Jacobs, his trainer since his amateur days, in his corner.

Jacobs had wanted Leonard to take a couple of tune-up fights before he met Duran again, but Leonard insisted on the rematch immediately. So Jacobs quit. The return fight turned out to be one of the most controversial in ring history. Red Smith, one of America's foremost sportswriters and a Pulitzer Prize-winner, reported for the *New York Times*, 'Not much was happening in the eighth round when Roberto Duran turned away from Sugar Ray Leonard and waved a glove at the referee in a signal to cease and desist. Leonard, aware only that the welterweight champion of the WBC was not defending himself, hit him a shot to the belly, but Duran did not respond.

'Roberto told the referee, "No mas, no mas", or "No more box". He walked to his corner, and when Leonard realised that Duran had surrendered the title to him he sprang up like a squirrel on the top rope in a neutral corner. It was 2.44 into the round, and suddenly the ring was the scene of utter confusion. One of Leonard's seconds charged Duran and took a swing at him. Swirling bodies eddied and elbowed. A report flew around that Duran had not quit but had merely misunderstood the referee about something, nobody knew what. There was another that Duran had told his corner he had cramps all over his body. Duran told José Sulaiman, president of the WBC, that when he threw a right hand in that round, something happened to his shoulder.

'Still later, Duran said, "I don't want to fight any more. I've been fighting for a long time." In fact, it has been almost 14 years. He said that in the fifth round he began to feel cramps in his stomach and that the pain spread and grew progressively worse.

'This was the first time a champion had voluntarily surrendered his title since Sonny Liston quit to Muhammad Ali, then Cassius Clay, in 1964, claiming a shoulder injury. He ratified the action a year later by taking a dive for Ali in Lewiston. A much more similar denouement, however, took place in 1949 in Detroit when Marcel Cerdan, the middleweight champion, tore the supraspinatus muscle in his right shoulder defending his title against Jake LaMotta. Cerdan, though, fought on left-handed until his seconds persuaded him to retire.

'None of those was so startling as this, for Duran was known as the most dedicated, intense warrior in the ring. He had held the lightweight championship for years and had lost only one decision in 72 bouts before taking the 147lb title from Leonard last June in Montreal.

'It was said that he could not conceive of losing, and his idolators in his native Panama believed he never would.

'When the match ended, officially a knockout in the eighth, Leonard was ahead on the cards of all three judges. Acting as his own judge, Leonard obviously felt that he had it all the way. In the third round when Duran lunged at him and fell far short, Leonard laughed and stuck out his tongue. In the seventh he thrust his face out toward Duran and taunted him with a grimacing, shoulder-shrugging boogaloo. He was not a spectacularly gracious winner.'

What did Leonard think of the fight and the shock finish? 'Many, many people, not only writers like yourself, have asked me that question over the years,' he said. 'I can only give you the same answer I've given everybody else. I was as shocked as anyone by what happened. I never bought Duran's story that he was beaten by cramps. I felt, and still feel, that he was just humiliated and quit. He had lost heart and that was it. He wasn't hurt or battered or anything like that. He'd just had enough. There were stories about a fix, and that Duran quit so as he could set up another big money rubber match fight in the near future. That was rubbish. Not with Duran walking out like he did.'

There are many people who regard Leonard's first fight with Thomas Hearns as his most spectacular performance. The two greats met on 16 September 1981 to unify the world welterweight title for the first time since Cuba's Jose Napoles in 1975. Leonard held the WBC belt and Hearns was the WBA champion. Unusually tall with a tremendous 78-inch reach, Hearns was born in Memphis, Tennessee, but he will always be associated with his adopted home town of Detroit, where his innate talent was developed in the sparring wars of the famous Kronk gym under the tutelage of one of America's greatest trainers, Emanuel Steward.

It was Steward who changed Hearns from a light-hitting amateur to one of the most devastating hitters in ring history. Known as the 'Motor City Cobra' but more famously as the 'Hitman', in time Hearns would win world titles in five different divisions. The Leonard–Hearns match was billed as 'The Showdown'. The venue was a specially erected stadium behind Caesars Palace in Las Vegas. It was quickly sold out and a crowd of slightly under 25,000 passed through the turnstiles in the 90-degree afternoon heat, with an estimated 300 million televiewers around the world. Everybody expected some real action, including the many celebrities in attendance including the original Sugarman, Ray Robinson. They got it – but not until after a slow, cautious start by both men.

Leonard fought from the third round on with an ugly swelling under his left eye which obscured his view of his opponent's punishing rights for a time. But he was able to score on the inside. As the rounds went by, it was a thrilling war of give-and-take, with one man and then the other gaining the initiative. Nevertheless, Hearns had a narrow lead after 13 thrilling rounds, but there were still six vital minutes to go.

In Leonard's corner before going out for the 14th, Angelo Dundee told his man, 'You're blowing this, son. Go out there and get him.' Leonard started fast and sent Hearns spinning into a corner under a sustained attack. Hearns tried to fight back but Sugar Ray would not be denied and while referee Davy Pearl gave Hearns every chance to fight back, the WBA champion had nothing left. After one minute and 45 seconds of the round, Pearl intervened. Leonard was undisputed welterweight champion of the world. All three judges had Hearns ahead on scores of 125-121, 124-122 and 125-123. Most ringside writers agreed that Hearns deserved his lead although the prestigious *Los Angeles Herald Examiner* called the scoring 'an absurdity of nearly felonious proportions'.

'Tommy Hearns was a really tough opponent and I respected him,' remembered Leonard. 'Even though he wasn't inflicting any punishment, he was winning the rounds but it was being difficult for me to get past those long arms to allow me to get my best punches in. Angelo saved the day. I had to get to him and my chance came in the 13th round. I put him down in that round and I felt I was finally getting to him. It happened in the 14th when I gave it everything I'd got. Lefts and rights, lefts and rights and Tommy was all in. The referee was right to stop it. Tommy is a good guy and we're still the best of friends.'

If Leonard's 1981 fight with Hearns was his most spectacular, and the one in which he proved he was not merely a skilful boxer but a powerful hitter as well, the stiffest test was still to come. This would be when he challenged Marvelous Marvin Hagler for the world middleweight title on 6 April 1987 at Caesars Palace, Las Vegas: 'The Superfight'.

Hagler was a lean, mean fighting machine in every sense of the word. Looking menacing with his shaven head, Mandarin moustache and hard-muscles physique, Hagler looked every inch a ring killer. One of the few southpaw world champions, he had a tenacious streak and was a powerful hitter who could adapt his defence to any opponent's style. Although born in Newark, New Jersey, Marvin moved as a child to Brockton, Massachusetts, the town that produced the great world heavyweight champion Rocky Marciano.

Hagler had defended his world middleweight title 12 times, as against Carlos Monzon of Argentina who notched up 14. Marvin was now champion for seven years. Leonard had actually retired three years earlier due to an eye problem and concentrated on his work as a commentator for HBO and CBS, having stepped down as undefeated welterweight champion of the world. A purse estimated at around $12m no doubt persuaded him to return.

There was strong criticism of both boxers. Leonard was accused of jumping the queue as he was not the leading contender, while fingers were pointed at Hagler for dodging his number one challenger, Nottingham-born Herol 'Bomber' Graham, and was threatened with the loss of his title by the WBA and the International Boxing Federation. Nevertheless, the fight went ahead. Hagler climbed into the ring as a 4/1 favourite in the Las Vegas betting, as Leonard was considered, in the words of one scribe, 'a has-been on the comeback trail' and had boxed only once in five years. A poll in one Las Vegas newspaper found that 60 of 67 journalists from all over the world covering the fight favoured Hagler.

Before an attendance of 15,366 in the outdoor arena behind Caesars and every seat long being sold, Leonard sealed one of the great comebacks in boxing history to win a split decision over 12 rounds and become the tenth boxer to win world titles at three different weights. In a classic encounter, with both men gaining advantages, Sugar Ray boxed cautiously, aiming to get Hagler frustrated and careless. He blocked, dodged and held, while taking care to put in little flurries towards the ends of rounds to impress the judges.

From the fifth round things improved for Hagler, who delivered the harder blows but Leonard made sure he had enough reserves to score flashy combinations towards the end. At the finish, Sugar Ray was given the decision, two judges scoring it 115-113 and 118-110 for Leonard, and the third marking his card 115-113 for Hagler.

'I definitely thought I won fairly and squarely,' said Leonard about the match that *Ring* magazine named Fight of the Year and Upset of the Year. 'I felt the victory was a special accomplishment for me. The strategy worked out with my team was to stick and move, stick and move, hit and run, taunt and frustrate and it worked. People say my win over Tommy Hearns was my greatest victory but the win over Hagler was my proudest. I'm very sure about that. Everybody besides my camp and my family didn't think I had a chance but I fooled them. I know Hagler said I fought like a girl but losers say a lot of things after fights, don't they?'

When this writer discussed the fight with one of the best of the modern boxing scribes, the late George Kimble of the *Boston Herald*, on one of his many visits to Ireland, he said, 'I must say I had Hagler narrowly ahead at the finish but it was always going to be close. For reasons that have never been clear, Hagler attempted to confuse Leonard by abandoning his southpaw attack and attempted to box in an orthodox fashion. Still, you have to hand it to Leonard for doing what he always did best, box, box, box. Gil Clancy, on the close-circuit telecast, said Leonard came up with "the greatest performance I've ever seen by any boxer", and Richard Steele, the referee, called it "the greatest fight I've ever been involved in". Yes, the "Superfight" was just that.'

There was talk of a return fight but for one reason or another it never happened. Both boxers announced their retirements, but only Hagler made it permanent, moving base to Italy where he went into movies. Leonard made a comeback, won the world light-heavyweight title, and retired once again only to return to the ring for one last time on 1 March 1997 at the age of 40. Hindered by a torn calf muscle, he was knocked down and stopped in five rounds by Puerto Rico's Hector 'Macho' Camacho. He retired with a 36-3-1 record. In his retirement years Leonard has endorsed products and worked as a boxing commentator and analyst on television.

I asked him what boxers would be in Sugar Ray's top ten. 'As you are well aware, it's so difficult to compare the men of my day to those of the past,' he confessed. 'Boxing has changed so much, society has changed so much so that it's really impossible to argue that somebody from the 1920s or the 30s or any era might have beaten the moderns, or the other way around. However, this would be my personal pick of the top ten, and I would have to remind you that it's just a personal choice.

'Muhammad Ali would have to be number one, the greatest of all time, no question about that. He could box and he could punch. He had a deceptive defence even if he used to drop his hands by his side in his prime. He dominated the heavyweight division for so many years, taking on every contender. To me, he is very, very special. In my number two spot I would place Sugar Ray Robinson, and that's not because I borrowed the "Sugar" part of his name. Robinson was the master, a brilliant boxer, terrific puncher, possessing a solid chin and ruggedness when necessary.

'I could not place the next eight of my top ten in order simply because I cannot seem to be able to do it. I'll leave that to yourself and others. As for the top four heavyweights outside of Ali, Joe Louis would have to be there. He defended his world title 25 times in over 11 years and ducked nobody. Louis was an iconic fighter who would be on anybody's list. Jack Johnson, the first African-American to hold the heavyweight championship, too. He really started everything for black boxers like myself and others. His fine ability could never be questioned. He had a knockout punch in both gloves and was a master of defence.

'Rocky Marciano, the only heavyweight champion to retire without a single defeat, finishing up 49-0. That was some achievement if you think about it. Rocky cleaned up the heavyweight division, beating some of his opponents twice. He was not a skilful boxer by any means but, my! what a killing puncher and as tough as iron. Jersey Joe Walcott is in there too. You may be surprised at that but he was very, very underestimated in my view, and in the opinion of others I have met too. He was a tricky opponent, very wily, and with a deadly right hand punch. Don't forget he put Marciano and Louis on the boards, both notable achievements.

'Okay, that's the heavyweights out of the way. Salvatore Sanchez, the great Mexican featherweight, would have to be in my top ten. He was amazing. Look up your record book there. Yes, there he is – 44 wins with 32 knockouts, one defeat and one draw. Now that's some record. He was a pro at 16. If I was pressed into putting Sanchez in at number three or four, I might be tempted but I'll put him in the group of eight behind Ali and Robinson.

'Now where were we? Yes, three more to make up my top ten. Wilfred Benitez would have to be in there. He could slip a punch like the best of them and was a master counter-puncher. There would have to be a place too for Roberto Duran, a real tough hombre if ever there was one. You tell me in the *Boxing News* book about the 100 greatest boxers of all time that Duran is in the sixth spot. There you go. One of the all-time greats, and he had the mentality of a killer. The third in my group of eight would have to be Thomas Hearns, the "Hitman". I don't want to be accused of favouring men who fought me but Hearns, Duran and Benitez were truly greats. Nobody can dispute that.'

Summing up his life and looking back on the sport he graced with such dignity, how would he like to be remembered? 'I would like to think I was a good boxer, contributed something to the sport in which I'm still involved and also a good family man,' he said. 'I'm a happy man, most importantly within myself.'

9

Earnie Shavers

The Acorn was a tough nut to crack

THE man regarded as one of the hardest-punching heavyweights in boxing history, the 'Black Destroyer', or 'The Acorn' as Muhammad Ali called him, took a sip from his coffee, placed the cup on the table and said, 'Did you say, "One of the hardest hitters, Thomas?" No, *the* hardest hitter. Only God hits harder and you can quote me on that.' The occasion was the British Boxing Awards lunch in a London hotel in 2003 where Earnie Shavers was an honoured guest.

In between signing autographs for eager fans, the retired contender chatted amicably, recounting stories of his early years growing up in Alabama, his days as an amateur boxer and his 26 years in the professional ring. During that span, from 1969 to 1995, he fought all the big guns and compiled a 73-14-1 record, with 67 by knockouts or stoppages, 23 inside the first round. Shavers was perhaps unlucky to be competing at a time when the heavyweight division was at its busiest – crowded with formidable champions and talented contenders.

In a different era, Shavers could well have been heavyweight champion of the world. He did get two shots at the title when he lost a 15-rounds decision to Muhammad Ali in 1977 and came within one punch of knocking out Larry Holmes two years later almost to the very day. Shavers had his limitations, too. Like many big hitters, he sometimes depended too heavily on his one-punch power and neglected combinations to finish the job.

Shavers's chin was also suspect too but if he got there first, it was all over. Those he nailed with his detonating punches, particularly with the right hand, generally stayed nailed, often waking up and saying, 'What happened? Where am I?' Muhammad Ali said after outpointing Shavers, 'Earnie Shavers hit me so hard he shook up all my kinfolk back in Africa.' Heavyweight contender Randall 'Tex' Cobb, an eight-round victim of Shavers in 1980, commented, 'Earnie could punch you in the neck with his right hand and break your ankle.' Ken Norton said, 'Anything Earnie Shavers hit you with, you would feel it. His punch was like photographers' flashlights going off in my head. When he knocked me down, I was out cold.'

Referee Mills Lane, who officiated Shavers's one-round demolition of Norton in 1979, called him 'the greatest one-punch hitter I've ever seen'. Not surprisingly, in 2003 Shavers received what he considered the ultimate accolade when *Ring* magazine ranked him at number ten among boxing's greatest punchers in ring history. 'It was real swell to be rated like that by your peers,' he said.

'You know, Thomas, and I can tell you this quite honestly, Joe Frazier wouldn't fight me. When I approached him one evening at some boxing function I said to him, "Why don't you and I get together in the ring, Joe? It'd be a good fight and the fans would go home happy," but he replied, "Sorry Earnie, no way are we going to meet each other, except socially." George Foreman too. When I put it to George when we were both ringsiders one night that we should fight each other some time and they could call it the "Battle of the Big Punchers" or something like that, he said, "I'd be happy to fight you, Earnie, except that you hit too damn hard for my liking." See what I mean?

'I was born on 31 August 1945 in Garland, Alabama, which is about 100 miles from the better-known Mobile. The violent Ku Klux Klan were big in Garland. For your younger readers, maybe I should explain briefly who the Klan were. The first Ku Klux Klan flourished in the southern United States in the late 1860s, then died out by the early 1870s. Members made their own white costumes: robes, masks, and conical hats, designed to be outlandish and terrifying, and to hide their identities.

'The second KKK flourished nationwide in the early and mid-1920s, and adopted a standard white costume, sales of which together with initiation fees financed the movement. They used code words as the first Klan, while adding cross burnings and mass parades. The third KKK emerged after World War II and was associated with opposing the Civil Rights Movement and progress among minorities. Though most members of the KKK saw themselves as holding to American values and Christian morality, virtually every Christian denomination denounced them.

'At first we moved to Warren, Ohio. Momma used to say that the day we left Garland, the Klan searched the house. I think it had something to do with dad not paying for a car from a Klansman, something like that. They would have killed him, no doubt about that. I worked on a farm and it made me strong. Chopping trees, tossing bales of wheat, all that increases your back muscles. I got into boxing when a friend, a former Golden Gloves boxer, invited me to his gym in Youngstown, not far from Warren. He said with my height and strength I could go places in boxing.

'I made my amateur debut as a heavyweight in the annual Golden Gloves competition in Youngstown a little later, January 1967, and won. I was over the moon. I won some more titles after that, including the National AAU championship, and finished up my amateur career with a record of 20-6. This was in the fall of 1969. I wanted to stay around as an amateur and try for the trials for the Olympics in Munich in 1972 but I was advised at the gym that my style was more suited to the professional ranks and I shouldn't waste my time hanging out for another three years.'

Shavers turned professional on 6 November 1969 with a second-round knockout over journeyman Silas 'Red' Howell in Akron, Ohio. It was an impressive start. Up to the end of 1970 Shavers had 20 fights, 20 wins, with only one opponent on his feet at the finish. Newspapers and magazines were taking notice of the fearsome hitter blowing away all opposition. *Ring* and *Boxing Illustrated* marked him down as a man to watch and a good heavyweight prospect. By the close of 1971 his record was 36-0, with 35 either by count-outs or stoppages.

Now for the big time. Shavers climbed into the ring at Madison Square Garden on 18 June 1973 against the slick Jimmy Ellis from the Muhammad Ali stable and a former heavyweight champion in an unofficial ten-round eliminator for new champion George Foreman's heavyweight championship. It opened dramatically, with Ellis getting through his rival's guard with a powerful left hook-right cross combination that sent Shavers reeling back into a corner. Ellis followed up and belted Shavers with lefts and rights to the head and body. Shavers covered up before unleashing his own smashing right uppercut to the chin and the Louisville boxer crashed down, landing on his back to be counted out. The time was two minutes and 39 seconds of round one.

'I had gotten good tips from Ali before the fight. He told me not to allow Ellis to get going with his smart boxing, force him into a fight, and in that way I would get him early,' recalled Shavers. 'Angelo Dundee, who managed Ellis as well as Ali, was going around before the fight telling everybody his man would be too smart for me but I would say that Ellis was just a blown-up middleweight. In that first round, after he sent me back with his sudden attack, I remembered Ali's words about going into the attack early. I saw a quick opening and just clipped him with my pet punch, a right uppercut, and down he went for good.

'I had hoped to get a title fight with Foreman after my quick win but it didn't happen. Then came an offer from Teddy Brenner, who was matchmaker at Madison Square Garden, to pair me with Jerry Quarry with the winner going in against Foreman. Brenner offered Foreman $1m to take on the winner.

Quarry was a New York-based Californian known as Irish Jerry Quarry and he was the new white hope of the heavyweight division.

'Quarry came into the ring on 14 December 1973 as a 12/5 favourite but I paid no attention to that. Odds mean nothing. The most important thing is what happens when the fight gets under way. Quarry had a 47-6-4 record and my tally was 46-2-0. I felt I could take him. After all, I had knocked out Jimmy Ellis in one round, and Ellis beat Quarry to win the WBA heavyweight title. Quarry came from his corner like a whirlwind which surprised me as I took him to be a slow starter. But I met him with some good right-handers. He countered with a left hook and I went down. I jumped up at two to take the mandatory count standing in a corner as the referee Arthur Mercante wiped my gloves.

'When Mercante gave the order to box on, Quarry rushed in again with both hands and kept up the attack, knocking me against the ropes. Just then Mercante stepped in and called it off. The time was 2.21. No excuses as Jerry was a very, very good fighter and unlucky not to be the heavyweight champion but I made one big mistake in that fight. I shouldn't have gotten up at the count of two. I should have taken full advantage of the mandatory eight count which would have cleared my head. If I had allowed my head to clear I could have lasted out the round and who's to know what would haver happened in the second round? I just got careless and that was it. But I considered it just a setback. I'd be back, and I was.

'Incidentally, despite getting that $1m offer to fight the winner, Foreman turned down a Quarry fight and signed to defend his title against Ken Norton, who had won and lost in two fights with Muhammad Ali. Foreman finished off Norton in two rounds in Venezuela, of all places. I guess big George had figured that Norton would be easier than Quarry and maybe he was right.'

Referee Mercante would remember the Quarry fight, 'I didn't expect Quarry to start so fast as Shavers was always dangerous, with tremendous punching power. His knockout percentage was simply incredible and many felt he hit harder than the reigning champion George Foreman, a monstrous puncher in his own right. Take it from one who has been watching fighters for nearly 75 years – Shavers's punching power was no hype. He was one of the deadliest punchers I ever saw and several years later in a title bout, Shavers had Muhammad Ali out on his feet but didn't realise it and lost his chance and the decision. Quarry was really on top form to take Shavers out so quickly.'

Shavers ran into another big hitter when he went in against Ron Lyle, the fifth-ranked heavyweight for the world title then held by Muhammad Ali who had sensationally knocked out George Foreman in eight rounds a year earlier. Shavers and Lyle clashed at the Denver Coliseum, Colorado, on 13 September 1975. Shavers had run up four wins and a draw, with one points loss, since the Quarry fight to take his record to 49-4-1 against Lyle's 30-3-1 sheet. However, Lyle, a local man and a former convict, had lost his two previous bouts, to Ali before Muhammad regained the title, and Jimmy Young, a former one-round victim against Shavers.

This is how Mike Hayes saw the fight for *Ring* magazine, 'The six rounds the fight lasted were an absolute brawl. Neither fighter tried to avoid mixing it up, and all boxing rules were dismissed. It was a war. Never had the crowd of 5,058 witnessed a fight with so many momentum changes. Lyle's perfect record of never having been knocked down disappeared in the second round when Shavers dropped the Denver fighter to one knee. He was on his feet at the end of the mandatory eight count, and as Shavers was moving in, the bell sounded to end the round.

'At the start of the third round Lyle, showing little effect from the knockdown, immediately carried the fight to Shavers. With the fight even going into the sixth round, Lyle took charge right off, and showed everyone he's a fighter who can survive a knockdown. He pushed Shavers to the ropes in the opening seconds and let loose with an intense barrage of right hands that completely destroyed the Ohio fighter. Five consecutive right crosses with no return fire ended the bout. Shavers fell forward and rolled over on his shoulders. Referee Joe Ullmer counted to ten but he could have counted to 50 and it took Shavers's handlers five or six minutes to get their warrior to his corner.'

Shavers remembered, 'Full credit to Lyle but when I floored him in the second round I thought they gave him a long count as the referee ushered me to a neutral corner very slowly. This allowed Lyle, the local fighter, to recover sufficiently. The local commission disputed this but I maintained, and still do, that he got a long count. There you go. But let me say that Lyle was a really big hitter, probably the hardest I ever fought. On the other hand, he told me after the fight that I hit him so hard that I untied his bootlaces. A tough guy, Ron Lyle, but a good guy.'

After five straight wins, four by count-outs or stoppages, Shavers finally got a chance at the heavyweight championship of the world when he faced the champion Muhammad Ali at Madison Square Garden on 29 September 1977. Ali, by now past his best, was still a considerable force and was on a nine-fight winning streak since winning back the title from Foreman. At the press conference to announce the fight, Ali nicknamed Shavers the 'Acorn' because of his shaven head, unlike his early appearances.

'Every boxer dreams of fighting for a world title and here was I fulfilling that dream,' said Shavers. 'I was two years younger and knew I was stronger too. I felt very confident I had what it takes and I wasn't going to let anything get in my way of winning the title. I was ready for Muhammad Ali.'

In a discussion about the fight with this writer some time later, John F. Condon, publicist for Madison Square Garden, said, 'Shavers was a very dangerous opponent, the hardest puncher in the heavyweight division now that George Foreman was off the scene. From our point of view, however, Ali was taking the whole thing too lightly. He was dismissive of the whole thing. He took off so many days from his training camp at Deer Lake, Pennsylvania, that I had to send him a letter saying that he had a duty to the paying public to enter the ring in his best physical condition.

'We also asked Floyd Patterson, the former heavyweight champion and at the time the chairman of the New York Commission, to visit Ali at Deer Lake and try to talk some sense into his head. It was to no avail. Floyd came back and told us that Ali did not want to be told how to train and that he knew what he had to do. It was quite clear that Ali was underestimating Shavers, a real banger who would always be dangerous.'

When Ali climbed into the ring, he looked flabby around the waist, weighing a bulky 225lb against Shavers who tipped the scales at 211 lb. Still, Las Vegas gamblers were not unduly worried about the likely outcome, a win for Ali, but they declined to lay odds. A crowd of 14,613 was on hand, with gate receipts totalling $722,217, with the main revenue coming in from TV. The scheduled 15-rounder was televised live throughout North America and broke all existing records with a viewing audience of 70 million.

It turned out to be the most exciting heavyweight championship fight since Ali stopped Joe Frazier in the 'Thrilla in Manila' two years earlier. Ali retained his title on a unanimous decision, with referee Johnny LoBianco marking his card 9-5-1 and judges Tony Castellano and Eva Shain, the first woman to judge a world heavyweight title fight, calling it 9-6. The verdict was greeted by a storm of booing by some sections of the fans. After such a dogged display by the underdog challenger, some crowd disapproval was expected, though no less a boxing authority than Red Smith, then working for the *New York Times*, said that Shavers deserved the decision by a narrow margin. Teddy Brenner, matchmaker for Madison Square Garden, also thought that Shavers won.

It was always an interesting fight and often an exciting one. Rounds were won by first one then the other, with Shavers pressing forward, looking for the chance to get through with his big punches. Ali got his left jab working well in the early rounds, and even when the action slowed down, there was always an air of suspense because Shavers had demonstrated he could hurt the champion. It was boxer Ali v fighter Shavers in the main, with Ali keeping his man at the end of his long left as the rugged challenger came in.

Ali clearly won the tenth, 11th and 12th rounds but the 13th and 14th belonged to Shavers as he battered his man with lefts and rights. Pat Puttnam of *Sports Illustrated* noted that, before the bell to start the 15th round, 'Ali was on wobbly legs.' In a furious last round, both boxers tagged each other heavily and often but Ali closed strongly and nearly dropped Shavers in the final 20 seconds. The fight made the cover of *Sports Illustrated* with the headline 'Ali's Desperate Hour' over a photograph of Shavers scoring with an overhand right. *Boxing News* said, 'Shavers put up the fight of his life. This was his greatest hour.'

'At the end of the 15th round I was sure I had won and you can imagine my disappointment when the result was announced,' Shavers said. 'Looking back now, though, I feel that the decision was probably fair but I think I scored a moral victory. Writers had been saying for years that I couldn't take a punch and that my chin would let me down. Others said I lacked heart and that I'd fold under real pressure. How wrong they were. What negative thinking! I left the ring in Madison Square Garden, boxing's most famous arena, upright and on my feet.

'Going back down the aisle on the way to the dressing room, Cus D'Amato, who trained champions like Floyd Patterson and Jose Torres, stopped me and said, "Earnie, tonight you became a man in all our eyes." I said, "Thank you very much, Cus." Coming from somebody like Cus, that was very special to me.

'In some ways, Ali came out of the fight a loser. His doctor Ferdie Pacheco had received a report that Ali's kidneys were damaged in the fight and urged him to retire there and then. Pacheco said the years of taking body shots and head shots were costing him his health and possibly shortening his life. Pacheco said he told Ali this but Ali being Ali, he wouldn't listen, not even to his long-time manager Angelo Dundee. Teddy Brenner, the matchmaker at Madison Square Garden, also advised Ali to quit and said he would not use him any more. Ali just wouldn't listen.

'I personally felt too that he should have retired after the fight. He took too many punches in the closing years of his career and sadly he is paying for it now with his illness. Boxing is a tough game and you can take so many punches but if you take too many, the cost can be great. Thankfully I came out all right. You just have to get out in time no matter what you yourself may feel abut the situation. Listen to others.'

Shavers would get another chance at the world heavyweight championship two years later when the title had passed to Larry Holmes. Meanwhile, Earnie was matched with former champion Ken Norton in a final eliminator for the title at the Hilton Pavilion, Las Vegas, on 23 March 1979. Shavers made short work of the ex-marine by blitzing him in the first round. Earnie came out fast and dropped his man with a smashing left hook to the head.

When Norton arose, Shavers was after him and unleashed his favourite punch, a sweeping right uppercut to the chin, followed by a hard left hook to the same spot to send the Illinois battler down on his back. He barely made it up at eight and fell over sideways into the ropes, at which point referee Mills Lane wisely called it off at one minute and 58 seconds. It was arguably Shavers's greatest win.

Shavers remembered, 'In the run-up to the fight, Norton's people had been looking for a chance to get another shot at the title after their man lost it to Larry Holmes a year earlier. Our match would now determine the official number one contender. I was very confident of taking him early on. I think Ken underrated me and maybe took me a little cheap. When I landed those two big punches I knew he was all through. He crawled up but he was finished. I was the top contender again, my 55th knockout in 65 fights and my 21st first-round win.'

Shavers ducked between the ropes at Caesars Palace, Las Vegas, on 28 September 1979 with world heavyweight champion Larry Holmes in the opposite corner before a capacity crowd of 4,500 and a TV audience of millions. Holmes had outpointed Shavers in a title fight in March 1978. Shavers claimed he made too many mistakes in the first fight and was depending on one shot to win but it did not work out that way. He vowed that this time it would be different.

The fight turned into a war of attrition, and far more exciting than the first match. For six rounds Shavers kept punching away but Holmes was ahead on his better boxing and sharper combinations. The fight exploded into action with just 30 seconds remaining in the seventh when the shaven-headed challenger floored Holmes with a thunderous overhand right to the chin as the crowd roared.

The champion got up and took the mandatory count on his feet and survived a charging attack to last out the round. Shavers never got a second chance and Holmes was totally in command, having won nine of the ten rounds, before referee Dave Pearl intervened in the 11th with the challenger almost out on his feet, cuts over both eyes. Holmes would say later, 'Earnie hits hard enough to knock over a mountain.'

'No excuses,' remembered Shavers. 'I was beaten by a better man. My moment of glory happened in that seventh round when, for a few seconds, I was heavyweight champion of the world. It was a great feeling, the best I've ever felt, but it was all too short. One more punch would have closed the show for me but Larry clinched and held on for dear life until the bell.

'Don King, my manager and promoter, was so dumbstruck he put a lighted cigar back into his mouth the wrong way around. Larry came out for the eighth round refreshed, thanks to sound corner work by his trainer Richie Giachetti, one of the best in the business. I worked out with Richie some years earlier and found him to be very good. At the finish Larry said to me, "You're a great fighter. I love you." I said to him. "You're a real man Larry. I love you too." All these years later, we're still the best of pals and that's exactly how it should be.'

Shavers retired from the ring in 1983 after retinal problems were discovered and became an ordained Christian minister. During the early 1980s while preparing for the feature movie *Rocky III*, Sylvester Stallone explored the possibility of using a real heavyweight boxer in the role of James 'Clubber' Lang and invited Shavers to spar with him. At first Shavers refused to hit Stallone with anything other than a soft jab.

'This was something that frustrated Stallone and he said to me, 'Come on Earnie, show me something real.' I responded by punching Stallone in the stomach and he doubled up. Stallone gasped and spluttered, "You nearly killed me", and he had to go to the men's room to throw up. I never got the part. That was the end of my chance to break into movies.

'I made many great friends through boxing, and met many famous ex-champions including the great Sugar Ray Robinson. I was working out at the famous Main Street Gym in Los Angeles when I was introduced to Robinson, who was then retired. He said, "I heard a lot about you, you're this great puncher from Ohio." He asked me about an old Youngstown boxer named Tommy Bell who he beat for the world welterweight title. I told him I knew Bell well and he used to say how proud he was to have gone the distance twice with Robinson. He just smiled.

'When I told Robinson that I was often nervous before fights, he felt that was a good thing. "When you stop being nervous before a fight, you are in real trouble," he said. "I myself was always nervous before a fight. It prevents you from being too overconfident. I don't care how long you are in boxing, you are supposed to be nervous and it's as simple as that. So you've nothing to worry about on that issue. Nothing at all." So that was good sound advice coming from the master, the man rightly considered the greatest of them all.'

Now 71 years of age and living in Las Vegas, Shavers makes appearances at boxing functions and celebrity dinners, and is often called on to take part in question-and-answer sessions. He has written an autobiography and published a video of the highlights of his ring career. 'Life's been good, and is still good,' says the old 'Black Destroyer'. 'I've no regrets.'

10

Joe Frazier

Smokin' Joe had fire in his fists

THEY called him 'Smokin' Joe' and it seemed an apt title. Joe Frazier always came out smokin' even when the odds were against him. Given the nickname when his trainer Yank Durham told his young charge in the gym, 'Let's see some smoke coming out of the leather, Joe,' Frazier fought the best of his day in the 1960s and 70s, arguably the most competitive era in the history of the heavyweight division. When the Philadelphian reigned as undisputed world champion in the early 1970s, his reputation as one of the greatest gunslingers that boxing had seen was intact.

By today's standards Frazier was relatively short for a heavyweight at 5ft 11.5in but he was able to turn that into an advantage by boring in against invariably taller opponents, head down, always moving forward out of a low crouch, bobbing and weaving to where he was in a position to deliver crushing blows to the head and body. This style was much in the Jack Dempsey and Henry Armstrong mould, and possibly to a lesser extent, Rocky Marciano.

It must be remembered too that Frazier was the first to defeat Muhammed Ali when both were in their prime years, and the only men to beat Frazier in 37 professional fights were

Ali and George Foreman. Even as an amateur he reached the ultimate heights, winning a gold medal in the heavyweight division in the Tokyo Olympics of 1964. Frazier's pet punch, a sharp left hook to the body, was characteristic of Philadelphian fighters. Smokin' Joe may have been born in South Carolina but he lived in the City of Brotherly Love since his teen years and always regarded it as 'my real home town'.

This writer met Frazier on two occasions. The first time was when he toured Ireland in 1972 with his band The Knockouts. It was during his reign as world heavyweight champion. The second time was in London the following year, shortly after he lost his title to Foreman, when he scored a 12-round decision over Joe Bugner, the Hungarian-born British and European champion.

'Never mind Frank Sinatra singing about Chigago being "my kinda town", Philadelphia was *my* kinda town,' he explained. 'Seriously, you may not realise it, or even know about it, but Philadelphia produced some of the greatest fighters of all time. Guys like Philadelphia Jack O'Brien, Tommy Loughran, Lew Tendler, Bob Montgomery, Harold Johnson, Midget Wolgast and so on and so on. Jack Blackburn, a great fighter in his day, although probably better known as the man who trained Joe Louis, also regarded Philly as his real home town, even though he was born in Kentucky. The city has a great boxing legacy.'

Joseph William Frazier was a child of the segregated Deep South. He was born in Beauford County, South Carolina near the US Marine base on Parris Island on 12 January 1944. Parris Island is a sleepy little town, clean but simple. It is a place of saltwater swampland, set in an area of old rice fields, watermelons and oyster creeks. In the backcountry, through thick pine forests and windy dusty roads, wooden shacks stand on cinder blocks.

It was in one of those shacks among the oak trees, Spanish moss and the sandy sea soil that Joe was born to Rubin and Dolly Frazier, the last in a family of 13 children. As can be imagined, the Fraziers were desperately poor, and their work consisted of scratching about the fields trying to grow vegetables.

'My folks worked their farm with two mules named Buck and Jenny,' he remembered. 'The farmland was what country people call white dirt, which was another way of saying it wasn't worth a damn. You couldn't grow peas or corn on it, only cotton and watermelons. After work, dad would make his way to the still where he made his bootleg corn liquor. He also grew what I discovered was marijuana. He was a good man, and on Saturdays he would go into town to buy the necessities that his large family needed.'

Four of Joe's brothers and sisters had died before he was even born. At the age of six he was at work on the plantation, putting in 12 hours a day and helping his father by picking radishes at 15 cents per crate. The senior Frazier had the handicap of losing his left arm in an accident before Joe was born, and Joe would describe himself as his father's left hand. 'He had the hammer and I held the nail,' Frazier would remember. 'Daddy had a Ford car which he affectionately called Billy. It was a real beast. He drove the hell out of it, over backcountry roads, and streets all over Beauford County, never breaking down. In Daddy's mind, the car stood for trustfulness and reliability, and that was what he said he saw in me. I was known as Billy Boy.'

In the early 1950s, Frazier's father bought a black and white television. The family and neighbours came to watch boxing matches on it. Frazier's mother sold drinks for a quarter as they watched boxers like Sugar Ray Robinson, Rocky Graziano, Willie Pep, Floyd Patterson and others on the snowy 15-inch screen. 'I was enthralled watching all the great boxers in action and I guess that was what started my interest in the sport,' he said. 'I didn't want to be a baseball player or a football player like lots of other kids, even though I liked those sports. I just wanted to be a boxer, like Joe Louis, who I had read about and heard about. Louis was my idol.'

Shortly after Frazier became world champion in 1968, his mother told the New York sportswriter and Frazier biographer Phil Pepe, 'Billy Boy was the love and joy of my husband. Rubin used to say that the boy would grow up to be another Joe Louis and be champion of the world. It all came true. Boxing was his life. At nine years of age he was fighting other kids. Billy Boy was a good child. I just couldn't say he was bad. He would never run around and do bad things, but of course, children are children and they do get into trouble at times. I thank God that he became heavyweight champion of the world, just like Joe Louis. It was something he always dreamed about, something to aspire to.'

One night Joe's uncle Israel noticed his stocky build. 'That boy there, that boy is gonna be another Joe Louis, mark my words,' he forecast. The words made a big impression on Joe. He would fill old burlap sacks with rags, corncobs, bricks, Spanish moss, leaves from the tree, grass, anything he could find and hang the makeshift punchbag from an oak tree in the back yard.

'For the next six or seven years, damn near every day Thomas, I'd hit that heavy bag for an hour at a time,' he said. 'I'd wrap my hands with a necktie of my Daddy's, or a stocking of my Momma's or sister's, and get down to it. I must have knocked that old bag out of shape. I would imagine I was Joe Louis against Max Schmeling or Jim Braddock or Billy Conn and I'd be going for the knockout.'

School bullies would keep clear of Frazier as they were aware of his boxing ambitions. 'Any scamboogah, in other words a disrespectful, low down or foul person, who got in my face would soon regret it,' he said. 'Billy Boy would kick anybody's ass and they all knew that. I had the reputation of being a tough kid, handy with my fists. Mind you, I never started any trouble in the schoolyard or anywhere else but if anybody started getting tough with me or tried to push me around, I could handle them.'

Frazier quit school at 13 and got a job with a construction company at $1.75 an hour, later moving on to become a mule driver for a slightly better wage. But it was not really what he wanted. Aged 15, Joe knew he would have to get to the big city, any big city, to make real money and maybe realise his ultimate dream – to get into boxing and become a champion. By this time he also had a wife to support, having married his childhood sweetheart Florence Smith, a local girl.

One night Frazier made up his mind. It was time to leave Beauford as he could only see hard times ahead and little money for himself and Florence. Even his parents could see it. 'If you want to leave home, then by all means do so, Billy Boy,' his mother told him. 'We'll hate to say goodbye to you and we'll shed many tears but we both agree it would be for the best. You're a married man now and hopefully will raise a family like your momma and poppa did.'

'The train fare from Beauford to cities up north was costly,' remembered Frazier. 'I understood the closest bus stop was in Charleston, 96 miles away. However by 1958 it seems the bus, or the Dog as it was called by locals, had finally made Beauford a stop on its South Carolina route. I had a brother Tommy in New York and he said we could stay with him and his wife Ollie in their three-room apartment on West 110th Street. First though, I had to get some money together for the journey and also have a little cash in my pocket to keep us going.

'I went to work at the local Coca-Cola plant in Beauford. The white guy would drive the truck and I would do the hard work, stacking and unloading the crates. That's how it was then. When I left I got a job in a construction company building houses for the marines stationed at Parris Island. By this time Florence and I agreed that she should stay in Beauford until I got myself settled. I didn't want to be hauling her around New York while looking for a job and eventually an apartment of our own.

'So one morning I packed my bags, kissed Florence and my folks goodbye and got the first bus heading northward. I climbed on the Dog's back and rode through the night. By now it was 1959 and I was all set for what I hoped would be a life-changing experience. I was on my own. New York was the biggest fight town in the world back then and that's where I felt I wanted to be. There was nothing in the South. The North was the place to be. It's a funny thing, though, Thomas. Once I got to New York I couldn't settle in. I just couldn't get focussed. Maybe I was born to be a restless guy.

'I even visited gyms in New York as I knew there were plenty there, like the famous Stillman's Gym we've all heard about and where all the greats trained. I don't know but I just wasn't happy in the city. In any event I didn't want to be leaning on my brother Tommy. Remember, I wanted to make it on my own. After about 12 months or so with Tommy, I moved to Philadelphia. I knew my aunt Evelyn had a three-storey house in north Philadelphia and she agreed to take me in until I got my own place. The move to Philadelphia completely changed my life around. I sent for Florence and we settled down in our new adopted city. Life was going to be good.

'I got a job in a slaughterhouse through one of my relatives James Martin. It was hard work but I enjoyed it, and the money was good too, about $25 a day. During the break I would punch sides of beef as they dangled from abattoir hooks. I guess I was working off my youthful energy and aggression, or perhaps getting ready for when I would become a boxer, which was still my ambition, and I would be punching opponents instead of meat. But in a strange way, I got into boxing through the slaughterhouse, well indirectly. It was the end of 1961 and I was just short of my 18th birthday. I looked in the mirror in my apartment and realised I was getting too fat. The next day at the slaughterhouse I stepped on the scales and the arrow pointed to 220lb. I was becoming seriously overweight. No, change that. I *was* overweight and I had to do something about it, and soon, or I would develop serious health problems.'

When Frazier enquired at work if anybody knew of a local gym where he could lose weight, somebody told him about the Police Athletic Gym on 22nd and Columbia. Joe made up his mind to give it a try. After all, he had nothing to lose. At the gym he met Duke Dugent, the boxing instructor and a former policeman. Dugent would later admit that his first sight of Frazier was anything but impressive. He said that when Joe told him he would like to be a boxer some day, Dugent laughed and said he was too fat, too short and too slow. His hips were heavy and his arms too short and stumpy. But Frazier was persistent and Dugent finally had him fill out a membership form.

'Much of my early success was down to Duke,' remembered Frazier. 'He was a wonderful guy and he showed me the way. Despite my size and my weight, he must have seen something in me after getting over the shock of his first impression. He put me on a strict diet, fat-free. I was eating green vegetables and steak but no sweets. Sweets and chocolates were out. Duke gave me a key to the gym and said I could get in after work anytime I felt like it. I often did, too. I loved the gym. I really did. I enjoyed the sessions, jumping rope, doing sit-ups and push-ups, hitting the heavy bag, sparring with some of the boxers there. I couldn't manage the speedball at all, missing it all the time but Duke would say that if I practised I would get the hang of it eventually, and I did. I was in my element.

'I would be out of bed at five in the morning, run three or four miles, report for work at the slaughterhouse and after eight hours of hard work I'd be over at the gym and train until about nine in the evening. Later that year, 1962, Duke entered me for the Philadelphian Golden Gloves novice championships as a heavyweight and I won the final. I had ambitions to turn professional and Duke handed me over to Yancey "Yank" Durham, one of the trainers at the gym. Yank was a former boxer himself and sometimes manager and he took an interest in me. I was in good hands.'

Frazier's record as an amateur showed only one loss in three years, against burly Buster Mathis on a decision. Mathis would prove to be Joe's biggest obstacle in making the US team for the Tokyo Olympics in 1964. The trials were held during the New York World's Fair, and the two boxers to reach the heavyweight final were Frazier and Mathis. After three rounds, Mathis was awarded the decision, though several ringside reporters felt that it should have gone to Frazier. 'All that fat boy did was run like a thief and he wins the fight,' said Frazier. 'He just pecked away at me and back-pedalled like crazy.'

Mathis wore his trunks very high so that when Frazier hit him with legitimate body shots, the referee took a dim view of Joe. In the second round Frazier was penalised two points for hitting below the belt. 'In a three-round fight a boxer can't afford points deductions like that,' said Frazier. Duke Dugent, who was in Frazier's corner, remembered, 'Joe was simply robbed of representing his country in the biggest amateur tournament in the world. It was a shame. When the decision was announced, Joe told me he was completely sick and wanted to quit boxing altogether. He said he'd had enough. I told him to wait until he got back home and then see how he felt.'

Frazier returned to Philadelphia feeling lower than he had ever been but Dugent and Yank Durham were able to talk him out of his depression and said that there might still be a chance to get to Tokyo. They suggested he might be able to travel with the team as a standby heavyweight, in case anything happened to Mathis. Joe reluctantly agreed but asked Duke to tell his boss at the meat packing company to keep his job open for him, which they did. The next move was to contact the US Olympic Committee requesting that Frazier travel to Tokyo as a sparring partner for the team, and while there, to be on standby as the relief heavyweight. They agreed. Frazier knew it was a long shot but was worth it. After all, he had nothing to lose.

On the day before the team was due to leave for Japan, they assembled at the Hamilton Air Force Base in San Francisco for some final workouts and to box several exhibitions for the troops. Frazier was paired with Mathis. In a fast exchange Buster fired a right that landed on Frazier's head. The impact broke a finger and Mathis was sensationally out of the team. The hand would be in a cast for a couple of weeks – meaning that Frazier was automatically named as America's official Olympic heavyweight representative. A dream come true for the boxer who had wanted to quit the sport altogether a little earlier.

In his opening bout a completely rejuvenated Frazier knocked out George Oywello of Uganda after 95 seconds of the first round. In his second contest he had another knockout win when finishing off the Australian hope Athol McQueen just 40 seconds into the third round. Frazier was now into the semi-finals, the only American boxer to get so far in Tokyo.

He would come up against the formidable 6ft 4in and 230lb Vadim Yemelyanov, one of the Soviet Union's best hopes to bring home a gold medal.

'I remember somebody describing my left hook as a heat-seeking missile, careering off the face and body time and again,' he said. 'That was a rather colourful description I thought. Twice in the second round I knocked him to the canvas. Just then I felt a jolt of pain shooting up my left arm. *Oh damn, the thumb*. I knew right away what was wrong. I knew it must be damaged, though I wasn't quite sure as to what extent. In the heat of a fight, be it for a world title or in this case the Olympics, with your adrenalin pumping, it's hard to gauge such things.

'Your mind is on different matters. Like, how I was going to deal with Yemelyanov for the rest of the fight, with so much at stake. Luckily my corner told me I was ahead and the other guy had little chance of victory. His corner threw in the towel after 1.49 of the second round and the referee raised my hand in victory.'

Now that Frazier was into the final, his corner said not to mention the injured thumb to anybody except his doctor. The doctor suggested an x-ray but Joe said the hand felt fine. A complete lie because the hand did hurt. When the doctor left, Joe soaked his hand in hot water and Epsom salts. 'Pain or not, Joe Frazier of Beauford, South Carolina and Philadelphia is going for gold,' he said. 'I had come this far by a lucky stroke and I wasn't going to let my big chance slip away. I would win the final with one good hand. I just couldn't let the folks down back home, no way, damaged hand or no damaged hand.'

Frazier's opponent in the final was the taller and heavier German, Hans Huber. Joe was used to fighting bigger opponents but he was not used to doing so with only one good hand. When the first bell sounded, he started swinging punches but was careful not to connect solidly with the left. Mainly he fired all rights to the head and body. Even so, every time he used his left, even light jabs, the pain would shoot up through his arm. Luckily, Huber and his corner were not aware of the situation and Joe continued to use light jabs but strong rights to the head and body. By sheer courage and determination, and a bit of bluff, Frazier landed enough punches and scored sufficient points to win the decision by the narrowest of margins.

Under Olympic rules in operation at the time, five judges were officiating and three voted for the American. Joe Frazier, the man who effectively got on to the Olympic team through the back door, was now the winner of a gold medal, the first US heavyweight to achieve this honour in the history of the modern Olympics dating back to St Louis in 1904. When Frazier returned home with the rest of the squad, he had immediate treatment on his injured thumb but there would be two operations several months apart. This meant he could not go back to work at the slaughterhouse. You would need two good hands for that. With a wife and two children to support, he was now in deep financial trouble – especially with Christmas coming up.

'Luckily a story in a local newspaper attracted some good publicity, and this brought in some badly-needed funds which helped us over the Christmas holidays. But I still needed to do some serious thinking about my future. I needed to turn professional when my hand healed to make some regular money, and with my Olympic gold medal, I had some kind of credentials, good credentials. Yank Durham agreed to become my manager as Duke Dugent was a police officer and his position prevented him from becoming involved. I also needed to get some financial backers the way Cassius Clay, as he was known then, had done. In the meantime the hand was responding to treatment, which was good news.'

Frazier had his first professional fight on 16 August 1965 when he stopped Woody Gross after one minute and 42 seconds of round one in Philadelphia. But he still had not found a backer. After several more fights, however, a group of businessmen came on board and agreed to finance the promising heavyweight. They formed a corporation called Cloverlay – 'clover' for luck and 'lay' for putting down the odds. They would pay Frazier $100 a week plus 25 per cent of his purses, later increased to $173 per week, then $1,000 per week, the rest to be invested.

The stockholders got 35 per cent, out of which they paid all expenses, and 15 per cent went to Durham in his role as manager-trainer-advisor, with no interference from Cloverlay. These men were not in it for the money. They had that through their various businesses. They were in it for the fun of it, and the chance to tell their friends over drinks at the local golf club that they had a top boxer as their friend, an Olympic gold medallist and a potential heavyweight champion of the world. They could sit at ringside and watch his fights while proudly pointing out, 'That's my boy.'

Frazier now had direction in his career. In the first two years he won all his 19 fights, all but two lasting the scheduled distance. Among the big-name contenders were the slick Californian Eddie Machen and the bruising Argentinian Oscar Bonavena. Then came a happening that would dramatically change the course of boxing history forever. On 28 April 1967 at the army recruiting centre in Houston, Texas, Muhammad Ali, having successfully defended his world heavyweight title nine times in three years, refused to step forward and wear a uniform. Ali maintained he was a Black Muslim and as such, members were forbidden to go to war. Consequently, he said, he could not go to Vietnam.

The World Boxing Association promptly withdrew recognition of Ali as champion and banned him from boxing in the US as well as overseas, having taken away his passport. They named eight leading heavyweights including Frazier to contest the vacant title but Yank Durham said Frazier would not compete on the basis that Joe was the leading contender anyway and therefore should not have to go through what he called a 'long-drawn-out and senseless tournament' to find Ali's successor.

The New York State Athletic Commission followed the WBA move by stripping Ali of recognition as champion, and to the surprise of nobody, proceeded to set up a championship fight between Frazier and his former amateur rival and two-time conqueror Buster Mathis to contest their version of the vacant heavyweight title. The bout was set for 4 March 1968 and it would be part of a double-header card to inaugurate the newest Madison Square Garden, the fourth incarnation.

'You will remember Mathis was the guy who opened the door for me to go to the Olympics when he broke his hand and I went over in his place but I never thought he was a good fighter,' said Frazier. 'To look at him you'd think he was an assassin. He was big and brawny. Surprisingly too for his size he moved well and had a fast left jab. But he wasn't a hard puncher. In any event I knew his style from the amateur days and I kinda knew what to expect. I felt he was fading around the ninth round or so because of my heavy shots to the body and head. I finally got him in the 11th.

'A left and right to the head dropped him and he went down on his back, his arms spread-eagled. I remember it well. He struggled to get to his feet at six but stumbled into a corner as the count reached eight.

'There was no way he could make it in time. Somehow, he struggled up but he was swaying like a yacht in a storm and referee Arthur Mercante waved his arms over his head and called it off. The time was 2.33. I must give full credit to Buster, though, for his gameness. He took all I could hand out and still kept going until the finish.

'I was now heavyweight champion of the world, at least in the eyes of New York and some other states who had supported New York such as Pennsylvania, Massachusetts, Illinois, Maine and Texas. Jimmy Ellis from Muhammad Ali's home town of Louisville, Kentucky won the WBA tournament so he was calling himself the champion too. Also, Ali was claiming he was the real champion, the rightful champion, on the grounds that he never lost the title in the ring – even though all America said he had been stripped of the crown. He was still under suspension in any event so he could be eliminated. The obvious match now was to pair me with Ellis and settle who the *genuine* champion was.'

The WBA and New York agreed that the winner of Frazier v Ellis would get their blessing as the official heavyweight champion of the world. The match was set for 16 February 1970. Ellis had one of boxing's most curious careers, going from obscure middleweight to WBA heavyweight champion of the world. The undefeated Frazier was a heavy favourite. Many scoffed at Ellis's ability, labelling him as merely an Ali sparring partner, a smiling nice guy in Ali's shadow. But the Kentuckian was a fine heavyweight, a smart skilful boxer even if he did lack a really heavy knockout punch. Few, however, felt he had the tools to end Frazier's run of 24 winning fights.

He had beaten the likes of Floyd Patterson, Jerry Quarry, Oscar Bonavena and Leotis Martin on the way to the WBA belt but the rampaging Frazier was a different matter. Ellis had never been floored as a heavyweight but that distinction ended in the fourth round when Frazier twice put him down. It was all over in the fifth when Ellis's manager Angelo Dundee pulled his man out of the firing line. It was his first loss inside the distance. 'Jimmy wanted to continue but no way,' explained Dundee. 'He'd taken enough.'

Frazier remembered, 'To be honest, Ellis didn't have much of a chance. I waded into him from the start and he backed up. I kept after him and by the end of the third round, I noticed that he hardly had the strength to keep his hands up. I kept pounding him in the fourth and I knew it was only a matter of time before I'd finish him off. It was no surprise when Dundee told the referee it was all over. I was now officially heavyweight champion of the world and it was a great feeling. Everything I had worked for, and my family had worked for, had paid off.'

Robert Lipsyte of the *New York Times* wrote, 'Frazier is no longer simply a shuffling, plodding, mechanical monster willing to absorb many punches until an opponent's arms are so tired they drop to expose his chin. His combination punching had become sharper. It was becoming a little harder to hit him. But when he does strike out, it is with a wide-eyed, smiling, joyful rip that sends shivers through the crowd an instant before the crunching sound of his glove against flesh.'

Frazier was now undisputed champion – undisputed that is except by the supporters of Ali, who had not fought for three years and was talking of retirement. Up to that point *Ring* magazine, acknowledged as the bible of boxing, had stubbornly and surprisingly proclaimed that Ali was still the true champion. Finally, editor and publisher Nat Fleischer bowed to public opinion and named Frazier as the real champion. Ali was gracious about the development. 'Far from being handed the title, Frazier had to fight the best around except for me,' he said. 'So I can't take that away from him.'

No sooner had Frazier settled into his role as king of the heavyweights than Ali burst back on the scene. His five-year sentence for draft evasion had been quashed on appeal and his licence to box reinstated. In late 1970, the undefeated ex-champion embarked on a comeback with impressive wins over Jerry Quarry and Oscar Bonavena, and both in faster time than it had taken Frazier to beat them. The stage was now set for one of the most anticipated matches in ring history – the 'Fight of the Century', as it was billed, except by those publicists who thought this tag was underselling it. They called it simply 'The Fight'.

'It was set for 8 March 1971 for where else but Madison Square Garden, the Mecca of boxing, where John L. Sullivan, the first of the modern world heavyweight champions had fought – in the first Garden in July 1882,' remembered Frazier. 'Tickets sold rapidly and with 42 days to go before we were due to climb into the ring, it was a complete sell-out. I was happy to be part of an event that ushered in a new era in financial and boxing terms. This wasn't an old-fashioned million-dollar fight. It was a billion-dollar extravaganza, and Ali and I picked up an unprecedented $2.5m each. It was incredible.

'Interest in the fight spread far beyond the world of boxing. Much of this was due to Ali. In the course of his nearly four years of exile there had been a remarkable transformation in the public persona of Muhammad Ali. In 1967, while a hero to the black community, he had been widely reviled by white America for his anti-war stance and for professing allegiance to the "alien" creed of the Nation of Islam. But in the intervening years there had been a sea change in opinion, especially among white liberals and the young generation who were becoming more vocally anti-war by the day.

Riding the crest of his popularity with the swelling anti-war movement, Ali had become a campus favourite, delivering lively lectures on everything from religion to philosophy, from race to war. He invariably ended his speeches by demanding that his audience remind him who the true champion was, and he could count on that familiar chant 'Ali! Ali! Ali!' In any event he *knew* he was the real champion and the match with Frazier was a golden chance to prove it.

'I remember the night as if it were only yesterday,' said Frazier. 'A crowd of 20,455 packed the Garden and the ringside was full of big names, from past champions including Sugar Ray Robinson, Joe Louis, Jack Dempsey, Gene Tunney, Willie Pep and James J. Braddock to celebrities such as Senators Ted Kennedy and Hubert Humphries, Diahann Carroll, Pat O'Brien, Ed Sullivan, New York Mayor John Lindsay, Count Basie and George Raft. Burt Lancaster was there too, ready to do the commentary for 300 million fans watching satellite and closed circuit TV around the world. Frank Sinatra, too, one camera strapped around his neck, another in his hands, waiting to click the photographs that would appear in *Life* magazine.'

The fight itself exceeded even its own hype and went the full 15 rounds. Ali dominated the first three, peppering the shorter Frazier with rapier-like jabs that raised welts on the champion's face. Frazier began to get into his stride from the fourth on his aggressive attacks. It was fairly close until late in the 12th when Frazier backed Ali into a corner and caught the ex-champion with a crushing left hook that very neatly put him on the canvas. Muhammad managed to survive the blow, and the round, but from then on, Frazier was in control.

At the end of round 14 Frazier was ahead on all three scorecards by 10-4, 8-6 and 7-6-1. Early in the 15th Frazier landed a powerful left hook that put Ali on his back. His jaw now swollen grotesquely, Ali got to his feet and back-pedalled until his head cleared but Frazier was giving him no rest. Soon the bell sounded, and the fight looked a lost cause for the man once billed as 'The Greatest'. Sure enough, all three judges marked the last round for Frazier. 'Smokin' Joe was the winner on a unanimous decision, dealing Ali his first loss in 32 fights. Frazier was now 27-0-0.

As Frazier saw it, 'I wasn't worried that Ali was scoring heavily with his jabs because I was forcing him to do so and making him vulnerable to my left hook. He was posturing a lot, like a guy whistling in the dark. He knew deep down I had his number and there was nothing he could really do about it. He had predicted that I would fall in six. Well, by the end of round six, I was still around.

'All the time I was looking for every opportunity to get through with the left hook, my main weapon and he knew that. Ali came out full of confidence for the 15th round but I knew the fight was mine. Secretly, so did he. Then the long-awaited opening came. Quickly I fired my pet punch, a looping left hook and it landed on the right side of his face. Down he went, one of the few times he had ever been on the canvas.

'Gamely he got up at four and took the mandatory eight count. Try as I might, I couldn't get another clean shot through before the bell went. It was all over. The two judges and Arthur Mercante, the referee, added up their scores and gave their cards to the announcer Johnny Addie. He read them out one by one and finally called out, "The winner...by a unanimous decision...and still heavyweight champion of the world...Joe... Frazier." I'd made it. I'd beaten the great Muhammad Ali and become undisputed champion of the world. It was Daddy who had predicted all those years before than I would be a world champion. My uncle Israel forecast it too. It was the greatest night of my life.'

What many consider the greatest world heavyweight championship fight of all time was going to be a hard act to follow. Frazier made two successful defences, both ending on stoppages in the fourth round, against Terry Daniels and Ron Stander. Soon the menacing shadow of George Foreman darkened the scene. The big Texan became the number one contender and they clashed in Kingston, Jamaica on 22 January 1973. Foreman became the new champion by extending his unbeaten run to 38 with a blistering win in two rounds. It was now painfully clear that Frazier's fire had gone out. He had been champion for only 22 months.

'The fight is still a daze to me,' said Frazier. 'Foreman had me on the canvas three times in the first round, and as the three count knockdown rule was not in effect, the fight continued. In the second round he had me down three times again before the fight was stopped. The reports said I was up and down like a yo-yo and I have to believe them. To be honest I haven't any clear memories of the fight and you'll have to check your files or the records to get the full details. But the six knockdowns are correct. I do recall that. There you go. You win some, you lose some. This time it was my turn to lose.

'I fought my old rival Muhammad Ali twice more, when both of us were contenders. We met at Madison Square Garden on 28 January 1974 and Ali won the decision over 12 rounds. It was unanimous but I still think he was lucky. He was lucky in several other fights too. You will remember Ken Norton beat him in the first fight, breaking his jaw. When they met in a return, Ali won the decision but I thought Norton should have got it. Ali was also fortunate to get the decision over Jimmy Young, too, and here he was now, lucky again with me. His punches were more of the pitty-pat variety, not hard, solid blows. But I didn't yell or complain. That's not my style, never was.

'We met for the third time in what was billed as the "Thrilla in Manila" on 1 October 1975. Ali was champion again by this time, having won back the title from George Foreman the previous year. I didn't like Ali's ranting before the fight, or any other fight for that matter. It's not sporting, and after all, boxing is a sport. He was shouting, "It's gonna be a thrilla, a chilla and a killa, when I get the gorilla in Manila." He said later that it was all for publicity but I'm not so sure of that. I had a serious problem with my left eye too because of a cataract issue. To be honest, I was virtually sightless.

'Ali won when my trainer Eddie Futch, who had taken over from Yank Durham who had died, pulled me out at the end of the 14th round. He told the referee, a Filipino named Carlos Padilla, it was all over. Padilla and the two judges all had me behind at the time. My left eye was closed shut. If I had been able to get to Ali I might have tracked his right hand but I couldn't see him. Eddie made the right decision to call it off, though at the time I pleaded that I wanted to go on. Looking back now, I've no regrets he made his decision. It was definitely the right one.'

Frazier had treatment for his left eye and returned to the ring eight months later but he was only a pale shadow, a very pale shadow, of his old self. His old rival George Foreman knocked him out in five rounds and he retired from the ring. On 3 December 1981, like many before him, Frazier attempted a final comeback, this time after a five-year absence, but could only draw with the limited Jumbo Cummings – and promptly retired again, this time for keeps. He managed and trained his son Marvis but the offspring seemingly lacked the will and the drive, not to mention the ability, of his famous dad and gradually faded from the scene without making any great impact.

Frazier died on 7 November 2011 in his adopted home town of Philadelphia at the age of 67. His great rival Muhammad Ali was among the 4,000 mourners during the two-hour service at the Enon Tabernacle Baptist Church. 'I will always remember Joe with respect and admiration,' Ali said. 'My sympathy goes out to his family and loved ones.'

The International Boxing Research Organisation rates Frazier among the ten greatest heavyweights of all time. In 1999, *Ring* magazine ranked him the eighth best heavyweight in history. Smokin' Joe is an inductee of both the International Boxing Hall of Fame in New York and the World Boxing Hall of Fame in California.

11

Billy Conn

The Pittsburgh Kid could run but couldn't hide

WHENEVER Billy Conn, the former Irish-American world light-heavyweight champion and heavyweight challenger, was interviewed, the subject of his first title fight with Joe Louis always came up. This was the 1941 match in New York when Conn had the championship in his grasp for 12 rounds before electing to slug it out with the hard-hitting 'Brown Bomber' and was knocked out with just two seconds of the 13th round remaining.

'Writers seemed to think that the first Louis fight was the only thing I ever did and that was all that interested their readers but I had a busy career before and after that fight,' Conn explained to this writer when he came to Dublin in July, 1972 to help the publicity for Muhammad Ali's bout with Al 'Blue' Lewis. 'However, I guess that the first match with Louis was the one most people remember me for so I couldn't blame them. I came so close to my dream of winning the heavyweight championship of the world that night, only to see it vanish like smoke with just two rounds to go. There you go. That's life.'

Conn's ring record is lined with famous boxers, champions and contenders, punchers and purists. They all came alike to the 'Pittsburgh Kid'. Besides Louis, there was Fritzie Zivic, Tony Zale, Gus Lesnevich, Teddy Yarosz, Young Corbett III, Fred Apostoli, Lee Savold, Bob Pastor, Al McCoy, Vince Dundee, Buddy Baer, Abe Simon and Babe Risko. Conn began as a lightweight and, as he grew, advanced through the welterweight, middleweight, light-heavyweight and heavyweight divisions.

Tall at 6ft 1in and rarely coming in at over 187lb, he had a good solid punch but his main attributes were fine boxing skills and fast footwork. When Warner Bros was shooting the movie *Gentleman Jim* in 1942 with Errol Flynn in the title role of James J. Corbett, it was Conn's fancy footwork that was used in the close-ups. Studio boss Jack Warner was reputed to have said to his associates, 'There is only one guy's footwork we can cut into, and which came nearest to Corbett's, and that's Billy Conn's. There is nobody else to match it.'

Gentleman Jim was not Conn's first foray into Hollywood movies. Two months after the first Louis fight in 1941, he starred in *The Pittsburgh Kid*. Made by Republic Studios, it was not autobiographical but based on a novel by Octavus Roy Cohen about a young boxer torn between a pretty girl and an unscrupulous manager. Several leading boxers appeared in the movie including Henry Armstrong, Freddie Steele, Jack Roper and referee Arthur Donovan. *The Pittsburgh Kid* never made it to any awards nights but it helped to keep Conn's name in the public eye.

In a poll of 20 world boxing experts conducted by *Ring* magazine in October 2014 to select the top 50 boxers pound for pound of all time, Conn came in at 25. A previous poll by the Associated Press news agency listed him as one of the top ten boxers of the 20th century.

Born in the tough East Liberty neighbourhood of Pittsburgh on 8 October 1917, Conn got into plenty of neighbourhood scraps as a kid where you had to fight to survive. 'I'm sure it was my fighting Irish spirit that got me through,' he recalled. Both Conn's grandfathers were Irish, from Co. Derry and Co. Cork. After the potato famine of the late 1840s, Irish Catholic emigrants flooded the north-eastern United States. By the start of the Civil War in 1861 it was estimated that one of every five Pittsburghers was an Irish Catholic immigrant.

'My dad was a keen boxing fan and used to hang around with the local boxers and often attended fights. He used to tell me about the great Pittsburgh fighters, but particularly about the greatest Pittsburgher of them all, Harry Greb. Greb was a world middleweight champion but he regularly took on light-heavyweights and heavyweights, and repeatedly challenged Jack Dempsey without success. They all came alike to Greb. They called him the "Pittsburgh Windmill". He lived just a mile away, in Garfield.

'Dad used to say that Harry was the most dashing boxing figure of the Roaring 20s. He dressed in all the latest fashions, expensive suits, shirts, shoes, that kind of thing. Harry had something like 300 fights. I was only nine years of age when he died in 1926 while undergoing surgery to repair facial damage caused by boxing and an auto accident. He was the man I worshipped. I wanted to be like him, and bring another world championship to Pittsburgh.'

Unlike most boxers, Conn never had an amateur fight but went straight into the professional ranks at the age of 16. Harry Pitler was a former lightweight contender who ran a busy gymnasium in East Liberty. Pitler, who was a member of a well-known Jewish sporting family which included famed Brooklyn Dodger baseball coach Jack Pitler, had changed his own name many years earlier to Johnny Ray because there were more Irish fight fans in Pittsburgh than Jewish followers.

One hot summer's day in 1928, a spindly kid of 11 walked into Ray's gym and said he wanted to be a boxer. Ray suggested young Billy get into the ring with a local, a preliminary pro who had three fights. Ray was impressed with the kid's enthusiasm and said that if Billy trained hard, learned the rudiments of the sport and looked after himself he could make it big in boxing.

'I went down to the gym regularly and sparred with experienced guys and picked up little tips. I didn't want to box as an amateur because I wanted to go pro but first I wanted to learn all I could in the gym with the help of Johnny. He was a good tutor, and taught me all I knew. Fighters who came to Pittsburgh would work out at the gym, big names like Joe Louis, Mickey Walker, Tony Canzoneri, Fritzie and Eddie Zivic, Freddie Miller, Babe Risko, Oscar Rankins and others. I often worked out with them.'

There was a story doing the rounds at the time, and confirmed by Conn, that when Max Baer, the world heavyweight champion, was passing through Pittsburgh in September 1934, he called into Johnny Ray's gym and said he would like to work out for a few hours. Johnny suggested he spar with Conn, and Baer agreed. Observers said that even though it was only a light sparring session, Billy, four inches shorter and 75lb lighter, brought a smear of blood to Max's nose with a lightning left and came out better in fast, hard exchanges. After three sessions, Baer grinned, 'My only advice to you, son, is don't grow up. At least not until I retire.'

That was the year Conn became a professional, 28 June 1934. He was 16. Johnny Ray felt he was ready for his first pro fight. Ray worked out a deal with a local fight manager named Johnny McGarvey, who would co-manage Billy, with Ray looking after his training. Conn would keep 50 per cent of his earnings.

'I never had a job other than boxing,' remembered Conn. 'In any event, America was being hard hit by the Great Depression and jobs were hard to come by. Thousands of workers were being laid off and those who stayed in employment in the big factories had to take massive cuts in their earnings. People queued to get food in the soup kitchens and things were really bad. Boxing seemed to be a good way out of the bad times and I was determined to give the sport a real go, and earn good money along the way. Johnny used to say, "Why should you box for cups and medals when you can earn money by doing the very same thing?" It made sense.

'As it happened, I lost my first fight, against Dick Woodward in Fairmount, West Virginia. It was over four rounds at 135lb, the lightweight limit, but he was a bit too experienced for me.

I was a raw kid who never had an amateur fight. Whatever I did, he seemed to do it better. Still, I wasn't discouraged. It was a learning experience. I would have better days, and I had. In my second fight a month later, in Charleston, West Virginia I knocked out Johnny Lewis in three rounds in a scheduled four-rounder.'

In 1934, his first year, Conn had five fights, winning three. In his second year, he had 15, with nine wins, five losses and one draw. In 1936, he climbed into the ring 18 times, all in Pittsburgh, and won all of them. Boxing writers were beginning to take notice of his young, handsome boxer with the flashing fists and fancy footwork and marked him down as a real comer.

'Let me tell you something about my final fight that year. I had now developed into a middleweight and felt stronger, more confident, even though I was only 18,' he said. 'Johnny matched me with Fritzie Zivic, who was also from Pittsburgh. I'm sure you know all about Zivic but for the benefit of your readers, he was one of the toughest, roughest fighters of all time. He hit below the belt, used his elbows, his head, rubbed your face with his open gloves. He did everything but bite you, or kick you. He was a real terror.

'Mind you, outside the ring he was a gentle soul but once that bell rang, he was a real demon. He gave no favours and asked for none. Zivic had 65 fights going into the fight against my 35 but I figured I could handle him. The match was over ten rounds. Zivic won the early rounds on his aggression and pressing tactics but I gradually got on top on my speed and by mixing my punches.

'I felt I gave as good as I got, and a little more. It ended in a split decision. The referee gave it to Zivic but the two judges marked it for me. It was my biggest win to date. Zivic would go on to win the world welterweight title from the great Henry Armstrong in 1940.

It was 1937 and Conn was now mixing with the top contenders. He had nine fights that year, losing two and defeating the likes of Babe Risko, Vince Dundee, Oscar

Rankins, Young Corbett III and Teddy Yarosz twice. The top New York writers were journeying to Pittsburgh to cast an eye over this bright young performer who, as one scribe put it, 'had Madison Square Garden written all over him'. Short pieces began appearing in newspapers and periodicals, including the influential *Ring* magazine. By 1938 Conn had developed into a light-heavyweight and *Ring* listed him in ninth spot in its top ten rankings.

'The fight that opened the way to appear in Madison Square Garden was my win over Solly Krieger on 28 November 1938. Some papers played up the Jewish v Irish angle but that would be usual in situations like this. Krieger had given me a bad hammering when we fought a few years earlier, busting me up all over the place.

'When we fought the second time, he had just won the world middleweight title a few weeks earlier which gives you an idea how busy champions and leading contenders were in those days, unlike today when they fight maybe a couple of times a year.

'Krieger had a big edge on experience over me in our first bout while I'd had only around 30 fights and I wasn't in the best of shape either. I'd gotten a bit overconfident too but I don't want to start making excuses over the loss. In truth he was too good for me. But I learned a lot by the time we fought the second time. Krieger's title was not at stake as it was an overweight match but I beat him on points over 12 rounds. The papers said I won the fight on my good left-hand work. I was making real progress.'

Back in New York, promoter Mike Jacobs, known as 'Uncle Mike', had been getting favourable reports about Conn from Nat Fleischer of *Ring* magazine. 'Who is this kid, Nat? Is he any good?' he enquired. 'He's pretty hot stuff, Mike,' replied Fleischer. 'They call him the "Pittsburgh Kid". He's Irish, good looking, smart and more importantly he can fight. He's a brilliant skilful boxer and we've just ranked him as the ninth best light-heavyweight in the world in our annual ratings. The way he's going he would give Joe Louis a scare or two for the heavyweight title. You could do worse than bring him to New York and feature him at the Garden.'

Madison Square Garden was the Mecca of boxing, not only in America but across the world. This was the third Garden, and between the three of them, every champion worthy of the name boxed there at one time or another – John L. Sullivan, James J. Corbett, Jack Dempsey, Joe Louis, Mickey Walker, Harry Greb, Benny Leonard, Gene Tunney, Barney Ross, Jimmy McLarnin, Jack Britton and many more. The fourth and present Garden would open on 7th and 31st Streets, opposite Penn Station, in 1968.

Conn made his debut at MSG on 8th Avenue on 6 January 1939. His opponent was Fred Apostoli, who had won the vacant world middleweight title two months earlier by stopping Young Corbett III, his previous conqueror, in eight rounds. The Apostoli–Conn fight was made over 12 rounds as Apostoli's title would not be on the line. Fred entered the ring as a 2/1 favourite, with the boxing writers feeling that Apostoli's greater experience would be the deciding factor.

'Apostoli was about the toughest opponent I had faced up to then,' said Conn. 'He had a good reputation and I knew I was going to be up against it, though the crowd was neutral, I being from Pittsburgh and Apostoli from San Francisco. He rushed from his corner at the first bell and showered me with all kinds of punches, hooks, uppercuts, crosses, aiming for a quick knockout but I survived by using my left jab and moving around. I had to figure out this guy's style.

'I gradually got my range as the rounds went by. But boy, was he tough! You had to be on your game to tackle Fred Apostoli and I'm really surprised he isn't rated today as one of the top six or seven great middleweights. In some of the rounds he belted me so hard that stars danced before my eyes. I kept up my boxing, jabbing and hooking him as he came in, though, and at the last bell I won the unanimous decision from the referee and the two judges.'

New York writers heaped praise on Conn the next morning. Bill Corum said in the *Journal American*, 'This was a story of

Conn-fidence and Conn-quest. This lad is an upstanding, handsome, cool and sharp punching young man – a bit of a throwback to the old stand-up fighters of old English print days. He has a left hand that would warm the hearts of old timers. Give him a bit of weight and maturity and two years from now he could well find himself in the opposite corner facing Joe Louis for the heavyweight championship of the world.'

Conn remembered, 'I beat Apostoli again a month later, once more at Madison Square Garden. Apostoli's people wanted the fight over 15 rounds because they felt that the longer distance would suit him better. That was fine by me, though like before, his middleweight title would not be on the line. Johnny Ray would shrug his shoulders and tell promoter Jacobs and the New York State Athletic Commission, "Ten rounds, 15 rounds, it makes no difference. Billy will beat him anyhow." Johnny always had great faith in me, right to the end.

'That second fight was another tough one. He stuck his thumb in my eye several times and I told him so but he wouldn't listen. He would say, "Come on, you Irish son of a bitch, quit beefing and fight. That's what we're here for." Apostoli butted me too in the second round, cutting my left eye. The referee Frank Fullam had a look at it but waved us on. It wasn't serious enough for a stoppage.

'To make matters worse, in the sixth round I slipped coming out of my corner which was soaked with water and sprained my ankle. Fullam gave me a few minutes to recover. I was behind at this stage so I stepped up my boxing, jabbing and moving, and won most of the rounds from then on. I won the decision. It's there in your record book – referee Fullam 8-7, judge Joe Lynch 9-6 and judge George LeCron 9-6, all in my favour. But boy, it was a tough one, believe me. That's what it was like in those days. Really good guys around and you had to be on your game to beat them, even take them on.'

Conn got his chance at the world light-heavyweight title at Madison Square Garden on 13 July 1939 against Melio Bettina. A tough, swarthy, all-action New York southpaw, he had won the vacant title four months earlier on the retirement of John Henry Lewis due to eye problems. Bettina beat Tiger Jack Fox, the favourite, on a stoppage in nine rounds and the Conn fight would be his first defence. A crowd of 15,295 filed into the Garden to see the bout which promised action. Conn was a 12/5 favourite to bring a world title back to Pittsburgh for the first time in three years.

'I really felt good answering the bell for that fight and there was a large party of supporters in the Garden, around 1,500 I was told later and I wasn't going to let them down. Bettina kept crowding me to the ropes but I kept up my boxing, hooking and jabbing and staying on the move. Bettina was a good fighter but I felt I had him figured out. He rushed in a lot, swinging those heavy shots, and while some landed, I slipped or countered most of them.

'Going out for the 15th round, Johnny Ray told me I had it all wrapped up but to take no unnecessary risks and that Bettina was still dangerous. He was, because he shook me with one of his heavy left hooks that sent me backwards across the ring. Bettina won the round but I won the fight on a unanimous decision. I was light-heavyweight champion of the world.'

The contracts called for a return fight within four months if Bettina lost. The second fight was held on 25 September 1939 at Forbes Field, Pittsburgh and again Conn won the votes of all three officials. At the last bell, Bettina sportingly put his hand on Conn's shoulder and told him, 'Good luck with the title, Billy. You'll be a worthy champion, and I'm sure of that.'

Waiting in the wings, to borrow a line from showbusiness, was Gus Lesnevich, a rugged campaigner from Cliffside Park, New Jersey with an impressive record of 44 wins, four losses and four draws. Always willing to mix it, Lesnevich was of Russian-Polish descent and as number one contender he felt he could 'take the title off this cocky Irishman and wipe the smile off his handsome face'.

The match was set for Madison Square Garden. The date, 17 November 1939. Conn was the 2/1 favourite and a crowd of 13,704 passed through the turnstiles expecting to see a good fight – the boxer v the puncher, a surefire draw. Having made his customary slow start, Conn gradually got his rhythmic style into action, jabbing and hooking at long range and using uppercuts in close. Lesnevich was constantly on the attack, seeking to smack Conn on the jaw with one of his big hooks but the defending champion never gave him a chance. Conn won the decision by wide margins. Referee Johnny McAvoy marked his card 8-5-2, with judge Marty Monroe making it 10-5 and Joe Lynch 9-6.

Lesnevich called for a return, although it was difficult to see how he could have reversed the result. The second bout was staged the following June at the Olympic Stadium, Detroit and ended with another decisive win for Conn, with all three officials giving the decision to the champion on scores of 8-5-2, 6-3-6 and 7-6-2. Conn had announced before the fight that if successful, he would relinquish the title and campaign for Joe Louis's heavyweight crown.

Both the New York State Athletic Commission and the National Boxing Association, the two major controlling organisations at the time, did not put any pressure on Conn to defend his title in the regulatory six-month period as there were no really worthwhile challengers around. Certainly the public would not go for another Conn–Lesnevich fight. Billy had proven his superiority in two fights. Lesnevich would go on to win the light-heavyweight title in May 1941 by outpointing Anton Christoforidis and would hold it for seven years, though his championship was officially 'frozen' for any challengers for five years during the war.

Conn said, 'I was hovering between 173 and 180lb around that time and with the light-heavyweight limit at 175, I reckoned I would be stronger in the heavyweight division. In any event, I figured I could give Louis a lot of trouble with my speed. Louis had shown he had trouble with boxers who moved around and that sort of thing. I reckoned that Louis would have to come after me if he was going to catch me and I wouldn't give him that opportunity. That's what boxing is all about, hitting the other guy and not letting yourself be caught.

Boxing is the art of self-defence, after all. The noble art. That was always my mantra.

'In any event, I had beaten the world's best middleweights and light-heavyweights. Mike Jacobs naturally encouraged me to move up among the heavyweights. Mike could see lots and lots of dollars dancing before his eyes with a big outdoor fight in a New York ballpark. Mike always had an eye for the dollar and here were the ingredients for a really big heavyweight championship fight. Louis was also running out of worthy challengers anyway. Up to the end of 1939, Joe had defended his title successfully eight times since winning it two years before from James J. Braddock, a really game guy I liked very much and with Irish blood like myself.'

To build up the gate for a Louis fight, Jacobs advised Conn and Johnny Ray to beat some good heavyweights to prove, at least to the public, that he fully deserved a title shot. Starting in September 1940, Conn had seven straight wins over the big boys, including the hard-hitting Lee Savold, nicknamed 'Lethal Lee', and two who had fought Louis in title bouts, Bob Pastor and Al McCoy. He was now ready for the 'Brown Bomber'.

Mike Jacobs set the big fight up for 18 June 1941 and a crowd of 54,487 piled their way into the horseshoe-shaped Polo Grounds, New York. Many gave Conn a good chance of taking the title from Louis who was making his 18th defence of the championship, and he entered the ring at the short odds of 18/5. Louis, though, would have a 31-pound pull in the weights, weighing in at 200lb against Conn's 169, six pounds inside the light-heavyweight limit.

Top writers such as Hype Igoe of the *New York World* and Willard Mullen of the *New York World Telegram and Sun* felt that, despite the weight difference, Conn's speed would be too much for the slower Louis, although both conceded that the champion's greater power would always be an underlying danger. When one writer asked Louis directly if he had anything to say about the swift-footed challenger, he replied cooly, 'Billy can run, but he can't hide.'

World champions such as James J. Braddock, Lew Jenkins and three former Conn victims Gus Lesnevich, Fred Apostoli and Fritzie Zivic plumped for the Irish-American to lift the crown. They felt that Conn could pull off what four previous light-heavyweights had failed to do – take the heavyweight title, the richest prize in all sport.

'I really felt I could beat Louis,' recalled Conn. 'Louis had trouble with clever boxers. Tommy Farr, the Welshman, moved from side to side as well as in and out, frustrating Louis and preventing Louis from getting a clean shot at him. Bob Pastor too, in their first fight. Pastor went on his bike and finished standing on his feet at the finish. If you elected to mix it with Louis, you were a goner.

'My plan, worked out in detail with Johnny Ray, was to jab away, pop, pop, pop, pop with the left hand and bam, shake him up with rights. I would keep on the move and never let him near my chin. Feint him out of position, confuse him. Take the lead away from him. That's what boxing is all about, isn't it? It's a skill. It's like chess. You have to out-think the other guy.'

For the best part of 12 rounds, Conn did just that. Louis did get occasional shots through, particularly near the end of the fifth round when he staggered Conn with a smashing left hook. Billy hung on and smothered Joe's follow-through but at the bell, the dazed Conn staggered to the wrong corner. Revived by smelling salts, Billy had recovered by the time the bell rang for the sixth and went back to his 'bicycle act', jabbing and hooking Louis at long range and staying on the move.

Conn won the 12th when he staggered Louis with a left hook and the big crowd were now on their feet, cheering for the underdog. Was there an upset in the offing? Was the four-year reign of the great Joe Louis about to come to a sensational end?

This is how Bert Sugar described the 13th round in a *Ring* magazine article, 'Louis came out of his corner hell-bent upon finding his quarry and bringing him to bay. Conn greeted the now purposeful champion with a right and a left to get his attention, the right cutting Louis's ear. As Conn waded in with a left to the stomach followed by a right that missed Louis' chin, the champion landed a hard right of his own. It caught Conn flush on the jaw, snapping his head violently back.

'Louis followed up with three more hard rights to the chin, but untrue to his pre-fight prediction that he would run away to stay another day, Conn fought back, out-slugging the champion at close quarters in a savage exchange. A right uppercut by Louis staggered Conn. Louis, now sensing the moment he had been waiting the past 38 minutes for, landed a volley of rights and lefts to Conn's head.

'Another right to the head spun Conn partway around and he fell, as if he were filmed in slow motion. Referee Eddie Joseph picked up the count over the inert form that had almost been heavyweight champion of the world. Conn tried to regain his feet but it was too late. Referee Joseph signalled the end, with two seconds to go in the 13th round. The fight itself was memorable, one of the best ever seen in this or any other era.'

Conn remembered it like this, 'Yes, I got a bit too cocky, after having the heavyweight championship all tied up neatly. In the 12th round I staggered Louis and it made me feel good. I knew I could win the last three rounds and take the title. I thought how much better if I could knock out the great Joe Louis, the unbeatable Joe Louis, and become heavyweight champion of the world. Although my corner advised me against it, I went out for the 13th round with the idea of knocking Louis flat on the canvas. He was ready to be taken.

'I remember cocking my left hand, around the middle of the round, for the final punch of the fight. I guess that's all I remember. When my corner lifted me off the canvas, they took me to my stool and Johnny told me I went in to mix it and paid the consequences as Louis had the reputation of being the greatest finisher in boxing. He said Louis opened up with a fast, hard combination and finished me with a big right hand. When Johnny said he understood that there were only two seconds of the round remaining, I told him that the fight shouldn't have been stopped. "It wasn't stopped," barked Johnny amid all the noise around us. "You were counted out." When I fully recovered my senses, I said I was terribly unlucky.

'You know Thomas, if I'd gotten up, the bell would have sounded. I feel I would have recovered during the interval and gone on my bicycle for another two rounds and I would have won the title. Louis would never have caught me again, I can assure you. Look at the scores. Referee Joseph had it 7-5 and judge Marty Monroe 7-4-1, both in my favour. I thought the other judge, Bill Healy, was a bit off with a 6-6 score.

'I would have made sure I did enough in the last two rounds to stay in front. I felt pretty bad about it. But there you go. A few years later, Louis and I met up at some function and I said to him, "You know Joe, if I'd won the title that night, I would have held on to it for ten years." Louis said, "Billy, how could you hold it for ten years when you couldn't hold on to it for another two rounds?" Louis was a good guy, a real gentleman.'

The boxing world looked forward eagerly to a return fight, especially promoter Mike Jacobs who had counted the receipts and found they had come to $452,743 gross. A second fight the following summer would draw an even bigger gate and he pencilled 25 June 1942 in his diary. It was the fight everybody wanted to see. Meanwhile both boxers kept busy without any great risk to the return fight. Louis stopped Lou Nova in six, knocked out Buddy Baer in one and Abe Simon in six. Conn won decisions over Henry Cooper, J.D. Turner and the reigning world middleweight champion Tony Zale in a non-title fight.

Two weeks before the scheduled date Conn broke his left hand in a row with his father-in-law, former Major League Baseball player 'Greenfield' Jimmy Smith. Conn's injury immediately caused the cancellation of the June rematch. Jacobs shrugged his shoulders, and rescheduled it for 25 September. The public would not mind waiting three short months.

Meantime, America had a bigger fight on its hands. On 7 December 1941, hundreds of low-flying Japanese war planes bombed Pearl Harbour in the Pacific, killing 2,335 US servicemen and 68 civilians. Eighteen naval ships and 170 planes were also destroyed in the attack. Within a week, after vowing vengeance against Japan, America joined the Allied Forces in Europe and declared war on Germany and Italy.

Secretary of War Henry L. Stimson told Jacobs he would have to cancel the bout on 25 September and leave it until the end of hostilities. He said any big fight, particularly one as important as this return match, conflicted with 'the standards and interests of the Army'. He ordered Louis and Conn, both of whom had joined up earlier in the year, to 'return at once to their military duties'.

It would be almost five years after their first fight that Louis and Conn fought each other again. On 19 June 1946 they faced each other at the Yankee Stadium, New York before a crowd of 45,265, some 9,000 less than witnessed the first battle. Boxing writers laid the cause of the drop on the robust price of tickets, the highest ever in ring history, with ringside seats at an unprecedented $100 – and these seats covered more territory than the immediate tier around the ring.

Jacobs was predicting a gate of 70,000 but the new novelty, television, took its toll on the attendance. It was estimated that around 100,000 fans watched the fight on TV in the limited area where it was available. A large part of this audience would have gone to the fight had it not been available for free. Still, the total receipts brought a wide smile to the promoter's face.

They came to $1,925,564, just falling short of the gate for the return fight between Jack Dempsey and Gene Tunney in September 1927 which brought in just over $2m. Louis–Conn II would remain the second-highest grossing contest in ring history for nearly 30 years, finally topped by the $2.4m taken in for the second Muhammad Ali–Ken Norton heavyweight championship fight in September 1973.

The Louis–Conn rematch was a big disappointment. The five-year absence from competitive action had robbed both men of much of their sharpness. Louis still possessed the power in his fists but a skilful boxer like Conn needed regular action to keep in shape. Almost eight pounds heavier that he was for the first bout, Conn boxed cautiously in the opening round, and when Louis came in strong with lefts and rights, Billy said to him, 'Take it easy champ, we still have another 14 rounds to go.' Louis just smiled.

'I have to admit that second fight was a bit of a stinker,' recalled Conn. 'I didn't seem to be able to get my old combinations working or my left jabs in shape. Louis seemed to be slower too but he still had his wallop, as the last thing a fighter loses is his punch. I had to watch that. Once Louis got you in his sights it was all over. Goodnight, Irene. I remember around the fifth or sixth round he caught me with a good left hook, a really big one. Still, I thought I did fairly well in the first seven rounds. I was still on my feet, though Johnny told me I was well behind on points.'

The eighth round started. Conn was still moving around and Louis was still stalking, like a jungle cat. Louis landed a solid right uppercut through Conn's defence and followed with a sharp, short left hook to the chin that snapped the challenger's head back. Conn went down on his back. As referee Eddie Joseph sent Louis to a neutral corner, Conn lay on his back, his left glove instinctively shielding his face from the blinding glare of the lights above.

Picking up the count from the timekeeper, Joseph tolled the seconds. Conn managed to struggle to a sitting position and was attempting to rise as the count reached ten. It was too late. Louis had made the 22nd successful defence of his title. The scoring showed how one-sided the fight was. All three officials – referee Eddie Joseph and judges Frank Forbes and Jack O'Sullivan – had it 5-2 in Louis's favour. Conn's performance earned him the *Associated Press*'s annual Flop of the Year award.

Conn laid off for nearly 18 months and returned on 15 November 1948 in Macon, Georgia, with a stoppage in nine rounds over Mike O'Dowd, who had won only five of his 14 previous fights. A week later he turned up in Dallas, Texas and knocked out Jackie Lyons in the ninth. Again, the opposition was weak, with Lyons having lost 17 of his 47 bouts. In any event Billy's heart was not in competitive boxing any more. He was getting out. Retiring from the ring as a boxer, however, did not mean leaving the sport completely. He was still a public figure.

Conn invested his money in oil wells as well as being involved in a lucrative car dealership and managing the Stardust club in Las Vegas. He also refereed big fights, did public relations work and made personal appearances around the country as well as being a guest at boxing-related events. He also participated in a number of television documentaries for Home Box Office. In addition, Conn and his wife Mary Louise were the subject of a lengthy article by the famed author and writer Frank Deford in *Sports Illustrated* in 1985 called 'The Boxer and the Blonde'.

Happily, Billy's boxing abilities never deserted him. In 1990 he stepped into the middle of a robbery at a Pittsburgh convenience store after an armed man punched the store manager. Conn moved in, fired a sweet left hook straight out of the memory bank and both ended up on the floor of the store. 'You always go with your best punch — a left hook,' Conn said. 'I guess I interrupted his plans.'

The robber managed to get away, but not before Conn pulled off his coat, which contained his name and address, making the arrest an easy one. His wife said that jumping into the fray was typical of her husband. 'My instinct was to get help,' she said at the time. 'Billy's instinct was to fight.'

Conn died of pneumonia in a Pittsburgh hospital on 29 May 1993, aged 75. Three years earlier he had been inducted into the International Boxing Hall of Fame in Canastota, New York. Nor is he forgotten by his old home town. A section of Craig Street in Pittsburgh's Oakland district was renamed Billy Conn Boulevard in 1998. It is near the site of the old Duquesne Gardens, where Conn had defeated six world champions.

12

Muhammad Ali

Poet, prophet and pugilist

T HE triumphant US boxing team returned from the 1960 Rome Olympics with an impressive haul of four medals – three gold, from Cassius Clay in the light-heavyweight division, Edward Cook in the middleweight class and Wilbert McClure at light-middleweight, and bronze from light-welterweight Quincey Daniels.

Seven other boxers from around the world left Rome with gold medals but none made such a personal impression in the Eternal City than Clay. The young man from Louisville, Kentucky had come through four tough fights against the best boxers in his division, emerging both triumphant and unscathed. He got on well with the world's media with his outgoing personality. As one said, 'He would light up the whole room.'

Clay would turn professional inside two months in a blaze of publicity as the golden boy and would win the heavyweight championship of the world just over three years later, proclaiming himself as 'The Greatest' and subsequently changing his name to Muhammad Ali.

Amid all the razzle-dazzle of America's affluent society in the Swinging 60s, he stood out as the strictly commercial

211

sportsman with all the up-to-date attributes for success. He had the good looks, a magnificent physique, a slick line of patter and, most important of all, he could fight, and fight well. As poet, prophet and pugilist, he was the super showman and salesman of the noble art.

Ali transcended sport. In purely boxing terms he was the most original and creative performer of his time, perhaps of all time and arguably the best heavyweight champion in history. But his impact on the wider world was immense. He became a symbol of black pride just as Joe Louis had been in the 1930s, and through his opposition to the Vietnam War and his principled, not to mention expensive, stand he took against it, he surely pricked America's conscience and contributed significantly towards the war's end.

In several interviews with this writer in London and Dublin in the 1960s and 1970s, Ali was always very courteous and not surprisingly very talkative. He called me Mr Myler at first but later it was always Thomas.

So how did it all start? 'My first great ambition was to own a bicycle back in Louisville,' he remembered. 'My folks got me a brand new one and I treasured it. Then one day, and I would have been about 12 at the time, it was stolen and I was just heartbroken. I reported it to the local police and told the officer what I would do to the culprit if I ever caught him. The policeman, whose name was Joe Martin and who happened to run a boxing programme to keep kids off the streets, said it might be better to learn how to box before setting out on the thief's trail.

'I went down to his gym and before I knew it, six weeks I think, Martin got me my first amateur fight. I did just enough to win but I still told Martin that I was going to go places in boxing. "I'll be the best in the world," I told Martin. I know he didn't believe me but I guess he admired my confidence. By the time I was 18 I had put together 100 wins in 108 bouts and qualified for the Rome Olympics of 1960. I was now a light-heavyweight. Martin told me that if I was going to get anywhere in boxing, I would have to win a gold medal in the Olympics. I managed to achieve that and I knew then that I was going to make progress in professional boxing. That was my aim.

'You know, before heading for Rome, I debated with Martin whether or not I would go there in the first place. I had a fear of flying. It was only when Martin pleaded with me to go on the plane that I agreed. I won through to the final and faced the favourite, a really tough Pole named Zbigniew Pietrzykowski. Don't ask me to spell his name. You can look it up in your files. Ziggy, as everybody called him, was in front after two rounds and I knew I had to win the third to get the verdict. I did, on a unanimous decision, and won the gold medal. It was a proud moment when I stood on the rostrum with the silver medallist Ziggy and the two bronze medallists, Giulio Saraui of Italy and Tony Madigan of Australia.'

When Cassius returned to America, there were all kinds of offers awaiting him but he opted for a consortium of 11 businessmen, seven of them dollar millionaires. They paid Cassius $10,000 to sign a contract that guaranteed him a salary of $4,000 for two years and then $6,000 for four years. They would then review the contract. They signed Angelo Dundee as his trainer and while the consortium would eventually break up and the contract was cancelled, Dundee stayed on as the boxer's coach and later became his manager.

Dundee was born in Philadelphia of Italian blood but subsequently moved to New York and gained an eye for the 'sweet science' by watching the great trainers impart their knowledge at Stillman's Gym in the late 1940s. The first world champion he worked with was Carmen Basilio but his career really took off when he moved to Miami Beach and became chief trainer at the renowned Fifth Street Gym. In a long career he also worked with world champions such as George Foreman, Sugar Ray Leonard, Willie Pastrano, Jose Napoles and Luis Rodriguez but he will always be principally associated with Ali.

'You see, Thomas, when I first worked out with Ali, then known as Cassius Clay, I could see he had a natural speed of hand and foot but I worked with him on also developing his punches, how to place his blows for the most effect,' he recalled in an interview. 'He learned fast because he was a natural, and there was never any doubt about that. Champions are not made in the gym alone. They are made from something deep inside them – a desire, a dream, a vision. That's what makes a champion, a real champion.'

Drew Brown would come into the Ali story three years later. Officially Ali's assistant trainer, Brown also acted as his right-hand man and would be known as 'Bundini' Brown. He was apparently given the name by a Lebanese girlfriend, but he never knew what it meant. Despite his nominal capacity as assistant trainer, Brown's biggest input once he joined the team was as co-inspirator of the outrageous and often hysterical antics that his boss employed to psych out his opponents. It was Brown who coined Ali's famous phrase 'float like a butterfly, sting like a bee' in the days when the former Olympic champion was known as Cassius Clay.

Indeed Brown was little known in boxing circles until he met Clay in 1963 after Cassius outpointed Doug Jones over ten hard rounds in New York and the two quickly hit it off. Thirteen years older than the rising young heavyweight, Brown had spent time in the merchant marines after his discharge from the US Navy for attacking an officer. Bundini and Ali shared an emotional relationship and it was clear that Brown idolised his employer, always referring to him as 'the champ' even before he won the title. This devotion was clearly illustrated in the ring when, following Ali's famous victory over George Foreman in 1974, Bundini shed tears of joy.

Any interview with Ali would have to include the two most controversial fights of his 21-year career, against Sonny Liston. The first, on 25 February 1964 at the Miami Beach Convention Hall, saw Liston making the second defence of the world heavyweight title he had won from Floyd Patterson two years earlier and defended successfully a year later, again against Patterson, both fights ending inside the first round. Ali won when Liston retired at the end of the sixth round claiming an injured left shoulder. The second fight seven months later ended in an even more dramatic fashion when Liston went down from a right cross, with many calling it a phantom punch, in the first round and was counted out.

Liston had looked unbeatable going into that first fight and was installed as a 7/1 favourite, almost ridiculous odds in a sport where just about anything can happen – and so often does. A former jailbird, he spent so many years in the company of law-breakers that he seemed to have difficulty telling right from wrong, and throughout his career he was a constant companion of adversity. In the ring, though, he always looked menacing – and was.

How old was Liston going into the fight? Take your pick. Sonny's birthdate was always the subject of mystery, right to the end of his life. There is no official record of his birth. He was born on a farm in St Francis County, Arkansas, a state which did not require mandatory birth certificates. Liston once told sportswriter Jerry Izenberg that his date of birth was carved on a tree by his mother but the tree was later chopped down. When he was arrested for robbery in 1950, he gave his age as 22, which would indicate he was born in 1928.

When Sonny filed for a birth certificate for legal reasons in 1953, he said his date of birth was 8 May 1932. When he testified before a US Senate subcommittee investigating the underworld connection with boxing, he said he was born in 1933. His mother insisted he was born on 8 January 1932. He later said the date was recorded in a family Bible but the Bible 'was lost somewhere along the way'.

Liston had a respectable amateur record in the ring and made his professional debut in September 1953 when knocking out Don Smith in the first round in St Louis. After his first five fights, a sportswriter called him the 'Big Bear', and it stuck. Ali would refer to him as the 'Big Ugly Bear'. In his first year, he won all his three fights. In 1954 he had four wins with one loss, against Marty Marshall, which he soon reversed with a stoppage in six rounds. In 1955, six fights, six wins. In 1956 and 1957, nine fights, nine wins. In 1958, eight fights, eight wins. By 1959 he was moving in top company, winning all his five fights including impressive wins over contenders Mike De

John, who was finished in six and Cleveland 'Big Cat' Williams in just two rounds.

'Sonny's imposing appearance was artificially enhanced with towels under his robe when he climbed into the ring,' recalled Ali. 'His opponents would often be intimidated by the impact of his massive physique and baleful gaze. Mind you, he was a good fighter. Roy Harris, known as "Cut 'n' Shoot" Harris, who had gone 13 rounds with the world heavyweight champion Floyd Patterson, was beaten in one round and another top contender Zora Folley in three. But I always felt deep down I could beat him.'

Liston's run of impressive victories compelled the boxing commissions to demand a title shot, and he got it in September 1962 by flattening Patterson in one round, repeating the exact result a year later. When he ducked between the ropes to face Ali on 25 February 1964 in the Miami Beach Convention Hall in Florida, Liston had lost only one of his 35 contests, 25 ending inside the distance, seven in the opening round. Ali, then still known as Cassius Clay, had just 19 fights, all wins.

Liston, older by at least eight years depending on which source you believe, had an abnormal reach of 84 inches, two inches more than Clay's and his mighty fists, described by one writer as iron weapons of destruction, were two and a half inches bigger than his challenger's. Even those who could recall legendary fighters such as Jack Johnson, Jack Dempsey, Joe Louis and Rocky Marciano shuddered at the sight of him. To all intents and purposes, Liston looked unbeatable. He was chilling and simply scared the life out of opponents with his menacing stare. The difference this time was that Ali was not scared.

'No way was I scared going into the fight,' Ali recalled. 'I knew I would win. I reasoned he was no superman. Months before the fight was even signed I had bought a bus and my father painted it in orange, green, blue, yellow but mostly red. On one side it read, "World's most colourful fighter" and on the other side was "Sonny Liston is great, but he'll fall in eight". When the fight was announced, I taunted Liston at every opportunity, at press conferences, even going up to his training camp and telling him he was a fake. Sonny often threatened to hit me there and then but his handlers would intervene.

'When I got into the ring at the Convention Hall, I was wearing a short white robe with the words "The Lip" embroidered in red on the back. Following instructions from Bundini, I planned to "float like a butterfly and sting like a bee". Liston came out fast, like I thought he would, throwing wild punches. He wanted to finish me off quickly like he did with Floyd Patterson but I wasn't having any. I swayed back, made him miss, and I could detect anger in his eyes. From that moment I knew I had him and the heavyweight championship would be mine.

'By the third his eyes started to swell up because of my jabs and right crosses. I opened a cut under his left eye, the first time he had ever been cut in the ring, and there was a sense of desperation about him. He had never met anybody like this before. It was all new to him. He was used to his opponents falling down but here was I, still on my feet, moving, jabbing, hurting. At the end of the fourth I came back to my corner and told Angelo Dundee I couldn't see and that my eyes were smarting.

'I learned later that Liston's cornermen had been rubbing his injured eye with a liniment. They also rubbed some of it on his left shoulder which he claimed was hurting him. It seems that in clinches, some of it had rubbed off on me. I told Dundee to cut the gloves off and that I was quitting. He cleaned my eyes and told me, "Get out there, you idiot, you're on the way to becoming the champ." It wasn't too bad in the fifth, and by the sixth round it had cleared.

'I was still jabbing and hooking Liston. He was just lunging after me, throwing wild punches and he looked all in. When the bell rang for the seventh round Liston stayed on his stool, claiming an injured shoulder. I had tamed the "Big Ugly Bear". I was king of the world at 22, the youngest heavyweight champion after Floyd Patterson.'

The *Boston Globe* described the fight as 'a world heavyweight championship battle that ended in bizarre fashion that fits this tinsel town to the letter'. Writer John Ahern remarked, 'The crown changed hands at the end of the sixth round of a surprisingly good fight when Liston quit in his corner. This is not done in a championship fight where it is customary to go on until the champ has to be carried off. Especially it is not done by a fierce, tough, rough man like Liston who was called good enough to beat any of the heavyweight kings since Joe Louis. But that's what he did, abdicating the throne to a 22-year-old loudmouth who was fighting professionally only for the 20th time.'

There was the contracted return fight, and it was held on 25 May 1965 at the St Dominic's Youth Centre in Lewiston, Maine, which had a population of 41,000 inhabitants, less than the attendance figures for big fights in the past. This time there was a sparse crowd of 2,434, of which 1,500 were complimentary. Yet the revenue from television, radio and other ancillaries brought in yet another million-dollar gate – $1,602,192. It was all over before many people had settled into their seats. Half a century on, the fight, if it could seriously be called that, remains one of the most controversial bouts of all time.

It ended after two minutes and 12 seconds of round one when Liston went down from what many believed to be a light punch, a right to the jaw, and was counted out.

Boxing Illustrated still referred to Ali as Clay, and its ringside reporter Lew Eskin wrote, 'The fight was a comedy of errors from the word go. The weak-sounding bell sent them on their way. Liston moved forward in a half-crouch but it was Clay, arms dangling at his sides, who struck first. He pawed with his left jab and landed a crisp right to the side of Sonny's head. Darting out of range, he pranced around the ring with Sonny in pursuit. Sonny kept after him but Clay was too fast. He was always moving. Where Sonny's punches went, Clay had just been.

'A left bounced off Sonny's head. Switching directions again, Clay landed a clean right to the head. Liston's jab grazed Clay's face, the only blow we saw him land. Backing out of range of Liston's swings, or taking them on his arms, Clay stabbed with his left. Sonny shifted, trying to trap Clay in a corner but Cassius escaped. Then, as Clay was backing towards his own corner, he landed a short right under the ear over a pawing left by Liston. Sonny's legs caved in and he fell on his right side and rolled over on to his back, his arms outstretched full length over his head. "Get up, get up and fight, you bum," shouted Clay.

'Referee Jersey Joe Walcott tried in vain to send Cassius to a neutral corner but he started a victory dance over his fallen foe. While Walcott was trying to make Clay go to a neutral corner, Liston dragged himself up, this time making it. Walcott wiped Liston's gloves, Cassius moved forward and the fight resumed. Then suddenly Walcott turned his back on the two and ran over to the timekeeper Frank McDonough who informed him that he had already counted Liston out. Then Jersey Joe quickly jumped between the two and raised Cassius's hand in victory.'

In his report, Eskin lay much of the blame on boxing commissions for permitting return fights in the first place. 'We in *Boxing Illustrated* believe that no champion, after losing his title, should be given a return match until he has proven himself by facing and defeating one of the top three contenders. If he cannot or will not do this, then he doesn't deserve a chance to regain the championship. In the long history of boxing, few return bouts have lived up to the first in the way of excitement.

'Two outstanding examples of this were the second Marciano–Walcott and Liston–Patterson fights, and both were over in the first round. There were more deserving challengers than Walcott and Patterson who would have given their all for a title chance. Had Jersey Joe and Floyd been forced to fight another top man first, the entire division would have received a real shot in the arm, and the value of the title would have been greatly enhanced.

'Had Liston been forced to face one of the top contenders, it is doubtful that we would have had another black eye hung on the already battered face of boxing. Sonny was an old man. His flesh was loose on his chest and ribs. He no longer presented the appearance of strength that he once did. Although he was in top physical condition after many long weeks of training, he was just not in shape to stand up and fight against a young, vigorous, powerful Clay.'

When Eskin was in Dublin in 1972 to referee Ali's fight with Al 'Blue' Lewis, which he won on a knockout in 11 rounds, he told this writer, 'Long after the majority of the fans had left the Lewiston arena, we watched the re-run of the knockout on the small TV monitor but the camera angle, over Liston's shoulder, did not provide the answer to the legitimacy or otherwise of the finish. Later when both boxers faced the press at the back of the arena, Liston, unmarked, said that he could have gotten up but did not know what the count was. Clay kept shouting that he was "King of the Ring". The fight was the first heavyweight championship bout in which the referee kept no scorecard.'

This was how Ali remembered it, 'It's funny, and I haven't told this to anybody before, but three weeks before the fight I dreamt I got into the ring and after the bell I moved out fast, hit Liston with a good right hand and he went down for the full count. That's exactly what happened in the real thing. Liston, as usual, had lunged forward intent on destroying me. I swayed back before moving in with a right to the side of his head which lifted him off the canvas and down he went, flat on his back. I stood over him, yelling, "Get up, get up. It's not over yet." He never did and I was still champion of the world.

'I know there was a lot of talk afterwards, and still is, that Liston threw the fight, that he had no intention of getting up, but all I know is that there never was a straighter fight than this one. The punch that put him down was similar to the one I used before and after that fight, against Cleveland Williams for example, and others.

'Why did Liston fold up? Maybe all the pressure about rumours of me being assassinated, the FBI hovering in the background, gun-carrying cops with bullet-proof shields and all that just rubbed off on him and that if somebody was trying to kill me in the ring, they might miss and kill him. In the end, as I say, I hit Liston with a solid right hand punch and he went down. I called it the anchor punch, which the great Jack Johnson had used. It got the job done.'

Opinions were divided on the controversial ending. Former champions Joe Louis, Jack Dempsey, Gene Tunney and Floyd Patterson all considered the fight a fake, but former world light-heavyweight champion Jose Torres thought the blow was a 'perfect punch', as did Jim Murray of the *Los Angeles Times* who said, 'It was no phantom punch.'

Ring magazine editor Nat Fleischer, regarded at the time as the greatest living authority on boxing, always believed it was a genuine punch that knocked Liston out. This writer met Fleischer in London a year or so later. Asked for his views on the fight, and particularly the controversial punch, he explained, 'I sat next to the knockdown timekeeper Frank McDonough and had a clear view of what happened and there was certainly no "phantom" punch.

'There was a blow that definitely landed and reporters who say there was no punch were definitely wrong. The slow-motion movies shown after the fight clearly prove that a short right hand blow, a kind of corkscrew punch, landed on the left part of Liston's cheek. Now whether it was enough to put Liston down is a matter of conjecture. Maybe it was. Maybe it wasn't. I do know though that so often in boxing a punch looks light but is still accurate and hard enough to drop a man.'

Liston stayed out of the ring for more than a year. He was back with four consecutive knockout victories in Sweden before returning to the US where he won 11 of his 12 fights, losing on a knockout against third-ranked contender Leotis Martin in nine rounds. He had the satisfaction in his final fight of stopping Chuck Wepner in the tenth round in Jersey City in June 1970. Wepner, who would be the role model for Rocky in the Sylvester Stallone movies, needed 72 stitches and suffered a broken cheekbone and nose.

About a year before his death in Las Vegas in mysterious circumstances, and still referring to Ali as Cassius Clay, Liston admitted in a rare interview, 'It was a great punch from Clay that put me down. I really didn't think he could hit that hard. I certainly didn't quit. I got hit and hit good. His right hand caught me high on the left cheekbone and I felt all screwed up.

'I felt I could beat the count but you don't figure so good when you get clobbered. Cleveland Williams, the "Big Cat", hit me like that once before but that didn't help me any when this one arrived. It wasn't the hardest punch I ever took but it was hard enough. Don't let anybody tell you Clay can't punch. He sure can. I wouldn't like people to remember me for just this fight, or the first one but I'm afraid many will. Don't forget, I cleaned up the heavyweight division before Clay came along.'

While Liston always publicly denied allegations that he took a dive, *Sports Illustrated* writer Mark Khan claimed that some years later Liston told him, 'That guy Clay was crazy. I didn't want anything to do with him, and the Muslims were coming up. Who needed that? So I went down. I wasn't hit.'

As if to maintain his mysterious persona, Liston was found dead at his home in Las Vegas just after Christmas 1970. Officially the cause of death was listed as lung congestion and heart failure. Unofficially it appeared to be the result of a heroin overdose although some police officials and Liston's associates believed he was murdered by gangsters.

How good was Liston? In an interesting discussion this writer had with Peter Wilson of the *Daily Mirror* in 1972, Wilson believed he was vastly underrated. 'I saw all the heavyweight champions from the 1930s to the 70s and I would rate Liston at number six in my top 14,' he said. 'Liston would be behind, in order, Joe Louis, Rocky Marciano, Muhammad Ali, George Foreman and Joe Frazier. Unfortunately for Liston, he will be remembered for his two losses to Ali, which is rather regrettable.

'I feel that Sonny was much better than those two fights would suggest. The record of "Old Stoneface" between 1958 and 1963 speaks for itself – 21 wins, 18 by knockout, 13 in three rounds or less. I feel that unlike Foreman, he met and defeated all the leading American heavyweight contenders of this period. At his best, he really was the Grim Reaper of the heavyweight division.'

After all these years Ali has still declined to officially comment on Liston's death except to say that it was regrettable. 'All I know is that Sonny was a tortured man, for whatever reason,' he said. 'But he was a good champion. All that talk about what I said about him was all for publicity. You have to do these things to boost the gate and promoters love you for it. Maybe more boxers should rave and rant. It's good for business, believe you me.'

Ali's publicity man, Harold Conrad, admitted to me several years after the fight, 'Let me tell you, Thomas, that Liston was in deep trouble long before his death. I can tell you that he was deeply involved as a bill collector in a major loan-shark operation in Las Vegas. When he tried to muscle in for a bigger share of the action, as he felt he was being cheated out of what he was entitled to, they murdered him in case he ratted on them. Liston was a good champion, and a far better one that he is generally credited but he was never free of the underworld influence. That was his problem, I'm convinced.'

If the Clay–Liston fights lacked real action, the three bouts between Ali and Joe Frazier were totally different and are very much an integral part of boxing history. Ali was the challenger in the first one, on 8 March 1971. He had been stripped of his title three years earlier over his refusal to join the US Army on religious grounds, having converted to the Black Muslims. The war in Vietnam was at its peak and he caused uproar in America with the comments, 'I ain't got no quarrel with the Viet Cong. No Viet Cong ever called me a nigger. We Muslims don't bear weapons. We don't fight wars unless it's a war declared by Allah himself.'

Ali declared himself a conscientious objector but he still faced a five-year jail sentence for his action and was barred from boxing while his case was under litigation. Nevertheless he called himself the 'People's Champion' and delivered over 200 anti-war speeches. By this time Americans had become uneasy about the war in Vietnam. Young Americans burnt their draft cards and shouted, 'We won't go, we won't go.' Older Americans were coming around to the same viewpoint.

Suddenly Ali's stance seemed less controversial. There was guilt too, for the way he had been punished for his religious beliefs in a supposedly democratic country. Soon the Supreme Court, which had upheld his conviction, suddenly reversed a ruling to the effect that young men who opposed the war on strong ethical grounds should be exempted from drafting into the armed forces.

It was a surprise decision that delighted the boxing fraternity – and Ali's licence would be restored. After three years and eight months away from the ring, he returned with two wins inside the distance and was matched with Frazier in a match at Madison Square Garden billed as the 'Fight of the Century'. It was a classic.

'I was fully confident going in against Frazier,' he recalled. 'He was the fighter and I was the boxer, and the boxer was going to win this one. But it turned out to be a tough one. I don't know if my three and a half years out of the ring dulled my reflexes, although I'd had two good warm-up fights, against Jerry Quarry and Oscar Bonavena. Maybe the lay-off did hurt me, maybe it didn't. But I wouldn't make that out to be an excuse. Frazier was good. He kept coming in and swinging, and when Frazier hit you, you knew you'd been hit, particularly in the belly. I thought I took the seventh but he won the eighth.

'It was still fairly close but I knew I had to win the remaining rounds, and there were still five to go. Frazier was still full of fight. In one of the rounds, and I'm nearly sure it was the tenth, he landed what must have been the hardest left hook he'd ever thrown. It flung me back across the ring and I had to do all I could to stay on my feet. I was still in with a real chance by the 15th and last round. In that last round I saw an opening and shot through a good solid right to the chin but he took it and countered with a left hook straight from the floor.

'It landed on my chin and I was down. Full credit to Frazier. He hit me and hurt me. I regained my feet and managed to hold him off and then the bell rang. I heard the result loud and clear,

"The winner by unanimous decision and still heavyweight champion of the world, Joe Frazier." Okay, I'd lost, my first defeat in 32 fights, but there would be another day, another opportunity.'

It would be three years before they clashed again – on 28 January 1974 in New York. This time there was no title on the line. Frazier had lost the championship to George Foreman inside two rounds in a stunning upset in Jamaica and was campaigning like Ali for another championship opportunity. Both knew that victory would bring the winner close to a Foreman fight. Indeed, the winner was expected to be named the number one challenger.

Ali won the unanimous decision yet many in Madison Square Garden and watching it on TV felt that Frazier deserved the verdict, though you would not think so by his face which was puffed, lacerated and looking as though he'd had some facial surgery by a third-rate specialist. Ali just had a bleeding nose.

As expected, Ali got the title fight next time he stepped into a ring for serious combat, and sensationally knocked out Foreman in eight rounds in Zaire. He had promised earlier that if he won back the title he would give Frazier a chance to win it back. He kept his promise, on 1 October 1975 in Quezon in the Philippines and this time put out Smokin' Joe's fire after 14 rounds. It was a famous fight between two great champions and is considered one of the classics in ring history.

In what was billed as the 'Thrilla in Manila', Ali scored early on with whiplash lefts and rights but Frazier gained control in the middle rounds with powerful smashes to the body, and after ten rounds it was even. In the 12th, Ali unleashed a blistering two-handed attack which sliced Joe's mouth and swelled his left eye until it was nearly shut. Ali continued his onslaught in the 13th and 14th, and as Frazier started to get up off his stool for round 15, his trainer Eddie Futch put his hand on his shoulder and said, 'Stay where you are, Joe. It's all over. Nobody will ever forget what you did here tonight. You did us all proud including yourself.'

Ali recalled, 'Frazier was truly a game guy. In all three fights with him, two for the heavyweight title, we both had it tough, even the first one which Frazier won. We both gave it all we had, you can be sure of that. That third fight was the closest time I ever came to death. It was that tough. Frazier quit before I did, to be honest. After the fight I went into his dressing room and told him so.

'I also told him, "The age of the dinosaurs is over. That's three times we've had wars and we'll have to stop beating up each other. I don't think any men in boxing history have fought three fights like you and I so that's it. The finish, forever." Frazier nodded his head in agreement. After two more fights, I was glad to see that he retired. Frazier was a good guy and a great champion. Let's not forget that.'

What was Ali's view on his own greatest victory, the superb win in eight rounds over George Foreman in Zaire on 30 October 1974 when he became champion for the second time? 'Muhammad Ali knocks out George Foreman,' Ali muttered with his eyes closed. 'Man, that was a hell of an upset. It would be weeks before I realised the impact of it. I couldn't wait to see the papers and the magazines. They had to say I was the greatest then, the greatest of all time. They thought I would have had to keep moving around him, that my legs would go and I'd get tagged. George thought that too but I changed my tactics.

'The trick was to make him *think* he was the baddest man in the world and everybody had to run from him. Truth is, I could have killed myself dancing against him. He was too big for me to go dancing around. I was a bit winded after doing it in the first round so I said to myself, "Let me go to the ropes while I'm fresh, and where I can handle him without getting hurt." I figured, "Let him burn himself out. Let him blast off and pray he keeps throwing. Let it be a matter of who can hit first, and that's me."

'This was a real scientific fight, a real thinking fight. For me it was. Everything I did had a purpose. There he was swinging away and all the time I was talking to him saying, "Hit harder,

George. Is that the best you've got? They told me you had hard body punches but they don't hurt even a little bit. Harder, sucker, swing harder. You are the champion and you are getting nowhere."

'Then I'd hit him with the jabs, pop, pop, pop. You could see his head go wobbly on his shoulders. He didn't like getting hit with those punches. I'd give him a left jab, a right cross and then finish with the jab. These punches took the heart away from George. Joe Frazier might have taken them but they sickened George.

'By the fifth round, you remember when I leaned back on the ropes and gave him all the free shots he wanted and he couldn't do anything to bother me? By then I knew George had shot his load. I knew he was through and it was only a matter of time before I got him.

'When he got knocked down in the eighth round it was all new to him. Being down was nothing new to me. I'd been on the floor in previous fights and once had my jaw broken. I had so much trouble with my hands for seven years that the doctors were telling me to quit.

'For the Foreman fight they were very strong. I was able to hit the bag without having injections for the first time in years. I had been through all the tough times but this time I was fine. When George went down I knew it was all over. I was already heavyweight champion of the world again before the referee even started counting.'

The result completely stunned the boxing world, one of the great upsets of all time. George Kimble, fight writer and author of the best-selling *Four Kings*, was at ringside for the *Boston Herald*. In 2006 he recalled in an interview with this writer, 'Once the bell rang, Foreman approached his task with the same disdain he'd had for Joe Frazier and Ken Norton, and there is every indication that he expected to finish off Ali as he had those other two.

'It didn't work out quite like that. From Ali's corner Angelo Dundee kept shouting, 'Get off the ropes!' But even as Ali plunged ahead with what seemed a suicidal strategy, he was able to periodically emerge from his cocoon against the ropes to land sneaky punches of his own.

'Even though he spent most of each round pounding away without meeting much resistance, this happened often enough that Foreman's face grew increasingly puffy as the night wore on. On several occasions Foreman was able to land punches that seemed as solid as the ones that had put Frazier and Norton on the floor. Ali not only took them but sneered back, "Is that all you got, George?" and, "They told me you could punch." By the fifth it was apparent that Foreman's punches were losing their steam. He continued to pound away but Ali seemed unaffected. I thought Foreman had beaten the count in the eighth round but by then he was through anyway.'

Ali reigned as champion for another four years and made ten successful title defences before losing his title to Leon Spinks and then regaining it from Spinks. After that, he announced his retirement. Alas, he made an ill-advised comeback on 2 October 1980 against the new champion, Larry Holmes, who had once been his sparring partner. 'I just wanted to go out on top,' was Ali's philosophy.

The fight was billed as the 'Last Hurrah' and resulted in a heavy defeat for Ali. At 39, and nine years older than Holmes, all that was left of the former great champion was his mystique. After two painful rounds on the receiving end of Holmes's powerful labs, Ali took a pounding before Angelo Dundee threw in the towel before the bell went for the 11th round. Holmes admitted later that he had often held his punches back out of sheer respect for his idol and former employer.

Ali claimed after the fight he was not fully fit and would prove it with another fight, not necessarily against Holmes. It seemed inconceivable that Ali would even get a licence again but on 11 December 1981 he climbed into the ring against the rising contender Trevor Berbick in Nassau in what was billed as the 'Drama in the Bahamas'. It went the full ten rounds and while Ali knew what to do, he couldn't do it fast enough. The ghost of the man they used to call The Greatest lost a unanimous decision and never boxed again. Had he any regrets about his life? 'No, except that I never got to raise my children and be a real father to them because of divorce,' he explained.

In the words of writer Joyce Carol Oates, Ali was one of the few athletes in any sport 'to completely define the terms of his public reputation'. Sadly, today he is a victim of Parkinson's. The former three-time world heavyweight champion, who boxed in Dublin in 1972, was back in Ireland in 2009 for the first time since then to trace his ancestral home in Ennis, County Clare where an enthusiastic crowd of over 10,000 greeted him, proving quite clearly that the man once known as The Greatest had not lost his tremendous popularity, or indeed ever will.

During the trip he was also guest of honour at a charity function in Dublin. On both occasions, this writer preferred not to meet him, rightly or wrongly. It had been nearly 40 years since we last met and as time passes perhaps it is often better to remember your heroes as they were and not as pale shadows of their former selves.

13

Evander Holyfield
The Real Deal held all the aces

EVANDER Holyfield went from being the hard luck story of the Olympic Games in Los Angeles in 1984 to becoming the first member of that US team to win a world title as a professional. Then, not satisfied with being called the greatest cruiserweight ever, the man known as the 'Real Deal' and the 'Warrior' would go on to win the world heavyweight championship a record four times – and very nearly five.

Holyfield was considered very unlucky not to have come away with a fifth heavyweight championship after his fight with Nikolai Valuev, on Christmas week in Zurich, Switzerland in 2008. Holyfield clearly outscored the plodding Russian, who had advantages of 96 lb, ten inches in height and seven inches in reach, but the majority decision went to Valuev, a verdict which was greeted with prolonged booing.

Holyfield's status as one of boxing's all-time greats is nevertheless secure. Besides his ability to handle all styles of skilful boxers and aggressive fighters, his courage and longevity alone make him a stand-out. He participated in 25 major world title fights, winning 16, losing seven and drawing two. Now retired, Evander competed in what is generally considered the most competitive period in modern heavyweight history, the 1980s and 1990s. What was the secret formula for his success? 'I think physical fitness, determination, hard work and a positive attitude will get you there,' he explained to this writer when he was in Dublin to promote his autobiography in 2008. 'And a little talent too, I guess.'

Evander fought and beat some of the most accomplished boxers of his era, including the fearsome Mike Tyson, the so-called 'Baddest Man on the Planet'. When Tyson bared his teeth and clamped them on to Holyfield's right ear in the third round of their heavyweight title fight at the MGM Grand, Las Vegas on 28 June 1997, he was paying his opponent a perverse compliment. Tyson knew he couldn't beat Evander any other way, and effectively surrendered his chances by getting himself disqualified.

The fight was one of those rare occasions when boxing moved from the sports pages to page one, and from sports news on television to the main news stories of the day, alongside reports of a massive volcanic eruption on Monserrat near Puerto Rico leading to total evacuation of the island, and an unmanned Progress spacecraft colliding with the Russian space station Mir.

'Tyson had already lost his World Boxing Council, World Boxing Association and International Boxing Association titles to James "Buster" Douglas but he still had his WBA title,' Holyfield recalled. 'I took this title off Mike in 1996 when I stopped him in 11 rounds and now we had a return fight because he demanded it on the basis that he took me too lightly the first time. Maybe or maybe not, but he got his return fight.

'The fight had been originally set for 3 May 1997 but was postponed for eight weeks when a sparring partner opened a cut over Mike's left eye. The sportswriters in general were going for Tyson to win back his title, one saying that, "Tyson should win in the first round." Mike was also favourite with the betting boys who made him 5/2. I could live with all that. I knew what I had to do and I intended to do it. I see you brought along our fight-by-fight records going into the fight, 46-2 for Mike and 31-3 for me.

'At the media conference before the fight, Mike refused to make eye contact with me. Later on, at a meeting of the Nevada State Athletic Commission, Mike's manager John Horne objected to the appointment of the referee Mitch Halpern, who had officiated in the first fight. Horne said Mike would be psychologically affected by having the same referee again and wanted somebody else. The commission was reluctant over a switch as Halpern had already been signed for a fee I believe was $10,000.

'However, Horne brought in lawyers for Team Tyson to fight Mike's side and the commission backed down. Both my team and Mike's agreed to accept Mills Lane as Halpern's replacement. Lane was from Reno, Nevada and he had been a prosecutor. He also acted as a circuit judge. Lane was a man who stood for no nonsense whatever job he was doing. We were told that he had refereed nearly 100 fights and he would be fair and impartial.'

Holyfield's trainer and chief second Don Turner, who had coached over 20 world champions and many contenders, told sportswriters before the fight, 'Tyson's character is going to let him down. He is accustomed to moving his head, but when he is doing that, he can't punch properly. Eight inches of movement and he's got to start all over again. I'm convinced he doesn't have the patience for that.

'It's character. Evander will expose his limitations just like he did the last time.'

Among the audience of 16,331 on the evening of 28 June 1997 was the usual cast for a world championship fight in Las Vegas – movie stars and hopefuls trying to break into the motion picture scene, showbusiness celebrities, high rollers, hot-dog-eating Midwesterners as well as politicians and civic leaders and pimps and prostitutes from the inner cities, all hungry for a slice of the action.

'Soon after the first round had gotten under way, I figured I had Mike's measure,' recalled Holyfield. 'He was throwing solid punches but I felt I was countering well. Mike was also resorting to getting into clinches a lot. Towards the end of the round, our heads clashed and Mike emerged with a cut over his right eye. He dabbed the injury with his glove and complained to Mills he had been butted but Mills indicated it had been accidental, which was true.

'My corner told me I had won the first round and this gave me even more confidence. I was forcing Mike to fight my style and it was clear he didn't like it. Over in Mike's corner I could see he was arguing with his seconds, no doubt telling them to watch my head as he later claimed that I deliberately butted him, which was nonsense. In the second round he hit me low but Lane didn't interfere, although Lane did tell both of us to break clean in the clinches.

'Before going out for the third round Mike must have been told that the fight was slipping away from him. All three judges had given the first two rounds to me by scores of 10-9. He started aggressively and drove me back. I countered and in a clinch Mike hit me with his right forearm, a definite infringement that Mills seemingly did not notice. The fight was really beginning to get physical now.

'With around 40 seconds of the round to go, Mike fired a left hook and followed through with a right uppercut. He then hooked his right arm around my neck and pulled me into an embrace on what they call the blind side of the referee. He spat out his mouthpiece and bit hard on the bottom of my right ear. Ouch! The pain was horrific, worse than anything I'd ever experienced in the ring before. I jumped high into the air, as one writer said later, like a scalded cat, and the blood streamed out of the ear.

'Mike spat out the torn flesh and it landed on the table of one of the judges, Duane Ford I believe. With my glove up to the injured ear I was in sheer agony. As I made my way to my corner Mike lunged at me from behind and pushed me. Lane rushed in, pulled Mike back and told him he was deducting two points from him and that if it happened again he would be disqualified. When the fight resumed, Mike made another lunge at me and coming out of a clinch, he left his teeth marks on my left ear.

'This was the last straw for Mills and he immediately moved in and sent Mike to his corner, disqualified. I was still heavyweight champion of the world. My! The headline writers sure had a field day with that one, with words such as "Bite of the Century", "Tyson Bites the Dust", "Chew On That", "Tyson is the new Hungry Fighter", "From Ex-Champ to Chomp", "Boxing's Hannibal Lecter", "Tyson makes Meal of the Real Deal", and so on. The *New York Post* had a one-word banner headline across page one – "Dracula".

'Mike didn't apologise for his actions right there in the ring, nor immediately afterwards but later on he did, and we shook hands over it. We're the best of friends today and sometimes meet at big fights. He's a good guy. Do I forgive Tyson for biting my ears? Of course I do. If not, I would be a very angry person and I'm not. The incident doesn't bother me at all. You have to forget such things and move on. Momma brought me up to forgive and forget. But I don't think Mike has forgiven himself. He still thinks he's a bad man but he's not.

'It's a great pity we didn't fight again but Mike didn't want it. It would have taken in $200m. Still, I picked up $35m for three rounds, which wasn't bad. Mike's a good guy and don't let anybody tell you otherwise. Mike and I were in camp together when we were both trying to qualify for berths on the US boxing squad for the 1984 Olympics in Los Angeles. Mike was 17 then but he didn't make it on to the squad.'

Born in Altmore, Alabama on 19 October 1962, Holyfield grew up the youngest of nine children. 'The local kids always told me I was going to be nothing and that I couldn't do anything,' he remembered. 'I was the kid who cried. I was the kid who was very sensitive and all the other kids would talk about me and poke fun. They would talk about my clothes and they would talk about my momma.

'They used to make me so mad that all I wanted to do was fight everybody. When I was around eight years of age I wanted to be a professional footballer player and when we moved to

Atlanta when I was 12, I had a dream that I was lining out for the Atlanta Falcons. Momma urged me to get fit and work hard and I would achieve my goals.

'It was tough being a poor, black, single mom raising a large family in the rural Deep South. Momma supported her family by working 12 hours a day, six days a week as a cook and it cannot have been easy. At times I wanted to give up on my dream but momma would have none of it. "Keep going," she would say. When I joined the local boys' club and got into amateur boxing, I was beaten by a guy called Cecil Collins. He was a white kid and he beat me twice. I beat him in our third fight but after that second fight, I wanted to quit. I was around 11 then.

'Momma wouldn't hear of it. She told me she raised no quitter. "You go out now and work harder and you'll beat this guy," she said. When I beat him in our third fight, she said, "You've gotten the best of him so now you can quit if you want to." I said, "Why should I quit now? If I can beat a tough guy like Cecil Collins, I can beat anybody." She replied, "That's the spirit. So go for it." That's why I owe my success to momma.'

By the time he was 21, in 1983, Holyfield had won a silver medal in the Pan American Games in Caracas, Venezuela but he really came to prominence in the Los Angeles Olympics in 1984. This was the year the squad won a record nine gold medals, America's dream team, although Holyfield, rated the most 'professional' of the side, was not among them. With celebrities like Kirk Douglas, Jack Nicholson, Dustin Hoffman, Andy Williams and Diana Ross in attendance, Holyfield was disqualified before he even reached the finals.

'After winning my early bouts I went in against Kevin Barry of New Zealand in the semi-final,' he recalled. 'A win would get me a silver medal at least and allow me to qualify for the final against Anton Josipovic of Yugoslavia. I almost had him out in the first round with a left and a right, and the referee gave him a standing count.

'In the second round Barry swung a long right which just grazed by chin. We clinched and I broke away and fired a left hook which landed smack on his chin and he went down. He struggled to his feet, dazed and confused, and I knew it was all over. The fight would automatically be stopped. I had the silver medal at least. The next thing the referee, a Yugoslav named Gliogorije Novicic, pointed to me to indicate I was disqualified. "For what?" I said, but he didn't answer.

'It seems that the referee had ordered "break" just before the knockdown but I didn't hear him. Barry told me later that he didn't hear the command either, what with all the noise. I told the referee, "You can't do this. This isn't American justice. We'll sort it out." But he just left the ring. Just like that. The crowd were booing and shouting all kinds of obscenities and throwing paper cups and anything they could find towards the ring. It was an ugly moment that cast a pall over proceedings.

'I was just plain robbed and American officials around the ringside just couldn't believe what had happened. They filed an official protest but it was rejected by the International Amateur Boxing Association's Appeal Committee. This meant that the Yugoslav, Anton Josipovic, got a bye in the final as Barry, under international rules, was banned from boxing for 28 days because he had been floored, officially, "by a blow to the head", in my case a punch to the chin. I had to settle for the bronze medal. By now I'd had enough of amateur boxing.'

Holyfield made up his mind to turn pro. He had been approached before the Olympics in any event but now it was decision time. He signed with Main Events, the promotional organisation run by Lou Duva, one of boxing's legendary managers and trainers, and his son Dan, for a signing-on fee of $250,000. This was considered small feed in the fight trade but Holyfield trusted the Duvas, which could not be said for the rest. 'With the right guidance, you can earn $2m over the next two years,' said Lou.

Leaving behind an impressive amateur record of 160 wins including 76 either by count-outs or stoppages and 14 losses, Holyfield made his debut in the paid ranks as a light-heavyweight in a scheduled six-rounder at Madison Square

Garden on 15 November 1984. His opponent was Lionel Byram, the light-heavyweight champion of Pennsylvania.

The nationally televised card was billed as 'A Night of Gold' because all nine American boxers who had won a gold medal in the 1984 Olympics three months earlier took part. Holyfield was the odd one out but Duva, as the promoter and Evander's handler, included him on the bill anyhow. Holyfield won the decision and his pro career was under way.

Holyfield made his first major breakthrough early on when, after 11 wins without a defeat, he was matched with the holder of the WBA world cruiserweight title, Dwight Muhammad Qawi, at the Omni Arena in Atlanta on 12 July 1986. Qawi's real name was Dwight Braxton and he had changed his name when he converted to Islam two years earlier. A busy, aggressive fighter, he learned his boxing in the toughest school imaginable – Rahway State Penitentiary, New Jersey. Qawi never boxed as an amateur but joined the boxing programme to relieve the frustrations of prison life.

'Dwight was a veteran when I fought him and he had a style and energy like Joe Frazier, always coming forward,' said Holyfield. 'He was a real dynamo and our fight was a real war. He took me to hell and back but I beat him over 15 rounds on a split decision. I knew then that I could go places in boxing. I had the confidence too, all important. After unifying the cruiserweight division in 1988 I moved up to heavyweight, with my eyes firmly on the world title and a match with the undefeated champion Mike Tyson.'

Holyfield remains the best of the cruiserweight champions since the division was set up by the World Boxing Council in December 1979 when Marvin Camel, a member of the Flathead Indian tribe from Montana, boxed a draw with Mate Parlov of Yugoslavia over 15 rounds. In a return bout, Camel, a southpaw, won the decision to become the division's first champion. There were several other title claimants but Camel held the WBC title on and off for the next eight years before losing it on a knockout in eight rounds to Holyfield in a unification bout.

'When the cruiserweight division was set up, many were wondering, "Why yet another division in boxing?"' remembered Holyfield. 'True, the sport was becoming overcrowded with titles. But in over 20 years, the physical dimensions of boxers changed somewhat dramatically, say between the reigns of Floyd Patterson and George Foreman. Patterson was in reality little more than a light-heavyweight and in his era a heavyweight weighing over 210lb would have been considered exceptional.

'By the time the massive Foreman was champion, 210lb heavyweights would have looked undernourished. Yet there was still a substantial number of good fighters who were too heavy for the light-heavyweight division, with its limit at 175lb but who would have been hopelessly overmatched against genuine heavyweights. There was an urgent need for an in-between division, and in 1979 the WBC instituted the cruiserweight class with a weight limit of 190lb.'

Three years later, the WBC raised the limit to 195lb while the World Boxing Association and the International Boxing Federation, which set up their own champions in 1982 and 1983 respectively, stayed with the original limit. It was not until Holyfield unified the titles on 9 April 1988 with a knockout of the Puerto Rican Carlos De Leon in eight rounds in Las Vegas that the limit was standardised at 190lb. Holyfield, however, did not intend staying at cruiserweight.

'I sat down one day and reckoned that every time I was fighting at cruiserweight I was selling the place out and I get $200,000,' he said. 'Tyson sells the place out and gets $2m. I said to myself, "Now how come I get so little money and he gets such big money?" He was fighting guys that were afraid of him, and the guys I was fighting were not afraid of me.

'I was having to work harder against tough opponents like Dwight Muhammad Qawi for example, and his guys were just laying down. In any event, I had cleaned out the cruiserweight division. I was also the first man to unify the division. There was nothing more I could do there, except fighting the same guys over again. Also, during the Qawi fight, the heat was intense and we were working so hard that the sweat was flying off both of us with every blow.

'The canvas was soaking wet and as the fight wore on it was difficult to maintain footing. I lost so much weight that I required urgent hospital treatment. The doctors said I was in danger of suffering permanent kidney damage. I decided there and then that my days as a cruiserweight were over. From here on in, I would box as a heavyweight.'

Holyfield knew his real future, and boxing's greatest prize, lay in the land of the giants, a land ruled by an ogre called Mike Tyson. Just three months after unifying the cruiserweight class, Evander beat heavyweight contender James 'Quick' Tillis in five rounds, halted Pinklon Thomas in seven and stopped Michael Dokes in ten in a fight billed as being for the WBC Continental Americas heavyweight championship.

The only organisation that took the title seriously was the WBC but it was a heavyweight belt of sorts and it could well lead to a Tyson title fight. Holyfield made three successful defences and it looked like he might have a chance against Tyson, though Mike was clearly more impressive in his wins. It was 1989 and while Tyson was blasting out Carl 'The Truth' Williams inside the opening round, Holyfield was slugging it out with Alex Stewart over eight.

Nevertheless, Holyfield was the number one contender and promoter Don King announced in December that Tyson's connections had agreed to a title defence against the Alabama fighter. The date was set for 18 June 1990 in Atlantic City. It was sealed when both champion and challenger signed a few days later, with Tyson getting between $22m and $25m, Holyfield's fee being considerably less.

As a warm-up title defence, Tyson agreed to make a defence of his championship in Tokyo on 11 February against a man considered a 'no-hoper' – James 'Buster' Douglas, from Columbus, Ohio.

Douglas had been knocking around the heavyweight circuit for many years but nobody took him seriously. Yes, he was 6ft 4in and always in peak condition but he was not a heavy hitter, finishing off only 18 of his 35 opponents before the scheduled distance.

But could he beat the awesome Tyson? No way, said the experts. Mike, the 'Baddest Man on the Planet', looked simply unbeatable. He had won all his 37 fights, 33 by either count-outs or stoppages and hoped to better former champion Rocky Marciano's tally of 49-0-0. But the unthinkable was about to happen – boxing's equivalent of a Japanese earthquake.

As Tyson walked down the aisle leading to the ring in the sprawling Korakuen Stadium on that bitterly wintry Sunday afternoon, he was making the tenth defence of his prized title. He could afford a rare smile. After all, he was a prohibitive 42/1 favourite, the greatest odds in boxing history, to defeat the man who was considered, in Hollywood parlance, a 'bit player'.

The domed stadium, known as the 'Big Egg', had a capacity of over 60,000 but was only half-full, a clear indication of the lack of interest in the fight. But the disbelieving fans, and many millions of TV viewers around the world, saw Douglas, boxing's forgotten man of the heavyweight division, knock out the world champion in ten rounds. A powerful right-left-right combination dropped Tyson and he was counted out while groping around pathetically on all fours, trying to cram his gum shield lop-sidedly back into his mouth before making a brave attempt to stand up. Alas, it was too late. Boxing had a new heavyweight champion of the world.

'I was in the audience for the fight and I was as shocked as everybody else,' said Holyfield. 'But that's what boxing is all about. The unexpected. It's the uncertainty of the sport that makes it what it is. My big fight with Tyson scheduled for June was of course off and negotiations had to start now for a match against Douglas. Really, it didn't matter to me. After all, I would be getting a chance, my first chance, at the heavyweight championship of the world and that was the important thing.

'The bout was scheduled for Las Vegas. The town had been very good to me. I had won important fights there. I beat Ricky Parkey in three rounds in a cruiserweight title fight in Vegas and I unified the title there too when I beat Carlos De Leon in eight. I was ready for whatever Douglas brought to the table. Sure, he knocked out Tyson but he would be up against a different type of opponent this time. This was my big chance and I didn't want to pass it up.'

A crowd of 16,000 packed every available space in the outdoor arena at the Mirage Hotel on 25 October 1990, making the promoter Steve Wynn, also the hotel owner, a very happy man. Holyfield entered the ring looking very trim and hard-muscled at 208lb while Douglas appeared flabby at 246lb, a difference of 38lb. He had weighed 15lb less against Tyson. Holyfield's battle plan had been worked out well in advance by his manager Lou Duva and trainer 'Professor' George Benton, the former middleweight craftsman from Philadelphia.

'They had studied Douglas's fight with Tyson,' said Holyfield. 'They noted that while Douglas's left jab was the most effective weapon in his arsenal, when an opponent jabbed, he would not jab back. Thus, by pumping jabs at him, they reckoned that you could take away his best punch. George also told me that if Douglas threw uppercuts from the side, like he did against Tyson, I could counter with a left hook. Too, George said if Douglas threw the uppercut from a standing position, square on, then I should rock back and throw the right hand.'

Douglas however was a disappointment. He moved around the ring nimbly enough but when he did attempt to jab, it was usually out of distance. He was not making full use of his height, weight and reach advantage and Holyfield looked unconcerned when Douglas got through with a right to the head. After a minute of the third round, Douglas dipped his shoulder and threw a ponderous right in Holyfield's general direction.

The challenger moved back a pace and fired a short right hand counter, dropping Douglas to the canvas. He landed on his left side and rubbed his right glove across his brow before looking at his glove as if seeking traces of blood as referee Mills Lane was tolling the seconds over him. He seemed to make little effort to rise and the count reached ten with Douglas still on the floor. Boxing had a new heavyweight champion of the world, Evander Holyfield.

There was widespread criticism of Douglas's performance and particularly the finish. 'Douglas didn't try to get up,' said referee Lane. 'I'm not saying he could have gotten up but he didn't even try. His eyes looked good to me and he wasn't out. Look, you're born with a ticker. Nobody gives you one.'

Hugh McIlvanney of the *Observer* wrote, 'Douglas lay blinking placidly up at the ring lights like someone whose thoughts of throwing back the bedclothes have been discouraged by word that it's raining outside. Douglas certainly looked the part briefly against Tyson but there were unmistakable signs that Tyson presented only impersonations of his powers that night. No doubt it would be best now if Douglas took his extravagant earnings, including the $20m he got here, and retired, leaving the fighting trade to others.'

Holyfield remembered, 'When I knocked out Douglas with a short right to the head in the third round, I achieved my goal, the heavyweight championship of the world. All my life I wanted it and now I had it. Was the knockout a "fluke"? Some writers said it was. Some said I put him down with a "lucky punch". Over the next few months I guess my "luck" held up when I took on George Foreman and Larry Holmes and the like. But after the Douglas fight I still wanted Mike Tyson. He was my real target.'

The Tyson fight was arranged for the autumn of 1991 but was hastily called off when Desiree Washington, a beauty parade contestant, accused Mike of rape. He was convicted and sentenced to ten years in jail in Indiana but served just three on good conduct. When he resumed his career he won the WBC title by finishing off former victim Frank Bruno in three rounds in March 1996. He was stripped of the title in September for failing to defend it against Lennox Lewis – which is where Holyfield would come into the picture.

'Since I won the title from "Buster" Douglas, I'd lost it to Riddick Bowe, won it back from Bowe and then lost it to Michael Moorer, all in under two years,' said Holyfield. 'Tyson still had the WBA belt and he was the one I wanted. The fight was finally arranged and I trained hard for 15 weeks. One writer said I trained with a religious devotion and that was true. I now wanted more than anything else to finally settle it once and for all with Tyson, after all the delays for one thing or another.

'When I first saw Tyson, I was in camp with him when we were both trying to qualify for berths on the US boxing team for the 1984 Olympics. Now, I felt fully confident that I could beat him. I was bigger and stronger. My arms were longer. I was taller. My thinking was that if he could beat all these guys then I could beat them too. When you see somebody you're just as good as, you know you can beat him. I felt I could also box better than he could.

'I reckoned that Tyson won as an amateur because he trained so hard, and he took chances. He is the only boxer I know who would jump off the floor to hit an opponent. If somebody caught him in the air, they would knock him out but they were afraid of him because he was always throwing those vicious punches. Things started changing when he split with his trainer Kevin Rooney. He fought with a more predictable rhythm. But when I eventually got the chance to fight him in the pro ranks, I wasn't afraid of him.'

Holyfield and Tyson came face to face in the brightly-lit ring at the MGM Grand Garden, Las Vegas on 9 November 1996 before a crowd of 16,325. It would be the highest-grossing gate in Nevada boxing history up to then, more than $14m. The fight turned out to be one-sided. Holyfield dominated from the start, floored Tyson in the sixth with a heavy left hook and stopped him in the 11th.

Under headings 'Fright Night In Vegas' and 'Evander Proved Us Wrong', Jim Murray reported in the *Los Angeles Times*, 'It was supposed to be an execution, not a fight. Tyson, one of the most awesome creatures you ever saw when his opponent is paralysed with fear, was supposed to leave Holyfield in a pile in a corner within a minute. It didn't work out like that.

'Beating Tyson to the punch almost from the outset, Holyfield's unyielding power opened a cut over Tyson's left eye in the sixth, then took the struggling champion apart in the later rounds. In the 11th Holyfield opened with a final flurry before referee Mitch Halpern called it off 37 seconds into the round.

'It was a great night for me,' recalled Holyfield, a deeply religious man. 'With God on your side, the things you choose to do, you can do. Only one heavyweight had ever won the title for a third time, and that was Muhammad Ali when he beat Leon Spinks, his earlier conqueror. At 45 I had become the second. It was a real thrill. I had upset the odds, too, as Mike was a 25/1 favourite.

'It was named Fight of the Year by *Ring* magazine. They also called it Upset of the Year. I must say that I didn't think it was an upset really. I knew I was going to win. I never went into a fight thinking otherwise. Sometimes it doesn't work out like that but it usually does. I hit him with some right hand shots and Mike proved his point. He takes a good shot but I knew I was at my best in that fight. It was one fight I had to win, and I did it.'

If Tyson or anybody else had any real doubts about who was the better man, Holyfield settled it seven months later in the infamous ear-biting debacle. Evander went on to retain his WBA title, and then added the IBF belt to his collection by stopping his old adversary Michael Moorer in eight rounds, dropping the Brooklyn fighter five times.

The two title fights with Lennox Lewis in 1999 also form a major part of the Holyfield story. The first one, on 13 March at Madison Square Garden, New York before a crowd of 21,284 would unify the heavyweight titles. After 12 rounds, it ended in one of the most controversial draws in the 107-year history of the world heavyweight championship under the Queensberry Rules. The scores of the three judges differed. Eugenia Williams marked it 115-113 for Holyfield while Stanley Christodoulou called it 116-113 for Lewis. Larry O'Connell made it 115-115.

'God knows, Lewis did not get the message that Holyfield would knock him out in the third round and delivered his own statement of stinging jabs and hard rights,' wrote Mike Katz in the *New York Daily News*. 'But while Holyfield's face got the point, the judges did not and in one of the worst decisions in a sport of terrible decisions, the heavyweight title was not unified. It is more fractured than ever.'

Rudi Giuliani, the mayor of New York, who sat in the front row, said, 'I'm embarrassed as a New Yorker. There is no way Holyfield earned a draw. I hope it doesn't hurt New York City because there were a lot of people here from England, 6,000 maybe 7,000, for the fight and they have to be going home thinking that we Americans are a bunch of cheats. It doesn't present a very good image of our city. It certainly doesn't.'

Colin Hart of *The Sun* was one of those who did not think it was a bad decision. 'Although I am among a small minority, I do not disagree with the judges' reading of the contest. It would be easy to say Lewis is the victim of an outrageous miscarriage of justice. But scoring fights is a subjective business and this fight was too close to be sure that anyone had got it 100 per cent right.'

Holyfield remembered, 'It was a close fight all the way. I thought I had won but when the decision was announced I didn't react or say anything about it. The sportswriters were falling over themselves to try and prove that it was an outrageous verdict and the worst since the Boston Red Sox decided to send Babe Ruth to the Yankees. Maybe it was a bad decision but these kind of things happen all the time and there is no need to lose your head over them.

'This fight was certainly not the worst in the history of the sport. If you lose or draw and think you should have won, you just accept it and move on. There's always the next time. I had my share of bad calls, most famously in the Olympics, but I didn't go around calling for the Olympics to be scrapped or anything as radical as that. Neither did I bawl after this Lewis fight. What the hell? It's not the end of the world. You can't lose your head over these kind of things.'

The return fight was held on 13 November 1999 at the Thomas and Mack Centre, Las Vegas. Not surprisingly it was another big attraction and there were 17,078 admissions to see the battle for the undisputed championship. Overall receipts would total a record for boxing in Vegas, the showbusiness capital of the world, $16,860,300. Again, the fight ended in controversy with Lewis winning a unanimous decision over 12 close rounds.

This is how Ron Borges of the *Boston Globe* saw it, 'The promised fireworks didn't begin until the fight was over. For 12 rounds Holyfield appeared to get the better of Lewis but the judges saw it differently, giving the World Boxing Council champion the undisputed heavyweight title. When they did, a flurry of fireworks shot into the air and confetti fell to the ground. It floated down as lifeless as the crowd, which seemed as stunned as Holyfield at the outcome.

'This time instead of investigating one judge, the federal government should haul all three up on charges, especially 83-year-old Bill Graham whose scorecard was an advertisement for retirement.'

Holyfield recalled, 'I thought I had won but so what! You win some, you lose some, you draw some. Indeed, I remember that I hadn't felt so good since I had won the cruiserweight title way back. Maybe I should have tried a little harder against Lewis. Maybe then I would have been sore and sick but I'd still have the title. Anyhow, I went over to Lewis's corner and congratulated him. That was all there was to it.'

The attempt by the 'Real Deal' to become the oldest heavyweight champion of all time at the age of 46 ended on 20 December 2009 at the Hallenstadion in Zurich, Switzerland when he faced the plodding, ponderous, seven-foot-tall Russian Nikolai Valuev for the WBA title. The verdict was considered 'blatant robbery'. The sell-out crowd of 12,500 booed the decision of the three judges. Italy's Pierluigi Poppi had it 116-112 for Valuev, Sweden's Mikael Hook 115-114 also for Valuev and Panama's Guillermo Perez Pineda marked it 114 for each.

Holyfield's trainer Tommy Brooks was shouting 'we were robbed' and 'this is outrageous' in the corner. Evander was not so vociferous but agreed that the decision went to the wrong man. Looking back, he said, 'I put him off balance for much of the fight and I felt I won more rounds than he did. I hit him with some pretty clean shots. I thought I fought the perfect fight, following Tommy's instructions. It took a lot of concentration to hit him clean because of his size rather than go toe-to-toe. But there you go.'

The 'Real Deal' had his last fight in Copenhagen, Denmark on 5 July 2011 when, at the age of 49, he stopped the local veteran Brian Nielsen in ten rounds. This brought his record to a very respectable 44 wins, ten losses and two draws. Twenty-nine of his victories were either by count-outs or stoppages. Holyfield has been inducted into the Nevada Hall of Fame and he will be a virtually automatic selection when his name appears on the ballot for induction to the International Hall of Fame Class of 2017 in Canastota, New York.

'I've no regrets in boxing,' he said. 'Nobody expected me to get anywhere. I was supposed to be too small. I was supposed to be too light. But I fooled the doubters because I always believed in myself. Too, I never did drugs or touched a steroid. I eat healthy, rarely drink and I've never smoked. I live a clean life. Momma used to say, "Look after yourself at all times." I've done that and still do. That's all you can do, I guess.

'Sure, I would have liked to have had a shot at the heavyweight title against the Klitschko brothers, Wladimir and Vitali. I felt I could have beaten either one and won the title for the fifth time, an all-time record, but it never happened. As we speak the heavyweight title hasn't been in the US for some years now but what's wrong with a foreigner like Wladimir Klitschko holding the title? America doesn't own the title.

'We had it for long enough, going back to the first heavyweight championship fight under Queensberry Rules when Gentleman Jim Corbett knocked out John L. Sullivan in New Orleans way back in the 1890s. A few Europeans took it away down the years but we always got it back. It's totally different today. Boxers from eastern Europe weren't allowed to fight for world titles for many years because of the communist ban on professionalism, and now that they can compete, they are making the most of their opportunities, and rightly so – and that's a good, healthy situation.'

What of Don King, for many years the world's greatest, and most controversial, promoter? 'I had a cordial relationship with Don and he's got to be the best in the modern age. I liked his style. He was flamboyant. True, he had his critics, and I was one of them at one time but I always tried to keep the peace with him. In any event, my people did all the dealings with him and I left it all to them.'

Ever the diplomat, Holyfield would not be drawn on who he felt was the greatest world heavyweight champion of all time. 'I don't allow my mind to get into discussions like that. Phantom fights are like that. Everybody has a different viewpoint and that's fair enough. We all have our time and you have to leave it at that. This is why I say that it's really difficult to even point to somebody and say, "He was the greatest."

'Muhammad Ali has his supporters but so has Rocky Marciano and so has Joe Louis and so have the others. I would put Floyd Patterson in there too. You have to respect all the great boxers who came from different eras. So in answer to your question, "Who do I think was the greatest?" I just don't know. Let's just say they were all great, and leave it at that,' he said, before adding with a smile, 'And Evander Holyfield wasn't too bad either.'

14

Jersey Joe Walcott

It started with an empty coal cellar

THERE was a big problem for the local promoter and matchmaker at the Armory Arena in Camden, New Jersey just before Christmas week in 1944. Business was bad and Vic Marsillo was looking for someone to top his bill for the last card of the year. He had contacted several boxers but they were unavailable, mainly because of the little money Marsillo was prepared to pay them.

He then remembered a veteran Camden heavyweight he had used down the bill a couple of years earlier but had now retired – for the sixth time, he believed. His name was Jersey Joe Walcott and maybe he would like to give the fight game one more shot, and more importantly as far as Marsillo was concerned, save the card. Marsillo made contact with Felix Bocchicchio, a local manager, and asked him to look up Walcott's whereabouts. Bocchicchio said he knew Jersey Joe and understood he had talent but wasn't getting the breaks.

He located the veteran and put the proposition to him. Walcott hesitated before saying, 'Look, Mr Bocchicchio, I've been in boxing before without getting anywhere. I have a reasonably good job with the local council, though the money isn't great. But we manage. My wife and six kids have enough

CLOSE ENCOUNTERS WITH THE GLOVES OFF

to eat and I don't want to take another chance on boxing. Our coal cellar is never full but we get by, I guess.'

Bocchicchio, who had a business card on which his name was spelt phonetically as 'Bo-key-key-o', had connections with the underworld and never seemed to be short of money judging by the way he dressed and drove around in a big car. 'Look,' he said to Walcott. 'Not only will I promise to always keep your coal cellar full but I'll give you enough money every week so as you don't have to worry where your next meal is coming from, even if you don't fight regularly. You can still keep your council job during the day and we'll concentrate on your boxing in the evenings. You have the talent to make the grade, I can assure you. How's that?'

Walcott looked at his wife and kids sitting around the fire, doing their best to keep warm, before turning to his benefactor. 'Okay Mr Bocchicchio,' he said finally. 'I'll give it one more shot, just one, and that's it.' They shook hands on the promise and the deal was done. The next day, a cartload of coal and a box of groceries were delivered. Bocchiccio recalled that when he got to the Walcott home, 'Even the chairs and the beds had broken legs. I had to get a carpenter to fix doors and windows so that they would stay shut. There was no coal in the cellar, no presents for the kids for Christmas and no meat in the house. Nothing. It was just terrible.'

So began one of boxing's greatest and most faithful partnerships, the old fighter and the racketeer with the soft heart. Within three years Bocchicchio had Walcott fighting for the heavyweight championship of the world, and four years on, Jersey Joe won the title. The Cinderella story had come true.

Walcott was one of the most remarkable men to wear the heavyweight crown. Possessing a clever defence with a 'punch and walkaway' style, clever, shifty footwork and knockout power in both gloves particularly in his left hand, it would still take him five attempts to win the title. His 23-year ring career took him through the reigns of no fewer than eight heavyweight champions; Max Schmeling, Jack Sharkey, Primo Carnera, Max Baer, James J. Braddock, Joe Louis, Ezzard

Charles and Rocky Marciano. Jersey Joe held the title between the tenures of Charles and Marciano.

The story of the man from New Jersey is one of perseverance over adversity, and a deep self-belief in himself. His situation would have discouraged many others. When Walcott was invited to a luncheon in London in 1969 to honour his achievements in the ring, this writer had the opportunity of meeting him and getting the story of his rise and fall. It was a fascinating tale, that of a man who came from being a nobody to a somebody, and to a treasured place in boxing history.

Walcott claimed he was born Arnold Raymond Cream in Merchantville, New Jersey, although this birthplace has always been questioned. While the *Boxing Registar*, the official record book of the International Hall of Fame, as well as Nat Fleischer's *Ring Record Book and Encyclopedia*, also list it as Merchantville, some historians say he was born in nearby Matchtown. They claim they have papers to prove it, although there is no record of a birth certificate apparently. His accepted date of birth was 31 January 1914 though some maintain he was born six or seven years earlier.

'I was one of 12 children and I quit school at 13 when my dad Joseph Cream died suddenly and I was sent out to work in a local soup factory to help support the family,' he recalled. 'My dad was always interested in boxing and he used to bring a few of us down to the local gym. It wasn't long before I was getting into the ring with other, more experienced kids and getting the better of them.

'Dad was originally from St Thomas, an island in the Caribbean, and he used to regale us with stories of the great old-time fighters. His favourite was the original Joe Walcott, who was born in Barbados in the West Indies and was known as the "Barbados Demon". He was welterweight champion of the world at the end of the 19th century and he was a good one by all accounts.

'Dad's cousin was the old "Joplin Ghost", Jeff Clark, a much respected black boxer of the past, so I guess boxing was all around dad. I remember Clark telling me about Walcott. He said he had such clever footwork that his opponents sometimes didn't know where he was in the ring and they would be thrashing away at thin air while Walcott was off dancing around them and firing punches from all angles. I guess I couldn't go wrong by adopting Walcott's name when I turned professional in 1930. I added "Jersey Joe" in reference to my birth state to differentiate from the original Joe Walcott.'

Jersey Joe started off as a middleweight at 16, winning his first fight by a knockout in the first round over Edward 'Cowboy' Wallace in Vineland, New Jersey in September 1930. In two more fights that year he won both inside four rounds apiece but various illnesses kept him out of the ring for long periods which meant he had only one fight in 1931, none in 1932 and three in 1933. Still, his record showed six wins and one defeat.

By 1934 Walcott had developed into a light-heavyweight and was spotted by Jack 'Chappie' Blackburn, a former boxer from Versailles, Kentucky. Blackburn claimed he packed 285 fights into his long career but never got an opportunity of boxing for a world title because of the colour of his skin. When his ring days were over he became a trainer and would be part of a stable managed by businessman John Roxborough.

'We're gonna take you on a trip down the alleyways of boxing and see what you got,' Blackburn told Jersey Joe. 'If you show promise and we like you, we'll take you down the big, bright thoroughfares and you'll be a big name and you'll make a lot of money. The old colour bar is beginning to break down and more black boxers are getting chances now than ever before.

'In my day it was different. Champions avoided black boxers. Me? I fought greats like Sam Langford and Joe Gans and Philadelphia Jack O'Brien and Harry Greb but I never got a title shot. Things are changing now. It's not perfect but blacks are getting there. You could be one of them.'

Blackburn started coaching Walcott, by now a fully-fledged heavyweight, in the finer points of the noble art and showed him how to punch correctly and get the most out of his blows. Soon, however, Blackburn was lured away to train a newcomer from Detroit called Joe Louis in the summer of 1934. Nevertheless 'Chappie' would invite Walcott to work out with Louis in 1936 when the 'Brown Bomber' was training in Lakewood camp on the New Jersey shore for his first fight with Max Schmeling.

'Lakewood was a decidedly upscale locale and totally different to anything I had been used to back in Camden,' Walcott remembered. 'At the turn of the century it was a popular winter resort for wealthy New York residents like John D. Rockefeller, and I believe that Rudyard Kipling had gone there to recuperate from an illness. Louis trained on the grounds of the luxury Stanley Hotel and had his quarters close by in a mansion. I remember one New York writer, I can't remember who, describing it as a "setting fit for the uncrowned king of fistiana". Certainly it was a class location.

'I was one of Blackburn's hired helpers to get Louis into shape for the Schmeling fight. Louis was an overwhelming favourite to win as the German was considered well past his best but as we all know now, it didn't work out as planned, with Schmeling knocking him out in 12 rounds. In the ring with Louis I found him open to a straight right or a right hook to the head. This is something Schmeling also exploited, having watched films of Louis's fights and seeing him in action from ringside.

'During one training session I caught Louis with a right hand shot to the head and he went down. Blackburn quickly jumped into the ring, checked if his valuable prospect was all right and told me that was all for the moment. The next day Blackburn came up to me, handed me my $25 fee and said I wouldn't be needed any more. Mind you, Louis and Blackburn both denied the knockdown ever happened and merely said that Joe had slipped and that's all there was to it. Blackburn said, "Joe hurt Walcott and he just never came back." That was their version of what happened and they stuck to their story.

'But the knockdown did happen, I can assure you. Otherwise why did Blackburn let me go? He hires me as a sparring partner and the next thing I'm sacked. Unfortunately there were no reporters on hand that day and nothing was ever recorded. When I would eventually get to fight Louis in 1947 and 1948 for the heavyweight title, I put him on the canvas three times with the very same punch.

'Does that not prove anything? Louis was always open to a right hand. Mind you this fault never stopped him from winning the title from Jim Braddock and holding it for nearly 12 years, which was a truly magnificent record, but he had that little weakness at the same time.'

Walcott had meanwhile married his childhood sweetheart Lydia Eleanor Talton and they would eventually raise six children. Jersey Joe now had to find regular employment, even if his boxing career had never really got off the ground. Before Blackburn came along, he hooked up with several trainers but he needed a manager to get him some meaningful fights.

'Several promised that I would be a world champion some day but I soon found them merely unscrupulous individuals looking for a cheap meal ticket,' he said. 'When I asked one particular manager for my promised purse money after one fight, I was told that the promoter had run off with all the purse monies and that nobody would get paid. Other managers showed me little interest and concentrated fully on their more established boxers. It was not an ideal situation to be in. I was now considered a journeyman, somebody who was mere fodder for rising heavyweights anxious to get valuable experience without any great danger and pad out their records.

'You have my record there in front of you. You'll see I had no fights in 1934 and in 1935 I had five, all wins but none of the opponents were big names or even reasonably near the top 15. In 1936, I finished with five wins, two draws and two losses, one on a stoppage in eight rounds. Look, I even began 1937 by being knocked out in eight rounds by Tiger Jack Fox. Things were looking really bad.'

There was one bright spot in November 1938 when Walcott decisioned the formidable Curtis Sheppard, billed as the 'Hatchet Man', over eight rounds in the Rocklin Palace

Arena, New York. But when Jersey Joe asked his manager at the time if they could capitalise on the win, he was told, 'Forget it, promoters only want white heavyweights. They're all looking for the Great White Hope who can take the title from Joe Louis.'

Now disillusioned with the fight game which had brought him only despair and heartbreak, Walcott drifted away from the sport and took any kind of jobs that were available. After all, he had a wife and a family of five at the time to clothe and feed. He hung up his gloves in 1941 for what he believed was for good. 'I never knew what an extra dollar was until I was in my 30s,' he said. 'I always had such a hard time getting along that I could never afford any kind of dissipation, not even cigarettes. Now take Joe Louis. Joe hit the big time very early in his life. He did well to last as long as he did, with all that easy living he went through. I was just the opposite.'

Walcott remained inactive through 1942 and 1943 and worked in New Jersey shipyards as well as for his local council. Offers of fights came up but nothing ever came of them. In any event he was tired of the fight game. He would follow the fortunes or otherwise of the big-time boxers but as far as climbing into a ring again, that was a definite non-event. Two meaningful fights, and two wins, came up in 1944 when Jersey Joe came in as a substitute in both cases. Then came Christmas and the meeting with Felix Bocchicchio, who turned out to be his fairy godfather.

In January 1945, Bocchicchio arranged two fights, both in the Camden Convention Hall. Walcott stopped Jackie Saunders in two rounds but was outpointed by the slippery Johnny 'Skippy' Allen over eight rounds. 'I was convinced that Felix would wash his hands of me at that stage but fair play to him, he told me he had made a promise to look after me and he planned to carry out that promise, come what may,' remembered Walcott. 'He told me the Allen loss was just a blip.

'In my third fight in 1945 I outpointed Austin Johnson over six rounds in Camden and then I got revenge over "Skippy" Allen over eight rounds. Things were definitely looking up but Felix felt, and quite rightly, that I would need a win over a rated opponent, someone in the top ten, to get some kind of recognition as a serious contender and not just an also-ran, which I had been up to now. Then a few weeks later Felix called over to the house and told me he had fixed up a ten-rounder with big Joe Baksi for the Camden Convention Hall.'

This would be a real test to see if Walcott had the goods. Trained by Ray Arcel, Baksi was originally a coal miner from Kulpmont, Pennsylvania. He left when his father met his death in a pit accident and took jobs as a dishwasher, fish cleaner and a bar bouncer. By the time he was 18 in 1940, he was living in New York and boxing four-round preliminary bouts on small cards and on the undercards of bigger shows.

Baksi broke into professional boxing that year and beat nine opponents, including the future Hollywood movie actor Jack Palance, who fought under the name of Jack Brazzo. Baksi was quoted as saying that he never had any intention of being a boxer, but he saw it 'as a ticket to a better way of life, out of the coal mines'. Early in his career he was compared in looks and style to the former heavyweight champion of the world James J. Jeffries. In his first 36 fights, Baksi dropped only one six-round decision and was now a leading contender for the heavyweight title, having beaten the likes of Lee Savold, Tami Mauriello and Lou Nova.

'Baksi's manager Nate Wolfson only accepted me as an opponent because he thought I was a washed-up old man looking for a quick buck,' said Walcott. 'Wolfson and his people were grooming him for an eventual shot at Joe Louis's world heavyweight title and a win over "old guy Jersey Joe" would put another name on his record. Happily for me, it didn't work out like that and I beat him on points over ten rounds. The referee Paul Cavalier marked his card 6-3-1 in my favour. Wow! With that win, my whole mental attitude changed.

'I felt I could make it as a real contender, and possibly even win the big title. It was all down to Felix's faith in me. When I was struggling in my early career I couldn't concentrate on my boxing. I had a wife and growing family to support and I always had them in mind, making sure they had enough to eat and so on. Fights were hard to come by. After the Baksi win, I had a good purse and things were definitely looking up. More importantly I had my confidence back, not that I ever really had it in the first place.'

Before the year was out Walcott had beaten two other heavyweight contenders, Lee Q. Murray on a disqualification in the ninth round and a totally impressive knockout in ten rounds over his old rival Curtis 'Hatchet Man' Sheppard, the only man to ever knock out the iron-chinned Joey Maxim in 115 fights. Opening 1946, Walcott gained final revenge over old rival Johnny Allen by knocking 'Skippy' out in three rounds but by year's end he dropped two decisions, to Joey Maxim, a future light-heavyweight champion of the world, and Elmer 'Violent' Ray, a contender for Louis's title.

'In between the "Skippy" Allen fight and the ones with Maxim and Ray in 1946, I had important wins over Jimmy Bivins, who had won the "interim heavyweight title" a few years earlier when Louis was in the armed forces, and Lee Oma, a skilful guy who later fought Ezzard Charles for the world title. In 1947 I beat both Maxim and Ray in return matches, Maxim on two occasions. Sol Strauss was now running the 20th Century Sporting Club while his boss Mike Jacobs, who had promoted all of Louis's 23 title defences up to then, was convalescing from a stroke. Strauss announced that Louis would defend his title on a big outdoor show in New York in the summer of 1947, though no challenger had yet been named.'

Strauss said the most likely opponent would be Joe Baksi. When Bocchicchio approached the promoter and pointed out that Walcott had already beaten Baksi and deserved first chance, Strauss said that despite his defeat, Baksi was a bigger attraction. Besides, Strauss was cautious about putting two black heavyweights into the ring and thought the fight might not draw. Louis had not defended his title against a black boxer for eight years, since he stopped John Henry Lewis in the first round. Was the public ready to accept another black challenger?

The point of course was that attitudes had changed in America. In any event Louis, by his demeanour and public persona, had altered the image of the black man from the turbulent days of the only previous non-white boxer to hold the heavyweight title, the arrogant if extremely talented Jack Johnson. The era of the despicable colour bar was now relegated to history. When Strauss approached Nate Wolfson, Baksi's manager, with the possibility of a Louis fight, Wolfson turned it down flat. He said his boxer was not prepared to get into the ring with Louis 'just yet', though he did not elaborate on what he meant by 'just yet'.

The problem was solved when Baksi went to Sweden to meet the local hope Olle Tandberg in July 1947 and lost the decision. With Baksi now out of the picture, Strauss turned his attention to Walcott. He announced that the event would not be a title defence by Louis but a ten-round exhibition later in the year while the promoter was waiting for a good drawing card to build up for a big outdoor match in the summer of 1948. The New York State Athletic Commission, however, ruled that any ten-rounder would have to be for the championship so Strauss went ahead with a full-blown 15-round bout with Louis's championship on the line. The location was Madison Square Garden and the date 5 December 1947.

Boxing writers scoffed at the match, with headlines such as 'Walcott does not deserve this fight' and 'Where did they dig up old Pappy Jersey Joe from?' Walcott trained hard but the betting people made him a 10/1 underdog. A company in Buffalo, New York, tried to rent the soles of Walcott's shoes as advertising space for when Louis would surely put him on the canvas. Not even the fact that Strauss's publicity people sent out press releases to the effect that Walcott had once dropped Louis on his back in a training session in the pre-war days, and was promptly sacked, stirred up their enthusiasm.

Nevertheless, Louis's name was enough to pull in the fans irrespective of who he fought and a crowd of 18,199 filled the famous arena, paying a Garden record of $216,477. But if the fans were expecting the demolition of a journeyman fighter, they were disappointed. Instead they saw the humiliation of the one-time 'Brown Bomber'. Walcott floored the champion in the opening round with a perfect right-hand shot to the head, and put him down again in the fourth as Louis desperately struggled to get into the fight.

When the bell ended the 15th round, Louis seemed to share the opinion of everybody present that he had just lost his title. Referee Ruby Goldstein awarded seven rounds to Walcott, six to Louis and two even. Judge Frank Forbes gave Walcott six rounds, Louis eight and one even. The other judge, Marty Monro, made it nine to Louis and six to Walcott.

Louis was still champion of the heavyweights – on a split decision. Disgusted with his showing, he tried to leave the ring before the official verdict was announced and had to be restrained by his trainer Manny Seamon, who had taken over after Jack Blackburn's death in 1942. The verdict was greeted by a storm of booing and jeering.

This is how Peter Wilson, then with the *Sunday Pictorial*, a forerunner of the *Sunday Mirror*, saw the fight, 'In my opinion this was the greatest robbery since Colonel Blood stole the Crown Jewels. Would Walcott freeze as so many of Louis's opponents had done? Would he hell! As round after round reeled off, Walcott bemused the champion. He would face him, then break stance, do a sort of jig, bob and weave or just walk away from him.

'By the 15th round, Louis had only three minutes to keep his all-time great record untarnished. He tried to do it – and oh, how he tried. Walcott ran unashamedly. Only fools and gamblers could blame him. He must have felt he had the fight on points. Then came the split verdict, Louis on points. But I'll swear on oath he was licked by the cagey, shifty, game guy they call Jersey Joe Walcott.'

Walcott remembered, 'Going out for the 15th round I was sure I had the title. Louis never hurt me once, and I even had him down twice. True, Louis was always coming forward but I was catching him with long punches, short punches, all kinds of punches. I knew I had to watch Joe's big right and how he came from behind to knock out Billy Conn in 13 rounds in 1941. I didn't want that to happen to me. I was always aware of his intentions. I don't want to put too much criticism on Louis as he was my idol growing up and since that fight in 1947 we've been the best of friends. We meet often at big fights and have a chat. But he never won that fight with me. I should have been named the winner and new champion.

'Naturally there was a demand for a return fight and this was held the following June at the Yankee Stadium. I figured I would take the title this time and I wasn't going to allow Louis to do the chasing. Mind you, I don't mean I would just go in there and mix it with him like the way Billy Conn did in their first fight and got himself knocked out. I would be careful. I would box *and* punch. I thought I was doing well and my corner told me two of the judges had me in front after nine rounds. Louis seemed to be getting frustrated at this stage because of his inability to get a good shot at me.

'While it may not have been a very exciting fight for the fans with no slam-bang action, there was a world championship on the line and both of us had to be careful. We both had our strategies. The referee Frank Fullam didn't help me, though. He kept shouting at me regularly to give the crowd some action, while he only occasionally spoke to Louis. In the 11th Louis saw the opening he had been looking for and knocked me out.'

This is how Nat Fleischer described the dramatic 11th round in *Ring* magazine, 'When Jersey Joe made one of his few offensive gestures of the fight, he gave Louis the necessary opening. The champion first nailed Walcott with three fast, numbing straight lefts to the head and then drove a crushing right to the jaw. All the fight left the Jerseyite. His legs became rubbery. He caught a right to the body that brought his guard down, and then came the hurricane of punches. He tried to hang on but nothing could save him from the fury of Louis' attack. Utterly defenceless, he was spared further punishment only by collapsing in his tracks. He was counted out in two minutes and 56 seconds of the 11th round. Joe Louis was still heavyweight champion of the world.'

Walcott recalled, 'I had no excuses. In the first fight I definitely felt I won and should have been given the decision and the title but this time Louis found the opening he was looking for and did his job. That was one thing Joe had all his career. A keen eye. He would spot an opening and drive in his best punches, particularly as I said to you earlier, against Billy Conn and now with me. As for losing my second chance at the title, what can you say? You met up with a better man. In any event, I felt another title shot could well come my way. You never know in this game.'

Sure enough, Walcott got his third opportunity of fighting for the championship sooner than he had expected. With rumours flying about like confetti at a wedding, Louis made his retirement official on 1 March 1949 when he called a press conference to announce he was stepping down as world heavyweight champion after a record run of 11 years and eight months, and 25 successful title defences.

Louis made a deal with the International Boxing Club, the leading promoters at the time, that the four leading contenders, Jersey Joe Walcott, Ezzard Charles, Gus Lesnevich and Lee Savold would get an opportunity to compete for the vacant title. Louis would be made a director of the IBC and get 20 per cent of the stock in the company, a down payment of $150,000 and an annual salary of $15,000, later increased to $20,000. On their respective records and performances Charles and Walcott were named the principal contenders of the four. Ezzard and Jersey Joe were matched for 22 June 1949 at Comiskey Park, Chicago. This was the same ring where Louis had taken the title from James J. Braddock 12 years earlier to the very day.

Ezzard Charles, a very underrated boxer in the sport, was born in Lawrenceville, Georgia, but grew up in Cincinnati, Ohio. He started boxing as a middleweight before moving up to light-heavyweight. Charles fought his way to the leading contender's position but was denied a title shot. Ultimately he graduated to the heavyweight division and earned a reputation as both a clever boxer and hard puncher.

Among those Charles defeated up to the time he fought Walcott were Joey Maxim five times, Lloyd Marshall twice, Archie Moore three times, Charlie Burley twice, Jimmy Bivins three times, Elmer 'Violent' Ray and Teddy Yarosz. Six months before the Walcott fight, he stopped the formidable Joe Baksi in 11 rounds. Essentially he was still a light-heavyweight and weighed only seven pounds above the 175lb limit.

'Charles and I would eventually meet four times,' said Walcott. 'That first one, in Chicago in 1949, was only recognised by the National Boxing Association, the NBA, as the rival New York had their own plans for a title fight, even though both Charles and I were the leading contenders. The fight went the full 15 rounds and I thought I won nine of the rounds. Charles was announced as the winner. By the time we met for the second time, in March 1951 at the Olympia Stadium in Detroit, Charles had gained full recognition as champion. This one also went the full 15 rounds and at the finish I was sure I had won but the decision went to Charles – again.

'I was disgusted and so was the crowd. They booed for six or seven minutes. Felix, my manager, was screaming at the top of his voice, "We were robbed, we were robbed." Full credit to Felix. He exploited the free publicity for all it was worth. There was only one answer. There would have to be a third fight to prove once and for all who was the better man – and this time I intended to make no mistake.'

Charles v Walcott III was set for Forbes Field, Pittsburgh. The date was 18 July 1951. While Charles was fully focussed on the fight when it was first mooted in March, he was in buoyant enough mood to take on the world light-heavyweight champion Joey Maxim in May. Although unable to stop the tough-chinned Clevelander, Charles won easily on points. It was his fourth win over Maxim. Ezzard now had just under eight weeks to prepare for Walcott.

A crowd of 28,272 passed through the turnstiles at the ballpark, home of the Pittsburgh Pirates, to see if the 37-year-old Walcott, seven years older than the champion whose birthday it was, could finally turn the tables on his rival. At the pre-fight press conference, both expressed full confidence in the outcome. 'I've beaten Jersey Joe twice before and there's no reason I can't do it again,' said Charles. 'Not this time Ez,' replied Walcott. 'This is going to be my lucky day. Sorry to disappoint you.'

Bocchicchio was convinced that Jersey Joe could do it this time, his fifth attempt at the title. The overall view of the ringside writers, and the crowd, however, was that Charles would hold on to his title. After all, the Cincinnatian had already beaten Walcott twice and there seemed no reason to believe he could not do it again, and probably on points. Going out for the first round, Walcott had told his corner, 'This is the big one, boys. I've got to do it this time. It's now or never.' Bocchicchio nodded in agreement.

'Unknown to the Charles camp, I had decided in secret training sessions that I would spring a surprise on Charles from the first round,' remembered Jersey Joe. 'I had previously relied on my right hook but for this fight I would concentrate on the left hook. Charles would not have been expecting that change of style and I'm convinced to this day that this is what won the fight for me. There's an old saying in boxing, and you've probably heard of it, "Concentrate on the body and the head will die." I had planned to do just that.

'Both of us were naturally cautious in the opening round, with a lot of counter-punching but by the third round I felt I was getting his measure. I definitely hurt Charles with a right to the head just before the bell ended the third round. I staggered him too in the fifth with that same punch. Charles was still very much in the fight, though, and to be fair to him, his counter shots were very good. Watch clips of the fight and you will see that. In the sixth I caught him with a good left hook and I could see a deep worried look on his face.

'In the seventh Charles came out fast and I gave a bit of ground. He opened up with short hooks but as we moved to the centre of the ring I caught him with a short, snappy left hook which some of the writers said could not have travelled more than ten inches. That's what they wrote. Charles fell and landed on his face. He attempted to rise and managed to get to his feet very unsteadily at the count of nine or ten, I'm not sure which, before he fell over backwards as the referee Buck McTiernan waved his arms. It was all over and I was heavyweight champion of the world – at long last, and in my fifth attempt.'

'Walcott's victory was one of the most remarkable achievements in ring history,' wrote Daniel M. Daniel in *Ring* magazine. 'Jersey Joe, Old Man River himself, had made it. Walcott rocked Charles at the close of the third round with a couple of smashing rights, and just missed knocking Ezzard down with a sneak right in the fifth. In the next round Charles appeared to realise that his time was running out and he was losing on points. He began to shoot left hooks and move about with more life. Then, in the seventh and before the customers knew what had happened, Walcott fired his left hook and became champion of the world. "I don't know what happened," said Charles as he sat in his corner, no longer the champion.'

Walcott and Charles would meet for a fourth time when Jersey Joe successfully defended his title a year later by winning a 15-round decision. He lost the title on 23 September 1952 on a knockout in 13 rounds against the younger, stronger Rocky Marciano after being well ahead on points. In a return bout the following May, Marciano knocked him out in the first round and Jersey Joe announced his final retirement. 'No excuses,' said Walcott. 'Rocky beat me fair and square, both times.'

Jersey Joe, however, did not go away from the celebrity scene. In 1956 he starred with Humphrey Bogart and Max Baer in the boxing movie *The Harder They Fall* and later tried professional wrestling. In 1965 he refereed the controversial second fight between Muhammad Ali and Sonny Liston which Ali won on a knockout in the first round.

'There is widespread belief that Ali knocked out Liston with a phantom punch and that Liston took a dive,' he explained. 'Phantom punch, hell! There was no phantom punch. It was a genuine right-hand punch to the chin, a devastating shot, and you can take my word for it. As the referee, I was closest to the action. What's more, I think Ali is the greatest heavyweight

264

champion of them all. Speed, punch, tough chin – everything. I'm convinced he would beat Jack Dempsey, Joe Louis, Rocky Marciano and a fellow named Jersey Joe Walcott. He puts his punches together better than any of the heavyweight champions.

'I know Ali didn't go to a neutral corner when he put Liston down so I had to push him away because I was afraid he was going to kick Liston in the head. He was acting like a wild man. He was running around the ring and shouting to Sonny, "Get up you bum, get up!" Can you imagine what they would have said if Ali had kicked Liston in the head? And he might have hit Sonny as he was getting up. If so, he could have injured Liston permanently. Ali never gave me a chance to start counting. I couldn't hear the count from the knockdown timekeeper. It was crazy.

'I finally saw the timekeeper waving his hands in front of his face. I ran over to him and he shouted up, "The fight's over. I counted to 12." Nat Fleischer of *Ring* magazine was next to the timekeeper and he confirmed it. It wouldn't have made any difference if I had picked up the count at four or five as most referees do because Liston was really knocked out. I could have counted another 15 or 16 seconds over him. You add that to the 12 seconds the timekeeper counted over him and you know that Liston was through. Ali made it tough on me the way he was carrying on, as I say, like a wild man. I think I did the right thing under the bizarre circumstances.'

Walcott later worked for the Camden County Corrections Department and served as director of community relations for the town. In 1971 he became the first African-American to serve as sheriff in Camden County and was chairman of the New Jersey State Athletic Commission from 1975 until 1984, when he stepped down at the mandatory retirement age of 70. Walcott was inducted into the International Boxing Hall of Fame in New York in 1990. He died in February 1994 at the age of 80. Assessing Walcott's career, esteemed trainer Eddie Futch told the author, 'Jersey Joe was one of the finest technicians in ring history – and a fine gentleman too.'

15

Georges Carpentier
*The aviator who flew
through eight divisions*

BOXING'S first matinee idol and war hero, Georges Carpentier was a handsome, debonair Frenchman who was responsible on both sides of the Atlantic for attracting not only those who would not normally be fans of the sport but hordes of female admirers to boxing tournaments leading up to World War I and after. Possessing consummate skills and a knockout punch in both gloves, he was known variously as 'Gorgeous George', the 'Idol of France' and the 'Orchid Man', the latter because of his habit of wearing a flower in his buttonhole.

Carpentier competed in every weight class in the days when there were only eight divisions, flyweight to heavyweight, and held the French, European and world championships at four different weights. By universal consensus, he is regarded by historians and fight experts as the greatest European boxer to ever lace up a pair of gloves. When the Irish playwright George Bernard Shaw first saw him in action, he wrote, 'I was startled by a most amazing apparition. Nothing less than Charles XII, the "Madman of the North", striding along in a Japanese dressing gown as gallantly as if he had not been killed almost exactly 201 years before.' The dashing Carpentier had that effect on people.

After distinguished and gallant service in the French Air Force, he won the world light-heavyweight championship in 1920 and eight months later was cast as the dashing hero to challenge the scowling Jack Dempsey for the heavyweight championship of the world. The fight drew the first million-dollar gate.

When Carpentier was in London in 1973 with Jack Dempsey at a special dinner to honour their achievements in boxing, I had the pleasure of interviewing him. He was friendly and chatty, answering any questions about his many great victories and equally his defeats in an open and honest fashion. Would he do it all again? 'Quite definitely,' he replied in quite good English. 'I met many wonderful people, and a few not too wonderful too, I could add, and saw a bit of the world. It was great to meet Jack here, and we always remained friends. It is a friendship I will always cherish.

'Boxing is a great game, despite its many detractors. Attack is only half of the art of boxing. Skill is the other half. You must always be fit and ready when you take part in the sport. Perspiration, dedication and direction would be the key. If you are going into boxing, you must put your mind down to it, and have a bit of luck along the way too. The rewards can be very good. Even when my career ended, I always managed to keep myself fit. It's a habit, a routine you never really lose.'

Before discussing his long career, I asked Carpentier who were the greatest boxers of all time in his opinion. 'I would have to say Jack Dempsey,' he replied. 'Dempsey would certainly be my number one heavyweight champion, and I'm not saying that just because he is here in London with me. Of the moderns, I could go no further than Sugar Ray Robinson, an all-rounder who disposed of the best and the toughest opponents who could be put into the ring with him. Robinson had elegance and class, and was a good friend of mine.

'Before Robinson there was Al Brown, or Panama Al Brown as he was known. He was bantamweight champion of the world for over five years as far as I can remember and he was very good too, though he enjoyed great advantages in height and reach over his opponents. There were a few good Frenchmen too, like Andre Routis, world featherweight champion, and Emile Pladner, flyweight champion. Marcel Thil, the middleweight champion too. I never thought Marcel Cerdan, another middleweight champion, was in the top class. A lovely man and a personal friend of mine, he was courageous and had a heavy punch but I felt his ring resources were very limited.'

Carpentier was born in Lievin, a small mining town just outside Lens in northern France, on 12 January 1894, the youngest of five children. A few months after Georges was born, the family moved to a miner's cottage in Lens, although his father was never a miner. Georges senior was of peasant stock and graduated from working in the fields to driving a horse and cart for a local brewery. Its light ale found its way into the Carpentier home and young Georges was weaned on the beer which he took from a feeding bottle and would develop a lifelong taste for it, although never to excess.

'I was something of a wild boy and often took four hours or so to walk the mile-and-a-half journey from school,' he recalled, 'the time being taken up by getting into mischief of one kind or another. I soon became tired of school and wanted to get out into the real world and leave my schoolbooks behind. I did love the physical training, though, and used to dream of being a boxer, and a good one. When I was about ten and during school holidays my mother took me to Paris as guests of a neighbour. I was gobsmacked with the city. It was a wonderful experience, something I'd never even imagined.

'The journey on the train, the majestic Arc de Triomphe, the magnificent Eiffel Tower, the fine buildings along the Champs-Elysees, the lovely cafes along the boulevards. The beautiful girls in their summer dresses, too. This was what I wanted. The good life, and I would work towards that end. It all didn't feel too far-fetched really. It could be achieved. It was now my goal. To see something of life in big cities, to make something of myself and be somebody. When I told my parents, the Lord be good to them, they said I would have to be careful but secretly I think they approved of my ambitions and would be happy if that's what I really wanted, which I did.'

One day Carpentier was getting the better of a street fight when his opponent's three friends joined in. He was about to get a beating when a man, who later introduced himself as Francois Descamps, saved him. Descamps ran a gymnasium in the town and he invited the boy to train at his gym as an alternative to fighting in the street. 'Learn to take care of yourself in the ring and you'll soon be more than a match for these bullies,' said Descamps. Carpentier not only learned something about boxing but also proved himself very skilful at gymnastics.

As well as training the boys at his gym, Descamps also gave lessons at the Sporting Club in Lens, not only at boxing but a French version of the noble art, called *la savate*, which also permits the use of the feet, as in kickboxing. When a German circus came to Lens, Descamps heard about an acrobat named Ali, an Algerian roughly the same age as the 11-year-old Carpentier. He arranged a *la savate* match between the two, with the result that his young protégé knocked out his opponent in around ten seconds. At this early stage, Descamps knew young Georges had real talent.

'I left school after what the family felt were good marks in my exams and had a variety of jobs including a riveter's mate and an insurance collector, but my dream was always to make it in the big city, Paris, and make something of myself. Boxing could do that for me. I was devoting a lot of time to the *la savate* training. I felt that the sport was excellent preparation for boxing. The suppleness you could gain, and the speed and strength you could acquire in your legs, would be invaluable.'

When Carpentier was 12, Descamps entered him in a regional French boxing tournament at Bethune, some eight miles from Lens. He was up against a much bigger man but he won impressively. Descamps soon put his name forward for a major championship tournament in Paris, where he reached the semi-finals. Descamps suggested Georges should forget about *la savate* and devote all his interests to what the trainer called 'English-style boxing'. 'This is where your talents lie,' he explained to the youngster. 'Always work at what you do best.'

With *la savate* now a thing of the past as far as he was concerned, Carpentier started training 'without the kicks' at the Sporting Club in Lille under the guide of Descamps. Georges would remember that it was at the club where he met 19-year-old Maurice Chevalier who came in for a workout. Chevalier was beginning to make a name for himself around that time as a singer/dancer and cabaret entertainer and in future years he would be a major international star of stage and movies, with his twinkling eyes, ready smile and wearing his familiar straw boater. Chevalier and Carpentier would become world-famous in their chosen fields and remained friends all their lives.

'When Descamps suggested I should turn professional, I told him he would have to see my mother first. She agreed and Francois became my manager and trainer. He was entitled to 30 per cent of my earnings and I had no problem with that, and later on when I started to become successful he reduced it to 20 per cent. You know, we never had a written agreement or had any sort of dispute throughout our relationship. He was that kind of man. We trusted each other implicitly.'

Carpentier had his first fight on 1 November 1908 at the Café de Paris in Maisons-Lafitte, a suburb of the capital, as a flyweight and defeated an English boy named Ed Salmon in a scheduled 20-rounder. Carpentier was doing well and looked set for victory when Salmon accidentally landed a low blow in the 13th round and was disqualified. A return match was set for a month later, again over 20 rounds, but this time Carpentier was well beaten. He was pulled out in the 18th round by Descamps after being down ten times in the previous three rounds. Georges pleaded that he wanted to go on but Descamps told him, 'You've had enough tonight. There will be better days ahead.'

Around this time Carpentier went to live in Puteaux, a suburb of Paris, while Descamps stayed on in Lille but they came together for fights. Carpentier made good progress and

13 months after his debut he won the French lightweight championship, and he was not yet 16. In 1911 he added the French welterweight title to his collection and while he had not yet developed the deadly and accurate punching power that would become one of his trademarks, he was gaining weight and getting stronger.

By 1912 Carpentier had become European middleweight champion but lost to two experienced visiting Americans, Frank Klaus, a future world middleweight champion, and Billy Papke, the reigning title holder who had knocked out the great Stanley Ketchel, the 'Michigan Assassin', in 12 rounds four years earlier.

Those were Carpentier's final two fights at middleweight. From now on, he would campaign in the light-heavyweight division, and often into the heavyweight class, two categories where he would achieve his greatest successes. With his earnings he bought himself his first dinner suit and car. At 19 his role as man-about-town in his favourite city, Paris, was about to begin. In the ring, he was also to become the scourge of British light-heavyweights and heavyweights.

Carpentier won the vacant European light-heavyweight title by knocking out Bandsman Rice in two rounds in Ghent, Belgium in February 1913 and the vacant heavyweight championship with a knockout in four rounds over Bombardier Billy Wells in London in June. He repeated his win over Wells with a one-round knockout six months later in just under a minute. Georges had a few scares in the first fight with Wells when the lanky Englishman had him down twice in the first round and slowed him down with a heavy body attack in the second and third before Carpentier landed a hard left hook to the body and a smashing straight right to finish off Wells.

'Slowly and limply, as though all the strength had gone out of his great body, the English champion staggered to the ropes,' said Victor Breyer in *l'Echo des Sports*. 'His legs gave way under him and he collapsed, an inert mass which did not even twitch as the chronometer ticked off the fatal ten seconds. The few

Frenchmen who were present were on their feet now, wild with enthusiasm. The English were silent, as though struck dumb.

'It took them at least a minute to realise that the incredible scene they had just witnessed was real and not a bad dream, that the incredible was a fact. But then they quickly recovered themselves and they gave Carpentier, who was now being carried shoulder high around the ring by his seconds, the ovation that English sportsmen give to a victorious guest in their midst. In the meantime Wells, whom Carpentier had helped carry to his corner, recovered consciousness. Then followed a scene I found as painful as any I have ever witnessed. When Wells got to his feet and went towards the centre of the ring, there was booing.'

Carpentier recalled, 'The great Welsh boxer Jim Driscoll was shouting from the ringside, "Coward! Coward! Coward!" but Wells was no coward or anything like it. He said from the centre of the ring that he had a weakness, which was his inability to take body shots, and that was it. I think he was the finest British boxer of his generation and that should have been respected. He was always a courageous and fair fighter and a gentleman out of the ring. Boxing crowds have short memories. You can go on and on winning, and then you lose, and all the wins are quickly forgotten.'

On 21 March 1914 Carpentier took on the great New Jersey heavyweight Joe Jeanette in Paris in one of the few white v black matches of the day. Jeanette was deprived of competing for the heavyweight championship of the world not through lack of ability but because of the colour of his skill. Racism, promoters' fear of riots and the economic climate of the time made it nearly impossible for black boxers to get bouts against top whites who refused to take them on.

As a result, black boxers were regularly matched against each other. Jeanette fought Sam Langford 15 times, Battling Jim Johnson nine times, Sam McVey five times and Harry Wills in three no-decision bouts. 'When Jack Johnson became champion, he forgot about his old friends and drew the colour line against his own people,' Jeanette lamented.

Carpentier conceded over 20lb in weight and seemed to have won easily over 15 rounds but German referee Frantz-Reichel had no hesitation in raising Jeanette's right hand at the last bell. In its report of the fight the next day, the *Auto* newspaper ran the headline 'A scandalous decision' over three columns, and continued, 'It was one of the finest boxing contests we have seen in Paris for many a long day but ended in an incredible and bewildering decision.

'Carpentier, in the pink of condition and in wonderful form, faster, more accurate and more scientific than ever, dominated the fight by a long chalk. In the first round he sent his opponent to the canvas with an irresistible right hook, and in the following 12 rounds he hit Jeanette again and again with lightning lefts, forcing the American to resort to more than one irregularity such as holding with one hand and hitting with the other.

'Three times during the fight the referee had to warn Jeanette and threaten him with disqualification. Carpentier, relying on his big lead on points, adapted defensive tactics in the last round, the only one that could have gone to Jeanette. It was a verdict that was as scandalous as it was incomprehensible. It was loudly booed by the large crowd, including even a good many people who had backed Jeanette, but were sportsmen enough to recognise that the French champion had beaten their man in a masterly fashion and that there was really no doubt about the true result.'

Carpentier's recollections of the fight were, 'I took command from the first bell and I was able to place my punches hard and accurately. Jeanette kept coming forward, although he often hit with one hand and held with the other. But I was doing all the work, and there was no way that Jeanette deserved the verdict. When it was announced, he seemed every bit as surprised as I was. Even the crowd was flabbergasted before they broke out in loud boos.'

Late in 1913 the US boxing authorities decided to set up the 'white heavyweight championship of the world' in opposition to Jack Johnson. While Johnson was the legitimate champion, he had enraged America because he lived by his own rules and did exactly as he wanted. He was beloved by blacks and some whites but thoroughly hated by those who saw him as a threat to America's divided society. A Philadelphian of Irish extraction named Edward J. Smythe, a former US Navy and Army heavyweight champion, changed his name to Gunboat Smith and duly won the 'white' title.

When the offer to meet Carpentier for the 'white' title in London on 16 July 1914 came along, Smith readily accepted. It was noticeable that among the 10,000 spectators, many were women. Georges had started a new fashion in boxing, and the ladies began attending the sport in large numbers. From the opening bell Carpentier skilfully danced and dodged Smith's big punches while countering with his own and dropping the American in the fourth. In the sixth Carpentier slipped to his hands and knees and on rising, the Gunboat struck him and was promptly disqualified.

Carpentier was in England in August when World War I broke out and he left immediately for France to enlist. He served in the French military as an observation pilot and by the end of hostilities in 1918 he was a decorated hero, having been awarded the Croix de Guerre and the Medaille Militaire. Resuming his boxing career in July 1919, he knocked out two more British heavyweights, Dick Smith in eight rounds in Paris and the native champion Joe Beckett in one in London. There was talk of a world heavyweight title fight with Jack Dempsey but an offer came to challenge Battling Levinsky for the world light-heavyweight title in Jersey City on 12 October 1920. It was too good to turn down.

'I had been campaigning as a heavyweight but a rather light one, around the 168lb mark or thereabouts,' he said. 'I could only win by a knockout as the rules in New Jersey stipulated that if it went the full distance, it would be a no-decision, and that would mean that he kept his title. He was pretty good, having been in the ring with the likes of Jack Dempsey, Harry Greb, Jack Dillon and my old opponent Gunboat Smith. 'He was a quick, clever boxer although not a heavy puncher and

I was confident I could beat him. I had a bit of trouble catching him in the first round as he was doing a lot of back-pedalling and he was as slippery as an eel. I caught up with him in the second round when I put him down twice, first from a left and right to the jaw, and then a right to the jaw. In the fourth I knocked him out with a left and right, again to the jaw. The round had gone one minute and seven seconds. I had made it at last and I was light-heavyweight champion of the world. My manager Francois Descamps told me that the next target was the really big one, the heavyweight championship, which at the time was held by the great Jack Dempsey.'

Carpentier got his big chance on the overcast, humid evening of Saturday 2 July 1921 at Boyle's Thirty Acres arena in Jersey City. It was an extravaganza that introduced sport as leisure for the masses at the beginning of the 1920s, the Roaring 20s, the Jazz Age. Dempsey's biographer Randy Roberts places the historic fight in the cultural perspective of the post-World War I era, 'In an age where man seemed to be guided by amoral forces beyond his control, the Dempsey–Carpentier fight represented man as master of his fate.'

Tex Rickard, the promoter, initially wanted the fight to take place at the Polo Grounds in New York City, an open-air venue. However, Nathan Lewis Miller, the governor of New York, opposed prizefighting and made it clear that he did not want it in the state. After a number of offers from other promoters, Rickard settled on a proposal from Frank Hague, the mayor of Jersey City, who had obtained 34 acres of land owned by John P. Boyle, a paper box manufacturer, and was prepared to hire it out to Rickard. The promoter hired 500 carpenters and 400 labourers to transform the land into a boxing arena.

It was constructed in less than two months, and completed a few days before the fight. The arena was initially erected to hold 50,000 fans but the demand for the international extravaganza was so enormous that Rickard had to expand it to hold up to 91,000 fans, making it the greatest seating capacity of any amphitheatre ever built. The official attendance was

80,183 and it grossed $1,789,238, well over twice as much as any previous fight. Boxing's first million-dollar gate.

In attendance was a roster of notables from all walks of life, with a tower for photographers. The occasion was also the first time boxing was broadcast on the radio, the new mass communications medium of the decade. Dempsey v Carpentier was billed as the 'Fight of the Century'. The sun came out as the boxers were being introduced and it stayed hot all through the afternoon.

Carpentier's fears of not being big enough to tackle the world's best heavyweights proved well founded. Dempsey out-weighed him by 20lb. The Frenchman did well at the start, getting through with hard shots to head and body. In the second round he crashed over a powerful right which made the champion wince but the impact broke Carpentier's hand. With the hand virtually useless, Dempsey was allowed to come forward with renewed confidence and by round four, Carpentier's chances looked hopeless.

The Frenchman could not possibly hold off the rampaging Dempsey with one hand, and a right to the chin put the Frenchman down on his face. Carpentier, still badly shaken, got to his feet at nine and tried to crowd Dempsey but a right to the body dropped him for the second time as referee Harry Ertle started counting. When he reached ten, Dempsey strode over to the centre of the ring and helped Carpentier to his feet. He half-carried the beaten challenger to a corner. On the way back to his own corner, Dempsey leaned over the ropes and said to the reporters, 'I'm really sorry I had to knock out such a good man, a really good man.'

In his report of the fight for the *New York Times*, Irving S. Cobb, borrowed from the *Saturday Evening Post*, wrote, 'Dempsey's right arm swings upward with the flailing emphasis of an oak cudgel and the muffled fist at the end of it lands again on its favourite target – the Frenchman's jaw. The thud of its landing can he heard above the hysterical shrieking of the crowd. The Frenchman seems to shrink in for a good six inches.

'It is as though that crushing impact had telescoped him. He folds up into a pitiable meagre compass and goes down heavily on his right side, his face half-covered by his arms as though even in the stupor following that deadly collision between his face and Dempsey's fists, he would protect his vulnerable parts.

'From where I sit writing this I can see one of his eyes and his mouth. The eye is blinking weakly, the mouth is gaping, and the lips work as though he has chewed a most bitter mouthful. The referee is close at hand, tolling off the inexorable tally of the count – seven, eight, nine, ten and out. Three things stand out as the high points of this fight, as far as I am personally concerned.

'The first is that Carpentier never had a chance. He trusted to his strength when his refuge should have been his speed. The second is that vision of him, doubled up on his side like a frightened, hurt boy and yet striving to heave himself up and take added punishment from a foe against whom he had no chance. The third and most outstanding will be my memory of that look on Dempsey's towering front when realisation came to him that a majority of the tremendous audience were partisans of the foreigner.'

Carpentier's recollections of the fight were, 'I never made excuses about my defeat and I am not going to make them to you here right now, half a century later. Jack was too good for me, too big and too strong, two points that often crossed my mind before the fight. Maybe if I had been a big heavier, who knows, but that's being theoretical. I did catch him with a good right shot in the second round but it smashed my hand and I was just a one-handed boxer from then on.

'Now it was hard enough to match someone like Jack Dempsey with two hands, never mind one, as you can readily imagine. Let me tell you a little story. Dempsey and I would often meet at boxing tournaments over the years but on one particular occasion I was chatting to him in his restaurant on Broadway and I said to him, "You know Jack, when I looked at you in your corner, you resembled a lion, and I can tell you now that I had no intention of getting killed by a ferocious beast." I'm happy to say that Jack and I have remained good friends all our lives.'

Carpentier took a break from the ring for several months to spend quality time with his wife and daughter. As far as boxing was concerned he also decided to stay away from the Dempseys of the world, at least for the foreseeable future and concentrate of his light-heavyweight championship. The boxing authorities were putting pressure on him to defend his title as there were several legitimate contenders waiting in the wings. However, five months after the Dempsey battle, he accepted an offer from London to face the Australian heavyweight George Cook at the Royal Albert Hall. The date was 22 January 1922. Carpentier needed to find out whether he could still deliver at the top level, at least under the radar of the likes of Dempsey.

During a globe-trotting career which would last nearly ten years, Cook took on all comers, with nobody barred. If a world heavyweight title opportunity were offered, George would have a pen in his hand ready to sign. He boxed in all corners of the world including the US, France, England, Germany, Argentina, South Africa, Sweden, Italy, Ireland, New Zealand, Canada, Wales and his native Australia, and that was before the aeroplane shrunk the globe. He fought many big-name heavyweights including Tom Heeney, Jack Sharkey, Primo Carnera, Johnny Risko, Paolino Uzcudun, Young Stribling, Walter Neusel and Larry Gains. He would win the Australian heavyweight title in 1926.

Cook put up stiff resistance against the Frenchman and was in real trouble in the opening three rounds as Carpentier landed frequently with stinging left jabs and fast, hard left and right hooks and uppercuts to the head and body. Carpentier forced the pace in the fourth round but Cook tied him up in the clinches and got through with smashing uppercuts to the body. The Frenchman broke away and suddenly shot over a piston-like right cross, the punch that made the great Dempsey grimace. He followed with a sweeping left hook which sent the game Aussie to the floor to be counted out. 'I felt I would get him in the end,' remembered Carpentier.

Now to get around a defence of his light-heavyweight title. The London contender Ted 'Kid' Lewis had been telling the English press that Carpentier could not be called a proper champion 'until he took on Ted "Kid" Lewis'. A gritty fighter who claimed he feared nobody, anywhere, Lewis was a former world welterweight champion and had a long-running rivalry with Jack Britton in the US, having met each other at least 20 times. Now campaigning as a middleweight, he entered the ring at the Olympia Exhibition Centre on 11 May 1922 weighing 150lb to Carpentier's 175. A problem for Lewis? 'Not a bit,' he told the newspapermen. 'I'll knock him out anyway.'

Lewis looked like carrying out his threat once the bell sent the two boxers on their way. He was all over Carpentier, bombarding him with punches from all angles. Georges moved away, jabbing and hooking but Lewis came on, still firing those big shots. At close quarters, Lewis was holding on to Carpentier and got a stern warning from referee Joe Palmer, a man with a reputation for taking no nonsense.

Lewis turned to Palmer and complained. Carpentier took full advantage of this distraction. He shot across a tremendous right to the jaw and Lewis went crashing to the boards to be counted out with his arms outstretched. The big crowd erupted furiously into a storm of booing with shouts of, 'Foul! Foul!' renting the night air. 'Yes, I felt cheated, but I don't want to bear any grudge,' said Lewis in the dressing room. 'I'm not that kind of person. I never was and never will be.'

There can be valid arguments that Carpentier landed a controversial blow when Lewis was complaining but in the unwritten rules of the game, a boxer is expected to defend himself at all times. Lewis did not do that.

What was Carpentier's view of the matter? 'Looking back now over 40 years on, I maintain that it was right and proper that I landed that punch, whatever the controversial aspects of it,' he said. 'The referee may have warned Lewis about holding but he got away with other blatant infringements such as sticking his thumb in my eye and jabbing his elbows into my stomach. What about those fouls? Lewis was careful to commit them on the so-called blind side of the referee. I decided I would get my own back so the next time the referee said "break", with Lewis still clinging to me like a leech, I hit him with a right. It was more of a flick.

'Lewis turned to the referee to complain and as he did so I hit him with another right, a lot harder this time and he went down. I thought the punch was legitimate and the referee obviously thought so too because he ordered me to a neutral corner and started the count. It was a formality and he reached ten and out. It was all over. But there were no hard feelings between us. Later in the evening at a banquet in a hotel, the Metropole as I recall, we chatted together and he said, "You certainly know your onions, Georges, and I'll hand you that." We embraced. We remained good friends long after that fight, as short-lived as it was. That's how it is in boxing. You try to knock lumps off each other in the ring and then when it's over, you are both the best of friends.'

Carpentier was determined to be a fighting champion and was prepared to give any reasonable contender an opportunity to win the title. Francois Descamps looked around for a good opponent, and even contacted Tex Rickard, who had promoted the Dempsey–Carpentier million-dollar battle a year earlier. Rickard called Descamps back and said that he was willing to put on a Carpentier defence, but only in America. Descamps cabled him back to say that Georges felt his native fans should get the next opportunity of seeing him in action.

Marcel Nilles, the French heavyweight champion, was suggested for a Paris match. Nilles was one of his country's finest products, with a good record. His powerful physique was even more imposing with gruelling training routines high in the mountains and deep in the valleys. However, he turned down a fight with Carpentier without giving any specific reason, with the French press suggesting that he simply did not think he was good enough to take on the world champion, and would have to weaken himself considerably to get inside the light-heavyweight limit of 175lb. Exit Nilles and enter Battling Siki.

Born Amadou Fall, with some sources spelling it Phal, on 16 September 1897 in the port of St Louis, Senegal, then known as French West Africa, Siki moved to France while still a teenager. He met a French actress who took a liking to him and made him her servant. In any event, Siki soon changed his first name from Amadou to Louis, and by the age of 15 began a career as a boxer. A local promoter changed his name to Battling Siki for boxing posters and fight programmes on the seemingly logical basis that he would draw more attention to himself.

From 1912 to 1914, fighting strictly in France, Siki compiled an unimpressive record of eight wins, six losses and a draw. With the outbreak of World War I, he enlisted in the French Army, where his bravery in battle earned him both the Croix de Guerre and the Medaille Militaire.

Siki resumed his boxing career in 1919 after leaving the forces. With renewed vigour, he won 43 of 46 fights in the ensuing four years, drawing twice, and losing just once. Promoters liked to use Siki because he was an exciting fighter. He would use his skill early on before opening up in the subsequent rounds in a whirlwind style which delighted the onlookers. 'When I had a man going, I would do my utmost to finish him off,' he told a reporter before one particular fight.

Descamps had heard a bit about Siki and his busy schedule in European rings but did not consider the West African any serious threat. Siki looked a 'safe' opponent. He approached the West African's connections and agreed for their man to tackle Carpentier. Moreover, the French boxing authorities, the Federation Francais de Boxe, said that Siki had proven himself to be the most worthy candidate and named him the official challenger. The big fight was on.

It was set for the afternoon of Sunday 24 September 1922. Sunday was a day of the week which Parisians set aside for entertainment. The venue was the sprawling Velodrome Buffalo arena on the outskirts of Paris. Siki would be the first black man in seven years to fight for a major boxing championship. Carpentier was a heavy favourite as he ducked between the ropes before a crowd of some 40,000 who had produced the first gate to reach a million francs in French boxing history. Celebrities from all walks of life were in attendance including a young Ernest Hemingway, a rabid fight fan, who was assigned to cover the fight for an American newspaper.

As Siki made his way down the aisle and into the ring, he was greeted with an ovation that carried a certain derisive ring. He clambered through the ropes, made an elaborate bow, a wide grin spread over his broad face. A few moments later Carpentier, a heavy favourite with the betting people, climbed up the ring steps and got a tumultuous reception. Smiling and looking in top condition, he waved to the crowd. The fans had been eagerly awaiting the return to French rings of their idol and now he would again display his natural boxing ability, albeit against a seemingly unskilled opponent.

'I found Siki relatively easy to hit, but I didn't try too hard,' Carpentier remembered. 'Descamps and I agreed with the promoter that I would carry Siki for a few rounds for the benefit of the movie cameras so I just danced around and playfully jabbed him with lefts, throwing the occasional right which I thought made him blink. He was inclined to keep his arms crossed over his face and body but I got through with what I thought was a light right hand and he went down on one knee. The referee Henry Bernstein called to him, "Get up, that wasn't a heavy blow." I certainly did not think so either.'

Shocks were to follow. Halfway through the second round, Siki went down again, once more from no apparent heavy blow. He took a count of six on one knee, then sprang up, and to the astonishment of everyone, not excluding Carpentier and his corner, sprang at the champion like a wounded tiger. Swinging both arms, Siki caught the Frenchman on the chin with a powerful right cross that sent Carpentier to the boards. He jumped up at two, a grim look on his face, and Siki came in again, swinging lefts and rights. At one stage he mocked the

Frenchman by saying to him in a clinch, 'You don't punch very hard, do you Mr Carpentier?'

'Siki had been transformed from a scared rabbit into a positive demon,' wrote Gilbert Odd in his book *Great Moments In Sport*. 'Carpentier made one carefully aimed shot with his right, missed, and was then overwhelmed by a deluge of whirling gloves. Siki was hammering in punches from all angles and Georges spent the rest of the round in avoiding another knockdown blow. The bell must have sounded as sweet music to his ears. He dropped wearily on his stool, while the Battling one trotted back, a look of intense satisfaction on his face.'

It was all downhill for Carpentier after that. There was no stopping this rampaging visitor, a human tank, whose vicious blows were playing havoc on the Frenchman's face. Blood was coming from his nose, mouth and a cut over his left eye. In the following rounds he fought back like the champion he was but there was no avoiding this whirlwind barrage of punches which were battering him into a state of utter helplessness. In the sixth, a powerful right uppercut caught the national hero beneath the chin, knocked him against the ropes and on to the canvas as the towel came sailing in. It was all over – or was it?

Officials at ringside were seemingly in a quandary. The fans were yelling for Siki to be announced as the winner and new world light-heavyweight champion. Instead, the loudspeakers suddenly boomed that Siki had been disqualified for 'tripping' his opponent and that the beaten and bloodied Carpentier had retained his title. It looked like a riot was about to break out. Fans rushed to assault the referee and a horde of gendarmes had to surround him for protection while Carpentier had to be escorted to his dressing room by an armed guard.

Only when a further announcement was made to the effect that the referee and the three judges were in consultation with officials of the boxing commission was the disturbance partially quelled. Nearly an hour elapsed before the four officials, sensing a riot, satisfied the angry mob, and Siki in particular, when it was announced that the referee's decision had been rescinded and that the challenger was the winner. Justice had been done, and Siki became the first African boxer to win a world title, his stunning victory coming after one minute and ten seconds of the sixth round.

'What can I say about the whole thing, Thomas?' remembered Carpentier. 'It was all a blur from the second round when Siki put me down for the first time. I had broken my right hand on Siki's head in the fourth and it was simply useless from then on. Siki did trip me up in the sixth round, and I've no doubt about that, but the tumult was so enormous that the officials had to go into hurried talks and make a final decision. They did so and proclaimed Siki the winner. I shouldn't have allowed myself to be surprised by his wild swings but there you are. Was I on the downside? Was I coming to the end of the road? I chewed over the whole situation for days, weeks on end but decided to carry on.'

Siki seemed to lose the run of himself after the fight. He enraged the city's civic authorities by parading down the boulevards with a fully-grown lioness on a lead, and tried to kiss every pretty girl he passed. On another occasion, he danced on the pavement, while holding the lioness with one hand. He was also drinking heavily. A scheduled fight with the British champion Joe Beckett in London was cancelled by the Home Office who said they just couldn't tolerate such erratic behaviour. Siki was simply banned in Britain, a *persona non grata*.

Siki finally accepted an offer to make the first defence of his title in Dublin. With Carpentier at ringside, he faced Mike McTigue from Co. Clare on 17 March 1923, St Patrick's Day. The Civil War was raging at the time, with bombs and bullets going on all around the La Scala theatre, one blast going off a few yards away as the crowd was going in. The odds were quite clearly against him – an Irish opponent in the Irish capital on the national holiday. Honestly, what could Siki really expect?

Nevertheless, it was a close fight all the way. During one of the middle rounds, one enterprising McTigue supporter sneakily substituted a bottle of whiskey for the water bottle in Siki's corner 'to make him a bit woozy', as the fellow later explained. McTigue, a veteran ring man, won the decision over 20 rounds.

Sadly, Siki met his death in tragic circumstances. On 15 December 1925 his reckless lifestyle caught up with him in New York. He was stopped by a patrolling police officer who saw him staggering drunk on 42nd Street, not far from his apartment. Siki said he was on his way home, and walked off. Later, he was found lying face down in the wet gutter, shot twice in the back at close range. The 'Singular Senegalese' was dead at the age of 28.

Carpentier did indeed continue with his ring career and had impressive knockouts in 1923, putting away Marcel Nilles, the French heavyweight who had earlier turned down a fight with Georges, in eight rounds and the British hope Joe Beckett in one. Carpentier finally hung up his gloves in 1927 following an exhibition match and retired to run a successful cocktail bar on the Boulevard de la Madeline in Paris. It became a popular haunt for actors, singers and artists. The Frenchman also made regular appearances at boxing shows and functions up until his death on 28 October 1975. He was 81.

Index

INDEX